D1784708

STRATEGIC ISSUES IN EUROPEAN AEROSPACE

Strategic Issues in
European Aerospace

Edited by
PHILIP LAWRENCE
Director,
Aerospace Research Group, University of the West of England, Bristol

DEREK BRADDON
Associate Director,
Aerospace Research Group, University of the West of England, Bristol

Ashgate

Aldershot • Brookfield USA • Singapore • Sydney

Published by
Ashgate Publishing Ltd
Gower House
Croft Road
Aldershot
Hants GU11 3HR
England

Ashgate Publishing Company
Old Post Road
Brookfield
Vermont 05036
USA

Ashgate website: http://www.ashgate.com

British Library Cataloguing in Publication Data
Strategic Issues in European Aerospace
    1. Aerospace industries - Europe - Congresses
    I. Lawrence, Philip K., 1952- II. Braddon, Derek, 1949-
    338.4'76291

Library of Congress Cataloging-in-Publication Data
Strategic Issues in European Aerospace / edited by Philip Lawrence,
  Derek Braddon.
      p. cm.
  Papers presented at the AEROSPACE 2000, held in 1997 at Bristol,
  England.
  ISBN 1-84014-823-3 (hc.)
  1. Aerospace industries--Europe--Congresses. 2. Aircraft
industry--Europe--Congresses. 3. International division of labor-
- Congresses. 4. International trade--Congresses. I. Lawrence,
Philip. II. Braddon, Derek, 1949-
HD9711.5.E8S77 1998
387.7'094--dc21   98-41214
                                            CIP

ISBN 1 84014 823 3

Printed and bound in Great Britain by MPG Books Ltd, Bodmin, Cornwall

Contents

Preface

Strategic Issues in European Aerospace addresses the aerospace agenda in Europe for the new millennium. In particular it highlights the competitive challenge posed to Europe by the newly consolidated American aerospace industry. The book is a unique collection of perspectives provided by a mix of leading academics, industrialists and government officials on the challenges facing the European aerospace industry. It focuses on two interrelated, daunting challenges. The first is the competitive threat posed to Europe by the rationalised and consolidated American aerospace industry, which in the 1990s has undergone $100bn worth of merger activity. The second is the compelling task of rationalisation and consolidation required in the European industry itself. Through a mix of analytical perspectives and project oriented assessments the book provides an essential guide to the major strategic agenda for the European industry. A unique feature of *Strategic Issues* is the contribution of leading industry executives and project managers. These industry insiders outline the dilemmas and challenges facing the industry from the view point of those at the sharp end of the business. The book is an essential guide to aspects of the technical, political and economic agenda for aerospace in the next decade and beyond.

The catalyst for *Strategic Issues* was AEROSPACE 2000, an international conference organised by the Aerospace Research Group at the University of the West of England, Bristol. The topical theme of the conference - The Future of European Aerospace: Towards Global Partnerships - and its unmitigated success prompted demands for the publication of the contributions - this book is the result. By its very nature the conference produced speculation and prediction concerning the future of the industry. But history is not always kind to those bold enough to predict it. As events have unfolded the actual trend of European restructuring has not followed the expected pattern and global aerospace has thrown up many surprises. Thus, to mention a few, we no longer have AI(R), but ATR is resurrected, as yet we still have no Airbus SCE, but in the UK we now have a merger of British Aerospace and GEC Marconi. Daimler-Benz is now DaimlerChrysler etc., etc. As a structural backdrop the aerospace industry is also coming to terms with the Asian and Russian economic crises which were not evident in late 1997. In other words the dynamic and unpredictable character of the aerospace industry continues to surprise even the most sophisticated analysts. Despite this some of the contributors to this book were remarkably prescient in their analysis of future trends. Thus our readers will find that Michel Bieler's comments about the likely difficulties of amalgamating Boeing and MDC have proved uncannily accurate.

In the main this book does not, of course, stand or fall on the predictive powers of its authors. *Strategic Issues* spells out an agenda for European aerospace and reveals the concerns and policies of those who manage one of our key industries. We hope it will be of use to all those who seek to understand the inner logic of the European aerospace industry.

Philip Lawrence
Aerospace Research Group
University of the West of England
Bristol, England

Acknowledgements

The editors of this book owe a number of debts to those who gave their assistance to the project. Thanks are due to all the industry executives who were extraordinarily generous with their time. In addition we thank Karen Cox for secretarial assistance and Sean Rothman for technical assistance with the manuscript. Charles Stocks of *Storm Creative Design* is also thanked for his assistance with our artwork and graphics. Finally, we would like to express our gratitude to our publisher, John Hindley for his untiring support and enthusiasm.

Abbreviations

ACE	Airbus Concurrent Engineering
ACP	Advanced Composites for Propulsion
AECMA	European Association of Aerospace Industries
AI	Airbus Industrie GIE
AI(R)	Aero International (Regional)
AIA	Airbus Industrie Asia
ALN	Alenia Aerospazio
AMC	Airbus Military Company
AMET	Advanced Military Engine Technology
AMRAAM	Advanced Medium Range Air to Air Missile
ARPANET	DoD Advanced Research Project Agency Network
AS	Aérospatiale
ASRAAM	Advanced Short Range Air to Air Missile
ATO	Authorisation to Offer
ATR	Avions de Transport Regional
AVIC	Aviation Industries of China
AWACS	Airborne Warning and Control System
BAC	British Aircraft Corporation Limited
BAe	British Aerospace plc
BMW	Bayerische Motorenwerke GmbH
BVRAAM	Beyond Visual Range Air to Air Missile
BVR	Beyond Visual Range
C^3I	Command, Control, Communications & Intelligence
CAA	Civil Aviation Authority (UK)
CASA	Construcciones Aeronáuticas SA
CEO	Chief Executive Officer
CO	Carbon Monoxide
CO_2	Carbon Dioxide
DARPA	Defense Advanced Research Projects Agency (US)
DASA	DaimlerChrysler Aerospace AG
DASS	Defensive Aids Sub System

DDUTI	Defense Dual-Use Technology Initiative
DGIII	Directorate-General III, European Commission
DMSTP	Defense Manufacturing Science & Technology programme
DOC	Direct Operating Costs
DoD	Department of Defense (US)
DTI	Department of Trade & Industry (UK)
DVI	Direct Voice Input
EC	European Commission
ECU	European Currency Unit
EF	Eurofighter
EFA	European Fighter Aircraft
EMU	European Monetary Union
ESA	European Space Agency
EU	European Union
EuroFLAg	European Future Large Aircraft Group Srl
FAA	Federal Aviation Administration (US)
FBW	Fly-by-Wire
FCE	Flight Crew Environment
FDI	Foreign Direct Investment
FDR	Franklin D Roosevelt
FLA	Future Large Aircraft
FLASH	Fly-by-Light Advanced System Hardware
FLIR	Forward Looking Infra Red
FOREX	Foreign Exchange
FP V	Fifth Framework Programme
GATT	General Agreement on Tariffs and Trade
GDP	Gross Domestic Product
GERD	General Expenditure on R&D
GIE	Groupement d'Intérêt Economique
GNP	Gross National Product
GPS	Global Positioning System
HSA	Hawker Siddeley Aviation
HOTAS	Hands On Throttle And Stick
HOTOL	Horizontal Take Off and Landing
HSR	High-Speed Research
HST	High-Speed Transport
IBM	International Business Machines Corporation

IPR	Intellectual Property Rights
IRST	Infra Red Search and Track
ISO	International Standardization Organization
IT	Information Technology
JAR	Joint Aviation Requirements
JSF	Joint Strike Fighter
JV	Joint Venture
KCDC	Korea Commercial-Aircraft Development Consortium
LCA	Large Commercial Aircraft
LM	Lockheed Martin Corporation
M&A	Mergers & Acquisitions
MANTECH	Manufacturing Technology
MDC	McDonnell Douglas Corporation
MEADS	Medium Extended Range Air Defense System
MES	Minimum Efficiency of Scale
MIDS	Multifunction Information Distribution System
MITI	Ministry of International Trade and Industry (Japan)
MMS	Matra Marconi Space
MNE	Multinational Enterprise
MoD	Ministry of Defence (UK)
MoU	Memorandum of Understanding
MTU	Motoren– und Turbinen-Union München GmbH
NACA	National Advisory Council for Aeronautics (US)
NASA	National Aeronautics and Space Administration (US)
NASP	National Aerospace Plane
NATO	North Atlantic Treaty Organisation
NETMA	NATO Eurofighter and Tornado Management Agency
NG	Next Generation
NOx	Oxides of Nitrogen
NRC	Non-Recurring Costs
NSC	National Security Council (US)
NSI	National System of Innovation
OAM	Overhaul and Modifications
OCCAR	Organisme Conjointe de Cooperation d'Armement.
OECD	Organisation for Economic Cooperation and Development
OG	Old Generation ('Classic')
OPEC	Organisation of Petroleum Exporting Countries

P&W	Pratt & Whitney
R&D	Research & Development
R&T	Research & Technology
REL	Reaction Engines Limited
RFP	Request for Proposals
RR	Rolls-Royce plc
SAAB	Svenska Aeroplan AB
SBAC	Society of British Aerospace Companies
SCE	Single Corporate Entity
SNECMA	Société Nationale d'Etude et de Construction de Moteurs d'Aviation
SST	Supersonic Transport
STANAGS	Standardisation Agreement
STIP	Strategic Trade Investment Policy (US)
STPE	Singapore Technologies Precision Engineering
TIALD	Thermal Imaging Airborne Laser Designator
TNE	Transnational Enterprises
TPCC	Trade Promotion Coordinating Committee
TRP	Technology Reinvestment Project
UAV	Unmanned Air Vehicle
UNCTAD	United Nations Commission for Trade and Development
UK	United Kingdom
US	United States
USAF	United States Air Force
USG	United States Government
USTR	United States Trade Representative
VIP	Very Important Person
VTAS	Voice, Throttle and Stick
WTO	World Trade Organization

Part I

Strategic Issues

1 The World Aerospace Industry: From Internationalisation to Globalisation

KEITH HAYWARD
Professor of International Relations, Staffordshire University
Head of Research, Society of British Aerospace Companies

Introduction

The topography of aerospace has changed markedly since I last formally surveyed the world industrial scene.[1] However, while I did not predict the extent of US restructuring that has so affected the industry outlook over the last two years, the trends towards national consolidation and further internationalisation of business were already well in train. I ended that book with an open question; or rather posed two possible directions the industry might take over the next decade. One posited the re-affirmation of national cores (in Europe perhaps defined in regional terms); the other suggested the emergence of a 'genuinely transnational industry, where national characteristics and concerns will have less significance for companies than the demands of global technology scanning, production and marketing...'. In short, I implied that aerospace might become like any other high-technology, capital intensive manufacturing sector, with truly globalised structures and processes. This contained the further implication that aerospace would become less overtly linked to the state; not apolitical (no major trans-national industrial sector escapes politics), but nonetheless in some respects, de-coupled from its 'home' national governments.

This chapter will re-visit these themes, comparing the current stage of industrial development in the aerospace sector with 'traditional' multinational enterprise (MNE) structure and behaviour. We will then consider whether there are fundamental forces for change at work in the aerospace industry pushing the sector towards truly globalised manufacturing.   We will conclude by suggesting that ethnocentricity

3

remains the most powerful force determining industrial development and that any assumption of reduced state intervention would be somewhat heroic. This, in turn, raises questions about whether aerospace can ever capture the true economies of scope and scale sought by other companies operating in other industrial sectors without the constraints of political frontiers.

Globalisation Defined

Globalisation is becoming an over-extended concept, deployed often without thinking to describe 'something more' than 'mere' internationalisation. However, globalisation means considerably more than just internationalisation with something extra. At heart, it challenges the nation-state as the organising unit of political and social behaviour. It is best defined as 'a process in which the constraints of geography on economic, political, social and cultural arrangements recede and in which people become increasingly aware that they are receding'.[2] Globalisation has been loosely associated, but not co-terminus with, the spread of western, particularly US values and organisations. Its onset portends the de-territorialisation of social and especially political arrangements. The process has been led by economic-corporate forces, but is now determined by a much more complex set of factors including culture and fashion fuelled by international, media and personal contact.

One of the main consequences of globalism and global thinking has been to call into question the long term viability of the nation state as the primary form of political organisation and of traditional thinking about the international system which views it continually in a state of anarchy, preoccupied by the threat of inter-state violence. This line of thinking presents a major problem for an industry such as aerospace that depends upon the state for more of its funding and is linked so closely to national security. Even limited forms of international restructuring have raised questions about the automaticity of state aid for civil projects, and the development of an integrated defence market in Europe will have to be managed carefully if support for the regions' defence industries is not to be undermined.

Herein lies the aerospace industry paradox: it is clearly an international industry in terms of market and production, but it is relatively underdeveloped in terms of having globalised integrated production systems operating in frontier-less markets. Moreover, with its close links to the state, especially as one of the security providers, aerospace remains 'pre-globalist' in its essential territoriality.

A Worldwide Industry

The aerospace industry is widely spread, with collaborative and sub-contracting links covering North America, West and Eastern Europe, the Far East, Latin America and Southern Africa. However, the aerospace 'core' is heavily clustered in the northern arc extending from the Western Pacific to the Urals.

States in this arc possess:

- complete industrial capabilities;
- a systems integrative capability of the most sophisticated aerospace products;
- the bulk of innovative research and technology acquisition;
- the dominant firms;
- the main markets for civil and military products.

Even within the aerospace core, aerospace capabilities are not evenly spread. The primary structural features are:

- a US technological and industrial dominance, accentuated by the latest round of domestic mergers;
- a problematic European challenge centring on France, the UK and Germany, with a gradual movement towards regional integration;
- a Russian industry with a range of technological capabilities nominally equivalent to the US, and with a high potential for future civil and military expansion, but beset by financial and organisational crises;
- countries with strong competence in limited areas of activity, such as Canada, Sweden, Spain and Italy. They have some vulnerability to further rationalisation and, following Holland, would be at risk of market exit without access to state aid;
- a long history of state involvement, direct or indirect, in industry; but growing concern over the cost and relevance of sponsorship, especially in the military sector.

The core is flanked by the aspirants and the established niche manufacturers of the Far East and South America. They are largely dependent on the core states:

- Japan, still largely a niche manufacturer, dependent on US industry but with unrealised ambitions; however, potentially a very strong competitor in the equipment sector based on national prowess in electronics;
- China, a strategic investor in aerospace, with market and security reasons for heavy and sustained commitment to the sector - a strong contender for promotion over the next 20 years;
- the development-pull countries, Indonesia, Brazil, possibly India, Korea, South Africa and Taiwan, where aerospace is the focus of government inspired industrial and technology policies. Many will find it hard to stay in touch with the core, and will depend upon strength of government willingness to pay the cost of their aerospace ambitions.

All of these states can sustain limited competition for international business, especially while benefiting from state aid and preference. They can threaten individual firms in the core, especially those operating lower down the supply/sub-contract chain.

The Globalisation of Business as an Evolutionary Process

Explanations and Motives

The globalisation process was closely linked to the development of a world economic-trading system in late the 19th century. The spread of international business and markets was further stimulated by two periods of hegemony - UK and US. The latter was particularly important as it encouraged the spread of a liberal trade system and the expansion of US-owned MNEs.

The emergence of the modern MNE, therefore, has a long history and a wide range of generalised concepts for internationalisation seek to explain the process. These include:

- domestic market saturation;
- exploiting the benefits of international vertical integration, typically the oil giants;
- product cycles and first-user advantages, typically US consumer industries. Trade barrier avoidance;
- hegemonic explanations.

At the level of the individual firm, there are four main corporate motives for foreign production.[3]

The Resource Seekers

Firms are prompted by the availability overseas of resources that can be obtained at lower real cost than can be found domestically. There are three types of resource seekers:

- physical resource seekers;
- cheap labour seekers;
- technological, management or organisational seekers.

The Market Seekers

Market seekers look to sustain existing markets or to develop new ones.

- Imitation (Japanese auto component manufacturers following auto assemblers);
- adaptation to local needs/requirements;
- lower transaction costs;
- physical presence to match competitors;
- and still most important, tariff barrier avoidance and government inducements.

The Efficiency Seekers

Firms seek to rationalise the structure of established resource-based or market-seeking investment in order that they obtain maximum benefit from the common governance of geographically dispersed activities:

- to obtain economies of scale;
- coordinate local advantages to common end.

The Strategic Asset Seekers

Here, companies want to promote long term international competitiveness, usually through M&A activity. This motive is particularly associated with service providers.

Many of these motives are reflected in the aerospace internationalisation process, especially the latter three categories. They have underpinned collaborative behaviour, joint venture and international sub-contracting. However, the key difference between aerospace and 'normal' industry lies in the form of internationalisation and its subsequent organisational structure.

Form of Foreign Entry and Organisational Structure

Form of Entry

The exact form of entry for the classic MNE will differ, and may change over time as market conditions evolve and as the firm itself alters shape or direction. Typically the pattern will follow the path of export servicing and distribution, the creation of autonomous sales operations and licensing. At some point, for some firms, subsidiary assembly operation will be justified either by internal or external factors (host government action, for example). This may then lead to integrated assembly, product specialisation and interdependence.

A collaborative, joint venture strategy might also lead to a similar end; perhaps, by-passing some of the stages of growth. Over the last two decades, we have seen patterns of strategic alliances either involving same sector firms to capture global/regional markets (airlines, telecoms) or synergistic mergers to develop new products/services (telematics). To anticipate the argument below, internationalisation in the aerospace sector is largely centred on the alliance or subcontract form. The creation of interdependent, providentially-owned international manufacturing systems is rare, especially at the systems integrator level.

Organisational Forms

The typical MNEs will vary in organisational form. This can be summarised as one of three broad categories:

- international division structure;
- geographical structure;
- product structure.

There is no one 'right' model for a particular sector, but the more complex and numerous the end product, the more likely a firm is to adopt the product structure model where centralised finance, research, marketing and other functional activities feed worldwide product group operations.

The more globalised the firm becomes in its main functions, the more likely it will have to move away from hierarchical structures in order to achieve a balance between benefits of cross-border integration of operations and local responsiveness, and between geographical and product organisation.

A balance must also be struck on the locus of decision-making. Here four approaches emerge:

- the ethnocentric firm, mother country and colonies;
- the polycentric firm, a loose federation;
- the regiocentric firm, blending strategic interests with regional integration/national sensitivity;
- the geocentric MNE tries to adopt globally integrated approach to decision-making. This represents the genuine trans-national enterprise.

To date, there are no truly geocentric aerospace MNEs; I would contend the nearest we have to this form are Messier-Dowty and Bombardier. Both have European and North American locations, with some international integration of research and production. Several have some of the characteristics of the polycentric MNE (Rolls-Royce-Allison; Boeing, P&W and their Canadian subsidiaries). We are beginning to see the development of regiocentric enterprises - an Airbus SCE would fall under this heading. Eurocopter and MMS already do.

Internationalisation in the Aerospace Sector

Since 1950s, accelerating through the 1960s and 1970s, there has been a marked expansion of international supplier-sub contract chain and international joint venture/collaboration activity in the aerospace industry. There are also a significant number of MNEs in the equipment/component sectors and, as we have noted above, a few more sophisticated forms of MNE amongst airframe systems integrators and major sub-systems companies.

But aerospace is still characterised by a dominance of national cores. These are similar to an ethnocentric MNE; however, their internationalism may not even be 'colonial', but rather structured more like

9

diplomatic coalitions which vary in terms of partner equality and autonomy, remaining largely 'sovereign' in operation and ownership.

The reasons for this stem from the history of the aerospace industry and its role as a national security provider, but several factors have contributed:

- aerospace as a military and economic asset;
- close involvement of the state in determining supply and demand, ownership and organisation;
- national consolidation as the norm as answer to structural challenges;
- internationalisation largely through negotiation, often involving national governments as direct actors, for workshare, offsets and technology transfer objectives.

The result is largely sub-optimal internationalisation of development manufacturing and a limited degree of globalisation compared to comparable manufacturing sectors. In comparable 'strategic' industries, for example, airlines and telecommunications, rapid de-regulation has triggered globalisation effects. Sub-optimisation may be caused by negotiated worksharing, cumbersome decision-making systems, lack of competitive tendering, lack of continuity of products and the effects of multiple government intervention.

Forces for Change

There are clear forces for change in the aerospace sector. However, they are not always consistent; indeed some appear to be contradictory. This is usually attributable to different national and regional perspectives, particularly US vis a vis Europe, and the position and interests of the core vis a vis the aspirants. The forces for change may be summarised as:

- general market pressures, especially in the defence sector;
- the emergence of more open aerospace markets;
- but also tighter control over key markets, especially in the defence sector;
- continuing increase in development costs and risk, forcing more firms to internationalise;
- the structural crises affecting many national industries, including the loss of competition in several areas of the US industry;

- the increased need for international technology scanning and sharing;
- the spread of new manufacturing and industrial systems, increasing the incentive to draw supply chains closer to the prime.

Possibilities

It would be bold and probably inaccurate to suggest that aerospace is on the verge of becoming a 'normal', global industry, where capital, goods and technology flow freely, driven by objective, economic forces. Most technologically important industries such as automobiles, IT and even consumer electronics, are themselves subject to non-market forces in shaping decisions to internationalise, to invest or to disinvest. All forms of FDI activity assumes the existence of a powerful political input as MNEs seek the best locational deal from several governments. Moreover government-led offset agreements and negotiated access to key 'new' markets such as China, will be an integral feature of aerospace for the foreseeable future.

However, significant changes in world industrial structure are appearing, and in some respects, already have occurred. In particular, the creation of European aerospace TNEs is a more immediate prospect. As we have noted above, Eurocopter and MMS already have some of the characteristics of regiocentric TNEs. European guided weapons interests are coming together. The translation of Airbus Industrie to a SCE is imminent, M. Jospin notwithstanding. A subsequent re-grouping of European airframe activity, civil and military, then becomes more likely.

At the same time, however, an integrated European defence market is still necessary to match industrial re-structuring; and this process is lagging industrial change. Much the same could be said for the idea of a European technology acquisition policy.

Market and political forces have already led several European firms into TN activity. Rolls-Royce's take-over of Allison created an Anglo-American aero-engine firm. However, US security restrictions have blocked the flow of R&T that would be the case in a civil sector TNE. Rolls also forms half of the BMW-Rolls joint venture, where UK investment in small civil engines is now located in Germany. Lucas makes use of its Anglo-French identity to access two markets. Messier-Dowty has three primary locations, France, Britain and Canada. Investment decisions are shaped by which of the three locations offer the best mix of skill, market access and, significantly, government inducement.

11

Several of the US 'super primes' have begun to talk of globalisation. A number, Boeing, for example, have internationalised their supply chain and have embraced long term partnership-in-design strategies. Few, however, have entered into the kind of egalitarian joint venture agreements characteristic of European aerospace.

Outside of Canada, US-owned overseas aerospace subsidiaries are also rare (though one result of US domestic rationalisation has been the creation of de facto aerospace transnationals as overseas subsidiaries are randomly swept into a new corporate net).

Some US firms, notably Lockheed Martin, have taken on a European identity - mainly in the UK and also through parent company acquisition (Litton-Loral-Lockheed Martin). LM has been able to take advantage of the UK's relatively open policy on foreign ownership in the defence sector. But as the European defence industrial base and defence market consolidates and integrates, this may afford more opportunities and stimulus for US acquisition.

One could envisage the emergence of a North Atlantic aerospace industry - some of its elements are in place. However, the political climate - especially in the US, but also in some parts of Europe - is hardly ready to embrace its consequences.

Implications

If aerospace begins to follow the patterns of other higher-value manufacturing industries and to adopt authentically globalised structures and operations, there are several possible implications:

- increased levels of industrial efficiency;
- support for more ambitious technological goals and expensive products;
- sustainable competition;
- lower costs and lower prices to public and private customers;
- the de-nationalisation of aerospace sponsorship;
- increased risks of truncation and 'hollowing out' in the aerospace sector.

None of these are inevitable outcomes. The underlying assumption of sustainable competition, for example, implies limits to a long standing industrial trend towards oligopoly and the loss already of competition in several aerospace sectors.

The potency of military aerospace systems, both passive and active, will ensure that militarily active governments will want some security of supply and will want to maintain the ability to determine the direction of technological development.

De-nationalisation implies the progressive dismantling and/or commercialisation of national R&T infrastructure and bureaucratic structures supporting national aerospace interests. Even discounting strong residual economic and prestige reasons for hanging on to nationally (or regionally) located capabilities, there are still doubts about whether the corporate sector, even as globally operating companies, would be willing to, or would be able to accept responsibility *in toto* for its own R&T. Nevertheless, as competition increases (especially in the civil sector) and leads to further demands for production efficiency, the promise of 'Toyotaism' - the short hand for the global spread of new manufacturing techniques and industrial organisation - will increase the pressure on aerospace firms to capture the economies of scale and scope that are associated with globalised (or at least integrated regional) manufacturing and operation.

However, the implications of aerospace globalisation are especially fraught for national governments, especially those core industries outside the US - the periphery of the core. They will have to be increasing sensitive to the long term investment needs of 'their' companies and also begin to adopt policies that may attract inward aerospace investment. Where national governments routinely provide launch aid for civil programmes, a new relationship may be required to cater for national subsidiaries of international companies.[4] These are not new concerns of governments pursuing active industrial development strategies, but they are more unusual when applied to aerospace, especially by countries such as the UK, France and Germany, with hitherto relatively comprehensive aerospace interests. The strategy is more familiar to states such as Canada, Spain, Indonesia who have long targeted aerospace for indigenous development based, or helped by large elements of outside aid and assistance.

Final Words

I am rather conscious that I may have set up something of a straw man - the imminence of the global aerospace TNE - in order to knock him down. Despite the appearance of some of the classic TNE characteristics in aerospace, driven by significant forces for change, the links between aerospace and the nation-state remain strong and definitive.

There has been change, but not fundamental change. One might even assert a more ambitious argument, that while the nation state remains the pre-eminent actor in international relations with all of the security overtones that implies, such a de-coupling will be impossible. Breaking the links between aerospace and the state, even in Europe, is unlikely. Indeed, one of the problems facing European industry is to achieve a continental scale of effort without a continental polity and polices to match. There is a danger, therefore, that we may again have to confront Jean-Jacques Servan-Schrieber's famous warning of *The American Challenge* issued in the 1960s. Then he predicted that the second most powerful industrial force in the world will not be European, but 'US industry in Europe'. This could become an epitaph for European aerospace and a harbinger of US-led globalism in aerospace as it still is in much of world industry.

Notes and References

1   Keith Hayward, *The World Aerospace Industry*, (Duckworth/RUSI, 1994).

2   For a general introduction to Globalisation as a general concept, see, M Walters, *Globalisation,* (Routledge, 1995). The definition used above is adapted from Walters, p. 3. Chapter 4 discusses globalised production.

3   The analysis of MNE motives and structure is taken from, J H Dunning, *Multinational Enterprises and the Global Economy*, (Addison-Wesley Publishing), 1993.

4   One of the key issues associated with the formation of an Airbus SCE is the status of national commitments to the programme. The French government may seek to retain some form of holding in the new company; it is certainly demanding assurances from the Germans and British that they will continue to support the company's research and product development.

2 Widening the Scope of Aerospace Collaboration: Consolidation and Co-operation

CARMELO COSENTINO
Senior Vice President Business Development
Alenia Aerospazio

The Overall Trends in the Aerospace Sector

In the last few years, the aerospace and defence sectors have experienced several changes that are challenging our traditional business methods. The main trends leading to the need for industrial restructuring are well known and are summarised in the following:

- more costly and less numerous civil and military programmes, increasing the need for economies of scale;
- dramatic cuts in military expenditure in Western countries;
- growing importance of Asian countries both in the civil and military markets;
- reduced governmental financial support in Western countries;
- national systems are increasingly concerned about the specific rate of return on aerospace investment;
- changes in the structure of airlines (global airlines, mega-regional) that are shifting more power to the customers;
- a continuously increasing presence of newcomers, particularly from south-east Asia and the Pacific Rim area (China, Singapore, Indonesia, Korea, Japan, etc.);
- more demanding customer requirements (performances, economics, etc.) and tighter standards (certification, noise rules, etc.).

All these factors have caused a general industry over-capacity and a decline in profits in Western companies, particularly during the recession phase of the post-Gulf War period, and an increasingly fierce climate of global competition in the civil and military aerospace sectors.

The reactions have been different in Europe and in the United States: while the US aerospace industry has found a way for rapid and deep consolidation, for both the civil and military sector, in Europe the industrial rationalisation process is still at its beginning and is slower than in the US (for example: it will take at least two years to form an Airbus SCE, whereas Boeing and MDC have merged in a few months).

All of us - European aerospace managers, academics and politicians - agree that Europe can no longer postpone its decision to consolidate and streamline its fragmented industry, otherwise it will no longer be competitive in the long term.

But what kind of action do we need to take in Europe? Can the US consolidation model be pursued by European companies, or - taking into account European specificities - could a different solution be more suitable for our companies? This chapter outlines Alenia Aerospazio's point of view about these fundamental issues.

Let us look at the competitive situation between US and European companies both for the civil and military sector.

The Civil Aeronautics Sector

My belief is that Europe, considered as a global economic and industrial entity, must have an optimised and well coordinated civil aircraft industry, focused around its two outstanding and comprehensive entities: AI(R) for regional jets and turboprops, and Airbus for large transport aircraft and commercial jetliners.

AI(R), incorporated in late 1995 by merging the marketing, sales, and customer support activities of ATR, Jetstream and Avro, represents the first example of a true pan-European aerospace company. The establishment of this joint company, equally owned by Aérospatiale, Alenia and BAe, must be considered the first step towards a further integrated European structure. Now the first phase of AI(R) implementation has been successfully completed, a greater integration shall, in the near future, occur between the partners' activities including engineering, flight test and industrialisation as well. There is now a window of opportunity for other companies: an extension of the partnership to include other partners (European and/or non-European) is desirable to give AI(R) a more competitive and comprehensive presence in the regional aircraft sector.

16

In the commercial aircraft sector, European industry has been able to reach a strong position thanks to Airbus Industrie, but now, after years of commercial success, restructuring seems, to the four partners, necessary to transform the consortium into a stand-alone company. The Boeing-MDC merger is creating a company with a size, measured in terms of civil performance (turnover, deliveries and backlog), more than twice that of Airbus. In order to avoid losing competitive ground, in the near future Airbus partners must carry out an unprecedented amount of effort:

- the creation of an Airbus Industrie single corporate entity (SCE);
- the entry of new partners into the new company;
- enlarging Airbus product portfolio and competing with Boeing in each product segment (100-seater, A340 derivatives, A3XX), particularly in the large capacity segment where the B747 holds a monopolistic position;
- widening Airbus' market access and industrial base in Asia.

In particular, the monopolistic positions held by Boeing must be fought because they are disadvantageous for customers: fierce and fair competition in every market segment may result in technology advances, better aircraft performance and economics, lower prices, and air traffic growth.

In my view AI(R) and Airbus are both part of an overall strategy aimed at increasing European competitiveness, high technology and market penetration. The trend in Europe is towards more integration and coordination between AI(R) and Airbus, even if that does not necessarily mean the merging of the two entities. The enlargement and integration of AI(R) and Airbus will redraw the industrial map of Europe. An equitable balance among the various countries has to be considered as an objective within the overall framework rather than on a one-by-one basis. It is necessary to facilitate the convergence of interests of the national companies towards the two industrial entities by means of fair negotiations with their existing and potential partners.

There are now several specific programmes which give us the opportunities needed to speed up the restructuring process within the European industry. They are; the expected change of Airbus's legal form (GIE to SCE), the A3IX 100-seater programme, the possible launch of Airbus derivative models and of A3XX, the activities on the FLA programme, and the possible launch of a new regional jet family in AI(R).

In addition to these trends in Europe, now AECMA is gaining a greater representative role towards other bodies (EU, European and non-European authorities, etc.). This could be very important for the development and integration of the European aerospace industry, but only if AECMA represents the industrial interests of the whole of Europe.

The Military Aerospace Sector

In the military aerospace sector US companies have a substantial advantage over European companies, more than in the civil aeronautic sector; in the last years they have been able to restructure themselves at a pace unforeseeable a few years ago. The recent merger process has thoroughly reshaped the US defence industry: the acquisition and merging of large corporate units has been the American answer to the changing environment and as a result now US companies are larger, more efficient, competitive, and profitable than the European players. The process has created supergiants like Lockheed Martin and Boeing (with MDC) able to compete with a 'thorough strategic coverage' of defence markets in terms of technological, industrial, commercial, and financial capabilities.

In Europe we are far behind the US defence industry because industry restructuring is restrained by the presence of national barriers within Europe: fragmentation of the domestic markets, barriers to cross-border industrial integration and differences in regulatory environment (arms export policy, funding, etc.) represent the main factors to be overcome for the creation of an integrated European defence industry.

Moreover it is a matter of fact that the US market, in addition to being much larger than the European one, is virtually closed to non-US manufacturers, whereas the European market is largely open to US competition. During the 1992-94 period US imports from Western Europe amounted only to $2.7bn against $8.2bn worth of arms imported to Europe from the USA (three times as much). These figures are even more significant if one considers that total US military expenses in equipment ($188bn in 1992-94) are about 50% more than European ones (about $120bn).

In Europe, the past decade's consolidation has been at national level, and the trans-national industrial collaboration has been, until now, possible only by following the formula of consortia or J-V which are characterised by ineffective structures, duplication of efforts, and programme delays. Production allocation has often been based more on specific industrial policy than on lowest cost or best competencies. The Jaguar, Alphajet, and Tornado are examples of such past joint ventures, and in most of these programmes export sales have been very limited; Eurofighter is another example of an initiative set up on a 'programme basis' and not on a 'structural basis' (but export sales forecast for the EF-2000 are more optimistic than for the previous examples). Nowadays this cooperation model cannot be pursued any longer.

It is a common view that Europe is nearing a crossroad and needs a rapid consolidation process to ensure the future competitiveness of its defence industry, and it is quite obvious that this problem, involving not only industrial interests but also national political interests, requires rapid action and answers from governments as well as from industry.

We see that the role of states is now changing: as a customer (competitive tendering and the first moves towards the creation of a common European defence market), as a shareholder (privatisation processes are under way), as a regulator, and as a guarantor of strategic interests (territory, defence and autonomy).

Governments' role in the European rationalisation process is fundamental so that a European integrated defence market is created quickly to sustain a restructured defence industry, abandoning inefficient work-sharing and the *juste retour* formula. Defence ministries across Europe have to find ways to harmonise their requirements, to stabilise their military spending (as an example, in terms of a percentage of GNP), and to accept the principle of an European Sovereignty in the defence field (in terms of joint procurement, operations, etc.) rather than national.

The final aim, from the industrial point of view, must be that the European market is harmonised. But I think it is up to industry to speed up the process; all industrial aerospace managers try to approach the problem from the perspective of a more competitive European defence industry.

There are, on the industrial side, a lot of unanswered questions:

- What sort of consolidation must be achieved?
- Is it necessary for future consolidated European companies to attain the same size of US giants or have an industry structure made up of fewer more specialised companies?
- Which is the more efficient and competitive model to be followed by European companies: a vertical or horizontal consolidation?
- A single source model or a multi-source model?
- What kind of ownership structure?
- How to consider the existing relations within the civil aircraft sector (Airbus in particular)?

19

- Is it useful also to pursue transatlantic cooperation in some specific product areas?

It is easy to recognise that size (the overall company size) can give several advantages to a company ('broader is better'), especially if one considers the civil/defence linkages and related benefit effects. But what is really fundamental for having a competitive advantage is to have a significant size at business unit level (the so-called 'critical mass').

Nowadays in Europe we see some national champions with interests in several product areas (multipurpose companies) but they are not of a sufficient size to compete in each product sector with US companies (with few exceptions): BAe in UK, Aérospatiale in France, DASA in Germany, Finmeccanica in Italy, and Airbus and AI(R) in the civil sector see (*figure 1 World Aerospace Main Groups*).

In many sectors of the aerospace industry the future entities need to be so large that only one company in the whole of Europe is feasible: heavy combat aircraft, advanced trainer/ground attack aircraft, military transport aircraft, attack helicopters, S/A missile systems, are all examples of such sectors. In other aerospace sectors characterised by lower development and unit costs, such as TLC systems, avionics, UAVs, etc., the solution could be also to set up competing trans-national companies within Europe.

Thus, in my opinion, the answer to the needs of the European defence industry is the creation, in the medium to long term, of streamlined trans-national structures within Europe, each one devoted to a specific line of products, and in which the relevant operating units of each European company will join to develop, manufacture, market and support specific products. Therefore my belief is that European rationalisation must be achieved through horizontal mergers of the European aerospace main players, removing duplication and building an efficient cost base. Such new focused structures will have to be characterised by their own assets: a proper industrial structure, technological and commercial capabilities, and an agile and responsive management with great autonomy in strategic decision making (products launch, collaborations, etc.); in addition these trans-national structures must retain and preserve the national identities of the participants, equally distributing the areas of specialisation and allocating specific activities to specific countries, creating European centres of excellence starting from actual companies' competencies and involvement in military programmes. The approach to rationalisation must be multilateral and integrated, otherwise countries not involved in the process from the beginning could be tempted to seek closer ties with US players and the consolidation process will be delayed.

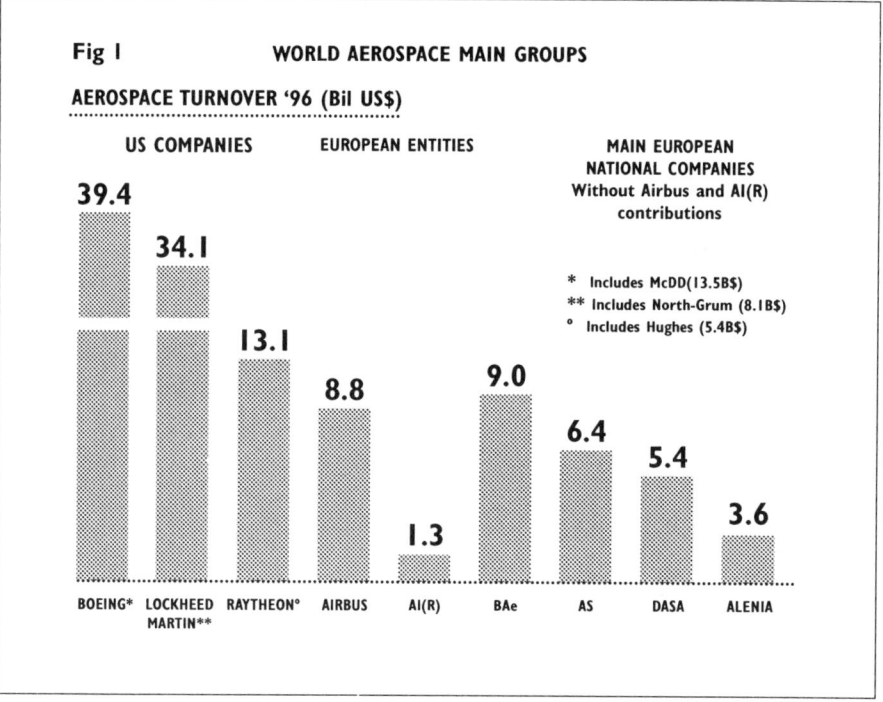

Fig I   WORLD AEROSPACE MAIN GROUPS

AEROSPACE TURNOVER '96 (Bil US$)

Future European military requirements and programmes can facilitate the creation of these trans-national companies by the reorientation and focusing of existing capabilities; in the short term I think it could be fruitful, in the absence of such specific requirements, to establish joint technological programmes in some critical areas in order to monitor technological advances and to form the basis for future consolidated and rationalised trans-national structures. The model should be that of 'technology demonstrator' or 'proof of concept' programmes typically used in the US military sector.

The combat aircraft segment is a priority area, otherwise Americans will be greatly advantaged in the post-2000 period thanks to their activities on the JSF programme, whereas Europeans have not yet planned their activities for a new fighter aircraft. It is fundamental to put in place these trans-national companies as soon as possible because in a few years time the US industry will benefit from its recent consolidation efforts and the competitive environment for European industry will be tougher.

The ownership structure that such an European integrated industry must have is a delicate one.

It is obvious that the shareholder base (and the control) of Europe's defence industry must be distributed throughout Europe; what would be a matter of discussion at several levels (government, industrial, legal, etc.) is the concept of a 'single holding company' controlling a series of focused and specialised units 'multiple holding companies' (two or more entities), each one with more limited interests and activities.

The Role of Alenia Aerospazio

Alenia Aerospazio (ALN), in the context of a thorough rationalisation of the Italian national defence industry, has recently passed through a painful restructuring and improvement process that has improved its industrial performance. The industrial reorganisation has been guided by the concepts of:

- more efficiency;
- leaner structures;
- centres of excellence;
- matrix organisation.

ALN participates in several cooperative programmes both in the civil and military sector.

As is well known, ALN was one of the founders, together with Aérospatiale, of the ATR consortium which is the leader in the regional turboprop aircraft sector with more than 500 sales. In the regional aircraft sector the trend is now to consolidate this strategic alliance in Europe.

As far as the commercial aircraft sector is concerned, recently, in the context of European rationalisation and consolidation, Airbus invited ALN to join the existing partnership and gradually enter the European consortium by participating in future new and derivative programmes. ALN will be involved in the A340-500/-600 derivatives and will be offered the role of full partner (along with AS, BAe, CASA, DASA) in the A3XX programme. Moreover ALN has set up a new European company with Airbus (38% ALN and 62% Airbus) called AIA (Airbus Industrie Asia) to collaborate with Asian manufacturers (AVIC of China and STPE of Singapore) to develop, manufacture and market the A3IX family (a 100-seater). I am very proud of this agreement because we have achieved a remarkable success by winning the competition against Boeing and MDC, and because it may constitute the beginning of a successful relationship.

I really believe that ALN's participation will help Airbus Industrie by means of its proven capabilities in the areas of engineering, manufacturing (Nola's facilities), technological competencies in composites as well as in fuselage structures, and its excellence in the overhaul & modifications business (OAM).

A check point of the progressive implementation of the agreement with Airbus is envisaged by next year.

In addition to its new role within the Airbus framework, ALN is maintaining its existing trans-Atlantic collaborations; in fact the agreement with Airbus Industrie, even if it has a strategic meaning for ALN, does permit us to continue cooperation, as subcontractor, with US manufacturers. Alenia's involvement in Boeing and MDC civil programmes will last therefore for many years, at least for the whole life of actual programmes. I would like to stress that the collaboration as a subcontractor with US companies is significant for us for two main reasons: because it will permit us to compare US companies' technologies and techniques, and because with the activities coming from US programmes it will be possible to exploit, to the greatest possible extent, the scale economies in our manufacturing plants allowing cost reductions and optimised capacity, and therefore manufacturing at competitive costs and with high quality standards. As a result all our partners, not only American but Airbus too, will directly benefit from this model of collaboration.

Also, in the military sector, ALN has a long tradition of cooperation with major players, mostly in Europe:

- Tornado and EF-2000 programmes in the heavy combat aircraft sector;
- AMX (with Aermacchi and Embraer) in the ground attack segment;
- FLA programme in the large military transport aircraft area;
- C-27J (in co-operation with Lockheed Martin) in the medium-lift military transport aircraft market.

Now we are ready to start activities for setting up an integrated European industry in which Alenia Aerospazio, thanks to its consolidated technological and industrial competencies, could play a primary role in several product areas: in light combat/advanced trainer aircraft, in the next European fighter aircraft, in military transport aircraft, and in maintenance, overhaul and modification of military aircraft.

Conclusion

I would like to emphasise the concept that the urgent and necessary consolidation on a continental base does not mean to deny transcontinental cooperation. In other words, the European companies, in their efforts to react to the market forces and environment changes (such as the Boeing-MDC merger), must not pursue a simple 'European strategy', characterised only by links and collaborations within Europe, but that cooperation must be extended as much as possible to other worldwide potential partners.

Nowadays competition is global, players and markets are distributed all over the world, and I am convinced that the best formula for the future integrated European companies is one in which partners and collaborations are searched for where there is more to be gained in the areas of:

- cost reduction;
- technological edge;
- markets access;
- financial resources.

I do not think that the future integrated European companies must be built upon the concept of a 'fortress Europe' against a 'fortress USA', but instead believe Europeans must be open to transatlantic and intercontinental cooperation (with US companies, Asian countries, India, etc.) if some sort of benefits are available. In particular, given the importance of the Asian market and the ambitions of the governments in that region, some form of collaboration with industries in the Far East seems to be logical. In this context, collaboration with US manufacturers in some product areas is welcome when specific business opportunities can be exploited.

I would like to cite as examples of rising trans-Atlantic opportunities:

- the on-going collaboration between Alenia Aerospazio and Lockheed Martin on the C-27J programme, for the joint development, production and marketing of a medium airlifter derived from the G222;
- the European cooperation with US companies on the MEADS anti-ballistic missile programme;

- the UK's participation in the JSF programme in which BAe has joined the Lockheed Martin team.

Following these guiding principles we will have a competitive aerospace industry in Europe in the global environment of today and tomorrow.

3 Europe vs America: Strategic Trade in Civil Aeronautics

PROFESSOR PHILIP LAWRENCE
Director Aerospace Research Group
University of the West of England, Bristol

'Throughout much of its history the American aircraft industry has benefited from a makeshift, but nonetheless effective industrial policy' (Laura D'Andrea Tyson, *Who's Bashing Whom? Trade Conflict in High Technology Industries*, International Institute for International Economics, Washington, 1992, p. 157).

'... unlike automobile manufacturing, which could be sustained by a middle-class consumer economy, aviation was always a super-luxury endeavour that could not thrive without massive government aid.' (Wayne Biddle, *Barons of the Sky*, Henry Holt, New York, 1991, p. 13).

Introduction

This chapter addresses key aspects of the de facto industrial policy of the USA towards its aerospace sector and its implications for the trade in commercial class aircraft. I argue that US trade in aerospace products is the *sine-qua-non* of strategic trade and that the success of this sector results from a powerful and effective industrial policy which subsidizes commercial aerospace manufacturing. In consequence I suggest that the numerous US complaints in the 1980s and 1990s about subsidy and the role of the state in the European commercial aircraft industry are based on a misunderstanding of the real character of the American aerospace industry and arguably the aerospace industry per se.

In my view the liberal characterization of the US economy in the post-war period is exaggerated and overblown. Some sectors, such as consumer electronics, have felt the chill wind of global competition, others

27

have not. Protection has been apparent in agriculture at one extreme and aerospace at the other. Judith Goldstein has outlined three models of trade relations based on an analysis of ideological and institutional factors which determine the prospects for political support. She conceives fair trade and redistributive trade as additional models to the orthodox free trade mantra.[1] But based on a realist perspective I would add a fourth category of strategic trade in products centrally linked to issues of national security. Post-1945 US trade in defense and aerospace has never simply been about commercial factors. Civil aeronautics exports have been closely linked to security issues and on occasion have arisen on the back of defense sales. In terms of assessing which industries are likely to receive aid and protection Goldstein noted how those prone to unemployment and those considered successful and highly competitive were most likely to obtain high level political assistance.[2] Again aerospace fits this categorization. As I shall argue below the more overt mercantilist policy of the Clinton era is related precisely to the competitive challenge mounted by Europe in civil aeronautics in the last 20 years and the high levels of unemployment experienced in the US industry after the end of the Cold War. According to Jens Van Scherpenberg the neo-mercantilist aspects of this process are becoming more pronounced as the constraints on conflict with allies in Europe are loosened. In his view aerospace exports are now at the centre of an executive steered advocacy policy which is seeking the rents and positive externalities due to the state which bankrolled the West's Cold War security policy. As Van Scherpenberg notes, 'Linking military dominance with an aggressive pursuit of economic interests has since become a core element of the US economic policy agenda'.[3]

The Enduring Nature of Mercantilism

Mercantilism is the oldest of the theoretical traditions in political economy.[4] In descriptive terms it arose as a characterization of the economic philosophy and trading practices of the states that arose in Europe after the treaty of Westphalia in 1648. In essence mercantilism amounts to economic nationalism. In the tradition's basic precepts military security and economic self interest are indivisible. Accumulated national wealth is the foundation of a strong state and such wealth is best stored in bullion or precious metals. According to mercantilist theory trading surpluses are the means for national wealth to grow and are best converted to reliable stores of wealth such as gold and silver.

The theoretical dominance of mercantilism was challenged by the classical laissez-faire economics of Adam Smith and the later liberalism of

David Ricardo. Both advocated a drastic reduction in the role of the state in economic affairs and the removal of tariffs, quotas and other restrictive trade practices. Because the modern period in the Anglo-Saxon world is associated with the philosophical dominance of liberalism it is all too easy to believe that the ideas of Smith, Ricardo and other liberals were actually embedded in the dominant social practices of Western states after 1800. But nothing could be further from the truth. After 1815 Britain enacted the Corn Laws to protect its agricultural interests and to secure self sufficiency in food production. In the United States leading federalist politicians such as Hamilton also recommended the mercantilist creed:

> It is well known ... that certain nations grant bounties on the exportation of particular commodities, to enable their workmen to undersell and supplant all competition in the countries to which those commodities are sent. Hence the undertakers of a new manufacture have to contend not only with the natural disadvantages of a new undertaking, but with the gratuities and renumerations which other governments bestow. To be enabled to contend with success, it is evident that the interference and aid of their own government are indispensable. [5]

After the repeal of the Corn Laws and other reforms in the 1840s Britain attempted to liberalize the world trading system in order to benefit its strong industries. But as Stein has persuasively argued this was a matter of degree.[6] Even in the heyday of lower tariffs in the 1860s Britain depended on import duties for 20% of its fiscal revenue.[7] Invariably moves towards or away from free trade policies have always had political causes and cannot be deduced from some inexorable market logic. Bilateral deals on trade have always been linked to discrete and particular political objectives. Stein notes, 'It is important to understand, therefore, that political rather than commercial or philosophical considerations motivated Britain's shift in its commercial practices'.[8]

From Mercantilism to Military Industrial Policy

Another era of trade liberalization was sought after 1945, but again this was a matter of degree. The USA did not unilaterally abandon all its trade protection legislation after the Second World War. In fact GATT enshrined the search for politically motivated bilateral and multilateral deals. The USA had a clear self interest in freer trade because of the strength of its own industries which produced half the world's manufactured goods.[9] But security loomed large in trade calculations. As Balaam and Veseth note, 'In many instances, the United States acted in a mercantilist fashion, when, for example, it used its trade and foreign aid as another weapon in the battle against communism'.[10]

In the post-1945 era in the Anglo Saxon world the philosophy and language of mercantilism has not sat easily with the ideology and rhetoric of liberalism. US global leadership ensured a rhetorical commitment to orthodox economic liberalism as countries seeking US aid were invited to celebrate the benefits of free markets and free trade. However, in Europe this was a socially engaged market liberalism. For the sake of social order Keynesian demand management policies were pursued in order to smooth out the effects of the business cycle and fiscal policy sought to compensate the disadvantaged through the assorted levers of the welfare state. Thus 'embedded liberalism' coupled Adam Smith to the disciples of social democracy. In the United States government direction of economic affairs was not designed to achieve social justice, nevertheless, it existed in the way the federal budget privileged large corporations whose outputs were considered vital to US security. With regard to government policy a strategic vision of economic interest was vital to a rational cold war policy. The main goal of the US government's foreign policy was the blunting of communist influence on the societies of the Western allies and the neutralizing of the general military threat from communist states, especially the USSR. Washington was in essence a military H.Q. As the historian Ernest May remarked, 'The main business of the U.S. government had become the development, maintenance, positioning, exploitation and regulation of military forces'.[11]

As I have indicated above a central contention of this chapter is that since 1945 the United States has had a de facto sectoral industrial policy in the form of a state directed orchestration of high technology production capacities and priorities in industries critical for defense. Pivotal here has been aerospace. Aerospace technology has been the physical backbone of a global policy which extended from the requirement of close tactical air support at one extreme to the capacity to wage inter-continental strategic nuclear warfare at the other. The same aerospace technologies also required and drove the systems integration that was the basis for the global command, control, communication and intelligence - C^3I - functions which provided the critical systems integration for this multi-layered world security system. Even the internet (ARPANET) was conceived by the Defence Advanced Research Projects Agency (DARPA) in response to the post-Sputnik Soviet missile threat in order to secure survivable and robust communications in the event of war. In US Air Force procurement strategy no possibility of falling behind the Soviet adversary was permissible, but such superiority had to be planned. As Hooks observes, '... the airforce could not rely on market forces to maintain the world's largest and most technologically advanced aircraft industry. National security had become equated with industrial policy'.[12]

The Emergence of US Market Dominance

The USA's post-war dependence on air power had been prefigured in World War Two. During the Second World War the US economy boomed on arms manufacture. In 1940 Roosevelt had called for aircraft production goals of 50,000 planes a year.[13] This was easily surpassed. During the War the US produced in excess of 300,000 aircraft and more than 800,000 aero-engines. As a matter of course corporations such as Boeing, Douglas, Martin and Lockheed earned enormous profits.[14] Between 1940 and 1945 the United States spent $185bn on armaments, with a massive $46bn bill for aviation weapons. Biddle notes, 'In order to win the war the United States spawned a weapons industry of titanic scope'.[15] Boeing, which is frequently perceived not to have had a large defence portfolio, developed its main expertise in producing heavy bombers, such as the B17 and B29, the last of which delivered the atomic bombs to their targets in 1945. The B17 Flying Fortress, arguably the most important aircraft in US World War Two air strategy, was launched in the mid-1930s when the US industry was in the doldrums.[16] But the return of big earnings for Boeing began in earnest in 1938 when mass production of the B17 started. By 1940 the US government wanted as many B17s as Boeing could produce. This emphasis on airpower symbolized a sea-change in military affairs; a process had been initiated which would transform the US aircraft industry. In 1939 the industry ranked 41st in output dollar value, in 1944 it was first.[17]

After 1945 the leaders of the US aircraft industry were fearful of cuts in federal expenditure as American military forces were de-mobilized and the economy was reshaped to concentrate on civil production. However, the dawning of the Cold War in 1947 and the Finletter Air Policy Commission of July of the same year soon promised a new era of plenty for the manufacturers. With respect to the Finletter report Biddle notes how '...the aviation industry got more than it could ever have hoped for - in effect, a pronouncement that the manufacturers were so vital to national security that they should be freed from the normal pressures of supply and demand'.[18] But now the resources and research and development required by the industry would be even greater as there were new and more complex technological ingredients in the equation. The arrival of the jet engine required enhanced levels of engineering precision and materials integrity, as well as access to a raft of critical strategic minerals. Jet aircraft could also fly faster and higher placing new demands on the airframe and the need for more complex structures and technologies to protect the crew. Most important of all aircraft would need to be designed according to radically different aerodynamic principles in order to accommodate the jet engine and make maximum use of its potential. Here Boeing were perfectly placed as their research for the Army Airforce's B47 jet bomber had given them access to top secret materials removed by the Americans in 1945 from the German Messerschmitt factory. Fortuitously for Boeing their chief aerodynamicist in the post-war period, George Schairer, had been a member of the special team tasked to obtain the research the Nazi regime had developed on jet powered flight. Thus German research on swept wings and tail-planes fell straight into Boeing's hands. At the same time US acquisition of the research of eminent scientists, such as Werner von Braun, gave America the capacity to develop missile technology and therefore to contemplate the future conquest of space.

The real fillip to the aircraft manufacturers came with the Korean War in 1950. Until then the Truman Administration had struggled to convince key sections of the US Congress that massive increases in defence expenditure were really necessary. But now the picture changed dramatically. In National Security Council document 68 (NSC68) Paul Nitze outlined and dramatized the communist threat and the new role required for US military power. The document had a dramatic effect and, coupled with the outbreak of war, was enough to secure support for Truman's new policy. Indeed, the President remarked that 'economy in defence policy was dead'. These words were apt. In 1950 Pentagon spending on procurement from the US aeronautics industry was $2.6bn, by 1954 it stood at $10.6bn.[19]

I have mentioned the central role of the Cold War in the rise of the post-1945 US aerospace industry in order to give a context to the dominance of the USA in commercial aeronautics. With regard to industrial policy the key is the fact that the huge expense of research and development was largely borne by the state in funding defense programmes. As Mowery and Rosenberg note, '... the history of technical development in commercial aircraft consists largely of the utilization for commercial purposes of technical knowledge developed for military programmes at government expense'.[20]

Today's market leader, Boeing, had already acquired invaluable research on swept wings and podded engines from its B47 contract. Clive Irving, author of a seminal study on the B747, noted its importance: 'no one at Boeing could fail to see the significance of this contract. Whoever built the Army Air Force's first jet bomber would have a commanding foothold in the dawning jet age'.[21] Following on from the B47 contract a string of military orders were secured in the 1950s that cross-subsidized Boeing's commercial aircraft manufacturing and allowed it to benefit from Department of Defence funded R&D for projects such as the B52. The table below indicates the massive scale of Boeing's military order book in the 1950s. A key point to note here is that Boeing's first successful large civil jetliner, the B707, began life as the KC-135 tanker first contracted by the Pentagon in 1955. This fact warrants emphasis as a recent and recurrent perception of Boeing has downplayed its post-1945 military order book.

In total Boeing was contracted to produce 4,422 aircraft by the Pentagon in the 1950s, the period when the foundations of its future global supremacy in commercial manufacture was being laid. In the 1960s the B727, B747 and B737 followed the B707, giving Boeing a family of aircraft with which to achieve global market dominance. In the early 1990s chairman Frank Schrontz acknowledged the benefits that the military contracts had brought, '[A] defense-commercial mix provides long term stability and a testing ground for new technologies lacking immediate commercial application. Financially there have been times when the defense side carried the commercial business'.[22]

Defence contracts help to alleviate conditions in the aircraft industry which make profitability difficult to achieve. The huge development costs of aircraft make a large programme essential if profit is to be realised. Defence sales ease the burden when commercial production has not reached the minimum efficiency of scale (MES) necessary for a particular aircraft's production run. Similarly, contrasting commercial and defence cycles offer potential buffers against market downturns. In addition economies of scope offer development and production savings when military and civil products have essential synergies. These benefits of cross-subsidy in the American industry are neatly summarized by Laura Tyson: All of the nation's commercial aircraft producers have been major defense contractors, at least at critical moments in their development.

Table 1 - Boeing Aircraft Military Orders 1950-1959.

YEAR	AIRCRAFT TYPE	VOLUME
1950	B-47 C-97*	82 14
1951	B-47/RB-47 TB-50 KC-97*	590 24 231
1952	B-47 B-52 KC-97*	788 13 231
1953	B-47 B-52 KC-97*	864 43 262
1954	B-52	25
1955	B-52 KC-135	77 29
1956	B-52 KC-135	133 68
1957	B-52 KC-135	213 118
1958	B-52 KC-135 VC-137 CH-46 Chinook	101 130 3 3
1959	B-52 KC-135 CH-47 Chinook	39 81 5

Source: *United States Navy/Air Force Serials*, ed Peter A. Danby, statistical analysis, Peter Cullen, ARG, UWE, Bristol.

The enormous flow of federal government contracts has provided profits (and even in some cases covered tooling costs) that could be applied to the development of commercial aircraft'.[23]

The problem of minimum efficiency of scale also puts a premium on export sales of aircraft. Even in the US, which has the largest domestic market, export sales are vital to maintaining the size of production run necessary for profitability. The politically significant issue of employment levels is also highly export sensitive. In a study undertaken in the late 1980s Lopez and Yager concluded that: 'at least 25,000 aerospace jobs are related to each billion dollars of exports including both aerospace employees and employees in areas that support aerospace'.[24]

The wider value of aerospace exports is also underlined when one examines the contribution of the industry to the overall health of the US economy. In the post-1945 period aerospace emerged as the key success story in US international trade. As Vicki Golich notes, 'Since the late 1950s aerospace has been the leading industrial contributor to U.S. export earnings. Since 1982, aerospace exports have increased at a rate of $1bn a year'.[25] Thus a product which is essentially 'strategic', because of its links to issues of national security and its dependence on high technology, is also one which is 'strategic' to US export success. Further, as many observers have noted, the global presence of US manufactured jet aircraft has been a compelling symbol of US power projection. To reiterate my earlier claim, trade in jet aircraft is the *sine-qua-non* of strategic trade. For the US this trade has been essential, as its oligopolistic advantages in aerospace allowed it to offset its growing trading weakness in other commodities, such as automobiles and consumer electronics.

A vital aspect of American success in trading aerospace products has been the US's role as a provider of security to friendly countries. As Anthony Sampson comments, 'the Pentagon has been relentless in making the connection between the commercial and diplomatic choices'.[26] With European industry shattered after the war and the Germans legally prevented from producing armaments, US dominance in NATO was an ideal springboard from which to secure overseas sales of military aircraft to friendly countries. With regard to aeronautics the Germans had been Europe's largest exporter of aviation products before the war and had led the world in wing design, jet propulsion and missile technology in the late 1930s. As we have already seen at the end of the Second World War most of the research upon which this was based fell into US hands.[27] In the late 1940s and through the 1950s Britain and France attempted to build an aerospace industry to match that of the USA, but with defence comprising 70% of the market it was difficult to compete with the large corporations funded by the Pentagon. On the commercial side Great Britain had an excellent opportunity with the de Havilland Comet, the world's first civil jet-liner, but a flaw in the design of the fuselage and the previously unknown phenomenon of metal fatigue caused a number of fatal crashes, which led to the plane being withdrawn from service. The potential of Britain's lead in jet propulsion was thrown away because inadvertently an inadequate design was put into production. For France the Korean War opened up possibilities for the newly restored industry and Dassault produced a number of fighter aircraft. But for the European industry the writing was on the wall; the domestic markets in Europe could not support a large industry on anything like the scale of the USA.

We have seen above the inventory of Boeing's military orders in the 1950s. In 1955 its civil supremacy was prefigured when Pan Am placed an order for the B707, the civil version of the KC135. This vindicated the company's decision to design an aircraft which had dual-use potential. In essence Boeing had ingeniously found a way for the Department of Defense to cover the cost of developing its civil jet through Independent Research and Development funds. Not surprisingly, as the years passed and the commercial market increased, as the public became used to the new form of transport, US manufacturers held sway, with Boeing and Douglas establishing the dominant positions. US airlines were also highly nationalistic in their purchasing policies. According to Golich, 'U.S. airlines were likely to consider foreign aircraft only if no domestically built alternative existed'.[28] But in reality airlines had virtually no alternative to US products. By the early 1960s, in the biggest market, the USA itself, US airlines were operating 2,136 aircraft and of these 2,076 were American manufactured. The USA established global hegemony by first dominating its large home market. [29]

The European Response to American Market Dominance

After the Second World War all the West European countries faced considerable obstacles in seeking to rebuild their aerospace industries. By the mid-1960s it was clear that these obstacles had not been overcome. Individual European nations lacked the resources to compete with the giant US aerospace corporations, whose order books had been swelled by the Cold War. On the commercial side the only rational response was for Europe's major aerospace nations to collaborate in partnership. After the mixed experience of the Concorde supersonic programme this move to collaboration bore fruit with the birth of Airbus Industrie in the late 1960s.[30] But national tensions and differences were not easily put aside and the rise of Airbus was not without its mishaps and conflicts. At the start of the Airbus initiative the British had negotiated a 37.5% work share, but the Wilson government pulled out of the project to build the A300, leaving British participation to Hawker Siddeley Aviation, who committed $30m towards the development of the A300 wing.[31] Fortunately for Hawker Siddeley, the German government, who were keen to have Britain on board, agreed to extend financial assistance to HSA and the project to produce the A300B moved towards completion in the early 1970s, with a roll out ceremony in Toulouse in September 1972.

It is worth pausing to consider Britain's lukewarm response to Airbus. Not only were the West Europeans inconvenienced by UK government ambivalence to the project, they were also frustrated by Rolls-Royce's attempt to provide engines simultaneously for the Lockheed L1011 as well as the A300. Having originally insisted on a 75% share of the Airbus engine, work at the Rolls-Royce Derby plant soon prioritized the US destined engine. In essence the UK appeared to be attempting to ensure that Airbus was stillborn. In the USA a unified state was fully supportive of its aerospace companies. But in Europe strategy was fragmented, as Britain continued its game of facing simultaneously across the Channel and the Atlantic. Compared to France, where the political elite had a coherent and integrated framework for industrial policy and a matching foreign policy, Britain had neither. Airbus did emerge and prosper, but in the early days this was despite rather than because of any British contribution. Not surprisingly dominance on the first Airbus project went to the French, '... consistent French support for and commitment to a truly European response to the American challenge in civil aerospace was translated into project leadership on the A300B'.[32] As a result Toulouse became the emotional as well as the physical home of the European aircraft industry.

The A300B was certificated in March 1974, a time that was extremely difficult for aviation as a whole. After the OPEC oil crisis of October 1973, which quadrupled the price of oil, the West plunged into recession and the era of stagflation began. From 1975 on it was clear that Airbus would have an enormous fight on its hands to establish a market. The A300B was a new concept, a wide bodied twin-engined aircraft for short to medium haul. It was a concept airlines liked, but the market was flat. Between 1975 and 1977 promotional world tours helped to sell just two aircraft. Then in 1977 Eastern Airlines agreed a deal to lease 23 A300s and a further 25 of the new projected A310. A real market battle had begun.

The EU/US Subsidy Dispute

In order to meet the huge costs of aircraft development the Airbus partner companies agreed loans with their governments known as launch aid. Such aid was a strategic commitment by the Airbus governments to the new collaborative venture. In the future these loans were to become highly contentious elements in the conflict which materialized between the EU and USA over allegations of unfair competition. But one thing needs to be crystal clear; without launch aid the consortium would not have had a chance to successfully enter the marketplace. As Laura Tyson notes, 'Given the industry's economics, Airbus would not have stood a chance against American producers without massive development, production and marketing support during it first 25 years'. [33]

The strategic nature of trade and manufacture in commercial aircraft was evident in the late 1970s when Airbus was aiming to develop its second product, the A310. Concurrently, the British government were seeking to merge the UK's two largest aerospace companies, BAC and HSA. They were also reconsidering the decision to remain outside the Airbus consortium. As the newly created British national champion emerged - British Aerospace - it was clear that its participation in Airbus would be welcomed in Europe. It was also clear that the new aircraft would require a different wing to the A300B, which British expertise could provide. Across the Atlantic Boeing saw a tactical opportunity. Now sensitized to the potential of Airbus, after the sale to Eastern Airlines, Boeing moved to recruit BAe as a major subcontractor on its rival to the A310, the B757. Boeing's aim was to '... prevent the return of the British to Airbus and draw in the British airframer and engine builder in constructing the B757'.[34] In general this was a non too subtle move to tie up British engineering expertise and capital and keep the UK estranged from Airbus. But the tactic failed and British Aerospace joined the Airbus consortium on the A310 project with a 20% workshare. [35]

The incident described above, which involved contacts at Head of State level, emphasizes and illustrates the high level strategic competition in the sphere of aircraft trade and manufacture. But this was just a foretaste of what would become an intense and acrimonious rivalry. In the late 1970s Airbus' orders for its new aircraft signalled the start of a global sales competition with Boeing and MDC which became increasingly bitter. By 1979/80 Airbus was taking a 20% share of the market for large commercial aircraft and had pushed one US company out of the civil business. The USA was now acutely aware that it had a serious competitor from Europe. Airbus also showed that it could outgun the Americans in the area of technical innovation. On the A300B the technology was not particularly innovative, but the overall concept was. On the A310, though, Airbus pioneered significant technical innovations, such as the forward-facing cockpit crew, wing-tip fences and a rear fuel tank in the horizontal tail plane in order that fuel could be moved to reconfigure the aircraft's centre of gravity, allowing improved trim and fuel consumption. In Seattle and Long Beach some of these innovations were met with scepticism, but they are now industry standards, as is Airbus' innovative vertical acceleration instrumentation.[36]

With a furious sales battle going on in sectors such as the Middle East the US industry chiefs began to take their concerns about Airbus to the federal government. On the US side a concerted effort was made to prevent the development of Airbus' third product, the narrow bodied, twin engined A320. The politics of this bear consideration.

In order to develop the A320 Airbus began looking for finance and potential customers in new environments. One approach was made to the Canadians through the government of the province of Quebec as Airbus were hoping to secure Canadian industrial participation.[37] But although not public knowledge the US authorities had been shadowing Airbus activity for some time. When the Canadian initiative came to light the United States Trade Representative in Canada, William E. Brock, sent a letter to the Canadian Minister of Industry, Trade and Commerce. The letter had a tone that was clearly threatening, 'Any implied or actual commitment on the part of Canada to purchase Airbus products or encourage their purchase, as an adjunct to industrial participation, would be a major concern to the United States Government'.[38] Ironically, USTR Brock justified his intervention on the grounds that Airbus Industrie was using government to government politics to secure project funding and sales. Clearly, using the same methods to block a project launch was seen in a different light.

As the decade wore on the US side increased the pressure on Europe through the lobbying of its USTRs and other diplomatic channels. But it became clear that the A320 would go ahead and American anxiety grew. In the market place blocking tactics failed as the DC9 derivative, the MD80 series, and Boeing's B737-300 failed to blunt the attraction of the new Airbus. After its launch in 1987 the A320 became the fastest selling commercial aircraft in history. In the US Boeing executives wanted a Cabinet task force to monitor Airbus and to co-ordinate export support in the United States. At the roll out of the 767-300 in Seattle in 1985, Boeing's Tom Bacher asserted that the company was, '... getting pretty damn mad'.[39] He then went on to give Airbus some friendly advice regarding an alternative area of comparative advantage for the Europeans, 'You build good train systems and things like that in Europe and we do not'.[40]

This comment of Bacher's may be a clue to the bitterness that has been widely expressed in the US concerning Airbus. When the consortium started manufacturing aircraft no one across the Atlantic was taking it that seriously. But as it began to eat into US market share, a sense of unease was apparent and a feeling was occasionally manifested that predominance in aeronautics was almost an American right. In consequence the assumption has been that Airbus' success must, by definition, represent some form of sharp or dubious practice. Thus, as the industry dragged government into the dispute, a certain ideological zeal was evident.

As the tension grew in the mid-1980s USTRs began to lobby European ministers directly on the Airbus issue. Moreover, as McIntyre asserts, the American side began to believe they were making some progress with their continuing call for the industry in Europe to be run on stricter commercial lines.[41] In order to increase the pressure in 1987 the US called for ministerial talks, with the target now the blocking of the launch of the A330/340. The US position was clear and hard-line, '... the US government was not going to stand idly by and accept the unfettered subsidisation of Airbus, particularly when that unfettered subsidisation was leading to displacement of U.S. exports by the number one export manufacturing industry in the United States'.[42] The tough line was echoed by Boeing, which began to crystallize its critique of Airbus's defects. In essence the US side began a process to try and undermine the consortium's credibility as a commercial organization and viable business. Using the assumptions of market economics and the legal framework of GATT the US policy was aimed to delegitimate Airbus through accusations such as the following: 'These subsidies lead to launch of new programmes without viability, incorporation of technologies that cannot pay for themselves, building of whitetails that are offered at fire-sale prices and widespread underpricing to gain market share'.[43]

To some degree these comments are understandable. In the 1970s, when the A300B came onto the market, new aircraft were stacking up on the tarmac and customers were in short supply. Further, no one in Europe was denying the role of state aid in Airbus's product development. But on the US side there was a continuing blindness to the role that defence procurement and publicly funded R&D played in the success of the American companies. Also by the 1980s the stereotypical American view of Airbus was outmoded. Airlines, including US ones, were buying the product because it met their requirements. Moreover, the European consortium's investment in high technology was reaping dividends in the growing perception in the marketplace that Airbus had some competitive advantages. Thus in the early 1990s it is not surprising that Laura Tyson noted how Airbus had 'achieved technological parity with Boeing...'. [44]

The Battle of the Reports and the 1992 Agreement

As we have seen US accusations of unwarranted subsidy were taken around European capitals in the late 1980s in an attempt to blunt the A330/340 programme. Ultimately though the issue was to end up under the jurisdiction of the GATT Subsidies Committee.

An issue which had long troubled the European side was that aircraft were traded in dollars. Thus the European manufacturer faced a form of double jeopardy. On the one hand dollar depreciation meant that the revenue from sales was deflated, on the other dollar appreciation meant larger real payments to the extensive network of American sub-contractors used by Airbus. In this context it needs to be borne in mind that an Airbus aircraft can have up to a 30% US work share. In this situation what the Europeans wanted was dollar stability. In response to this Deutsche Airbus agreed a deal with the German government in 1988 which would give them protection from dollar fluctuation. This FOREX deal was worth DM2.6bn. From the US point of view this was the straw that broke the camel's back. The issue was taken to GATT.

Prior to this the US Department of Commerce had commissioned a report into Airbus' funding by Gellman Research Associates, of Jenkintown Pennsylvania. The report, issued in September 1990, was a damning indictment of Airbus' financial arrangements. The brief had been to, 'deepen the understanding of the complex web of relations between the participating companies, the governments and the AI consortium'.[45] However, as Thornton points out, the report was in reality much narrower and dealt exclusively with the question of Airbus' credentials as a commercial organization. [46]

Using 1990 dollar values the Gellman Report claimed that Airbus had been the recipient of more than $13bn of government support since its inception in the late 1960s and that the real commercial market value of this subsidy was $26bn. The report's conclusions were highly critical and indicated that Airbus had distorted the US industry because of its state subsidy and ability to pursue ventures without regard to commercial criteria. In a wider context this pattern of thinking then became reinforced as scores of economists jumped on the anti-Airbus bandwagon. US textbooks on International Economics frequently cited Airbus as a clear example of the damaging effects of industrial policy and strategic trade.[47]

The US position was also bolstered in early 1992 when the GATT Subsidies Committee found in favour of the US on the issue of German FOREX compensation.

Airbus Industrie did not take this assault lightly. In response to Gellman the Toulouse consortium commissioned a report by Washington based lawyers Arnold and Porter on government support of the US commercial aerospace industry. Arnold and Porter identified three categories of assistance, DoD, NASA and benefits accruing from the US tax code. In the previous 15 years they estimated combined supports worth between \$33.48 and \$41.49bn in current dollars.[48] But more important than the specific identification of discrete elements of support was the overall and indisputable fact established by Arnold and Porter that the US industry was not a stand alone entity divorced from government policy and political supports. The Arnold and Porter study showed clearly that the US industry was embedded in an infrastructure for research and development, financing and commercial manufacturing assistance funded by the federal government, which greatly enhanced the competitiveness of American aerospace firms. As I have indicated above a key problem with this area of debate has been the presence of an 'idee fixe' in the US about the liberal nature of its economy. Hence the conviction that there was no corporate welfare, no industrial policy and no support for strategic trade in aerospace products. Since the Arnold and Porter report this misconception, at least, has been less easy to sustain.

In the early 1990s there seemed every chance of a trade war between the USA and EU in commercial aeronautics. In the end, though, this was obviated by the 1992 Bilateral Agreement on the funding of Future Large Civil Aircraft. In article four of the agreement the EU accepted a cap of 33% on government funding for development of future aircraft, with loans repayable over a maximum of 17 years. Conversely, article five put limits on indirect support in the USA. For the industry as a whole this was limited to 3% of turnover, while for specific firms a maximum of 4% was stipulated.

Renewed Hostility

The 1992 Agreement did not end the tensions over EU/USA trade in commercial class aircraft. Global recession and the end of the Cold War meant job losses and painful rationalization in the EU and USA. On the back of this the Clinton Administration chose to reopen hostilities with a series of public statements about Airbus. After the July 1992 Bilateral Agreement, USTR Mickey Cantor referred to the EU side as 'screaming pigs stuck in a gate'.[49] At the Everett Boeing plant in 1993 the President promised enhanced support for Boeing and blamed Airbus for US job losses. What was clear was that the new Democratic administration was going to pursue a more overt industrial policy, with strategies to bolster US high technology industries and a new brief for NASA to give its research more commercial relevance.

With regard to trade policy the Clinton era has seen more pronounced state involvement in export advocacy and more unilateral interventions in global trade issues, such as the threat to impose penalties on firms trading with Cuba.[50] Through the aegis of the Trade Promotion Co-ordinating Committee (TPCC), the Departments of Commerce, Defense and State have been orchestrating a more overt neo-mercantilist policy to use executive level state inputs in a global strategy to enhance export sales in high technology sectors.[51] The late Secretary of Commerce, Ron Brown, was tragically killed in the former Yugoslavia while on just such a mission to secure US export sales.

Another example of increased sales advocacy was the 1993 Boeing Saudi deal, which involved Presidential contacts with King Faud and other Saudi authorities and was announced to the world's media on the steps of the White House. This move should not engender surprise. President Clinton had been elected on a ticket to secure American jobs and improve living standards. His mercantilist instincts were also reinforced by his advisers. As Lynn notes, 'Around him were theorists and advisers who believed that it was time to start turning the military and political might of the United States into harder coinage: money, trade, jobs'.[52] According to some commentators political involvement may even have gone further. Press reports asserted that agents of the National Security Agency bugged the Airbus sales team at the time of the Saudi deal.[53] Strategic trade now almost certainly includes industrial espionage.

In Search of New Rules

As I have shown an early problem with many of these issues in commercial aircraft trade was a reluctance on the US side to see any government funded contribution to the performance of American aerospace companies, because of a blanket assumption that the USA did not operate industrial policies. However, the trade discussions of the last decade and the proliferation of reports into government funding and supports have now created a dialogue where at least certain parameters should be known. The 1992 Bilateral Agreement formalized an acknowledgement that indirect support did exist in the US system. Nevertheless, the EU side is posed with a serious difficulty. The real value of indirect support to US manufacturers is inherently contestable in terms of the precise contribution to the commercial viability and competitiveness of products that reach the market place.

Despite the July 1992 agreement members of the US administration continue to deny the contribution made by publicly funded R&D to the commercial aircraft industry. Moreover, the calculation of the worth of DoD and NASA programmes which benefit US firms is also difficult because some figures are hidden in black, secret programmes which are classified. For this reason policing adherence to the 1992 agreement on the US side is problematic. Because of the methodological problems in studies of indirect support in the US, reports often specify an enormous range between minimum and maximum figures.[54] In terms of establishing whether indirect supports are a given percentage of turnover of the US industry the EU faces a daunting task. In 1997 the EU Trade Commissioner, Sir Leon Brittan, sought to reopen the 1992 agreement. But not surprisingly the US side were not interested.

A Qualitative Analysis

This chapter has sought to propound two key propositions. First, that the US aerospace industry is the beneficiary of a huge supportive infrastructure which underwrites key elements of the manufacturers' competitiveness via NASA and DoD programmes. In my lexicon this comprises an informal or unrecognised (covert) industrial policy. Secondly, I believe that in the 1990s we can identify a policy orientation which can be meaningfully characterized as the new mercantilism. If traditional mercantilism meant general economic nationalism, the new mercantilism is more sectorally specific and relies heavily on trade policy as a surrogate for overt industrial policy. The new mercantilism reflects a new conjuncture where the structural and ideological conditions have materialized to encourage more overt executive support for high technology/export sensitive industries; classically aerospace. In essence the new mercantilism results from two key phenomena. First, the recognition in the United States that its preeminence in commercial aeronautics is under serious challenge and secondly, the realization that American security now depends on the strength of key commercial technologies.

Bearing in mind the arguments above the search for a viable model of how to quantify the extent and role of government support for the US aerospace industry must continue and will be a necessary precondition for trade agreements which are fair and can be policed. But in the meantime it is also essential to establish a qualitative interpretation of the structural characteristics of the US industry. This can be done by exploring the following areas:

- the historical development of the US commercial aircraft industry;
- the role of military procurement and R&D in the commercial success of the civil aircraft manufacturers;
- the use of trade policy as surrogate industrial policy in certain sectors of the post-war US economy;
- specific publicly funded projects and initiatives, where the value-added benefits to commercial aircraft manufacturers are incontrovertible;
- the contribution of executive level support for export sales of commercial aircraft.

In particular it needs to be recognized that publicly funded research and development reduces the technological and financial risk associated with the launch of new programmes. As I have indicated above one should also note a pronounced shift in recent years to a more overt industrial policy.

Seeds of the New Mercantilism

The US civil aeronautics industry is one of the jewels in the American industrial crown. As Mowery and Rosenberg comment, 'Judged against almost any criterion of performance - growth in outputs, exports, productivity or innovation - the civilian aircraft industry must be considered a star performer in the [post-war] US economy'.[55] In addition it is the largest exporter and a symbol of national prestige, which resonates with America's optimism about the role of technology in society. The belief that there has not been a national strategy to protect and foster this industry is vacuous. The only period when the US industry was left to the vicissitudes of market forces was in the early 1920s when it nearly disappeared. In the late 1920s and through the 1930s air travel was subsidized in order to provide a market for larger and more comfortable passenger aircraft and to secure a national mail service.[56] In 1938 the Civil Aeronautics Authority was created within the Department of Commerce to provide, 'direct subsidies to promote passenger travel, economic regulation of the airlines, air traffic control, and safety'.[57] During the war, as we have seen, a massive industry was spawned and civil designs, such as the Lockheed Constellation, Lockheed Electra and Douglas DC6 were prefigured in military forerunners. At the same time Boeing developed the skill base for manufacturing large military aircraft which had dual-use potential, such as the B-29 which formed the basis for the B-377 Stratocruiser. In 1954 Pentagon orders for the KC-135 allowed Boeing to utilize the benefits of its prior work on swept wings and podded engines (engines hung on pylons; not directly on the wings) on the B-47 and B-52 bombers. From its inception the KC-135 was conceived as a dual-use tanker and civil jetliner project.

Although the KC-135 story is 'old hat', it bears some rehearsal. A key advantage for the US manufacturers has been the synergies that exist between defence and civil aerospace technologies. As Eberstadt notes:

> The single greatest means by which U.S. government policy has affected the competitiveness of the commercial aircraft industry is in the procurement of military aircraft and funding of the related R&D... In some cases whole systems developed for the military have been 'spun off' to commercial applications, reducing development costs and risks to the commercial users.[58]

The KC-135/B707 linkage was a clear example of this defence/commercial synergy. Production of the two aircraft shared the same plant and 20% of the parts and tooling.[59] Both aircraft were derived from a common prototype and had concurrent development programmes. Regarding the prototype it must be remembered that the B707 was a revolutionary aircraft and that the military funded project helped Boeing iron out potential technological glitches. As Rodgers observes, 'any bugs in the basic design found in shaking out the tanker during its early days in service would be worked out at government expense'.[60] In addition common production runs increased the speed with which progress was made down the learning curve and hastened the arrival of economies of scale.[61] The learning curve is critical in aircraft manufacturing as learning elasticity is estimated at .2, i.e. production costs reduce by 20% with a doubling of output. Regarding the B707 the simultaneity of the commercial and defence programmes significantly reduced the financial risk of the aircraft's launch, with Boeing ultimately selling 820 KC-135s to USAF. To this day many Boeing officials deny the significance of the dual development, but in an authoritative study of the Boeing Aircraft Corporation by analyst M. J. Hardy we find the following:

> Without the huge KC-135A programme there would almost certainly have been no Model 707, as its unit costs would have

been too high, especially without the benefits of using some KC-135 jigs and tooling... and it was not until 1963, when just over 1000 of the 707, 720, and KC-135/C-135 series had been sold, that Boeing finally passed the break-even point on its jet transport programme.[62]

This is an old tale, but by retelling it one can balance the accusations against Airbus which point to the large infusions of state aid that helped the consortium survive in its early days. The point about the B707 is that it was the commercial product which helped initiate Boeing's dominance of the world market. Arguably Boeing's most critical and daring decision was to proceed with the development of the enormously successful B747. But even this product, Boeing's commercial trade mark, was originally conceived as a large military cargo aircraft. Development began in response to an Air Force procurement proposal. Although ultimately the contract went to Lockheed for the C-5A, the Boeing design teams working on the new heavy-lift wide-body jet gained the valuable experience that was necessary for producing a civil version.[63] Clearly, another advantage of the defence/commercial mix is the creation of expertise that can be used on both sides of the divide. Even if military orders are cancelled or slimmed down, engineers will have been trained who can be transferred to commercial projects.

Fortuitously for American manufacturers downturns in commercial orders, such as at the beginning of the 1980s, have frequently coincided with upturns on the military side. In short Pentagon contracts give the US market stability and help to subsidize commercial production, either when times are hard on the civil side or early in production runs when development costs have not yet been amortized. This point has been acknowledged by Boeing executives regarding the recent acquisition of McDonnell Douglas, which will increase the defence turnover of the company to approximately $14bn. But contrary to some perceptions this situation is not new. According to leading aerospace analyst Wolfgang Demisch, this process sustained Boeing through its loss making first 20 years of jet aircraft manufacture.[64]

In recent times Boeing executives have repeatedly claimed the spin-off synergies between defence and commercial products have reduced. Indeed, Boeing vice-president Ronald B. Woodard, asserted in 1996 that there are none.[65] He also posed the question that if defence helps the commercial side then why have Lockheed and MDC failed on their civil programmes? But this is a fatuous argument. The underwriting of the industry by the Pentagon did not guarantee which US manufacturer would come out on top in commercial aircraft manufacture. Moreover, the vast increase in aircraft development costs in the last three decades indicated market exit for at least one player, as the production run necessary for profitability approached 600 units.[66] As Tyson explains in the late 1960s all three major manufacturers were seeking a successful, new high capacity wide-bodied jet.[67] Ultimately only one was to succeed in commercial terms. But why was it possible for three firms to compete to over-supply the market place? 'Neither Lockheed nor McDonnell Douglas could have survived, let alone dared to undertake head-on competition in their wide-body designs without their military operations.'[68] It was precisely the largesse accruing to Lockheed and Douglas from the Pentagon that allowed them to engage in a costly head to head competition in the same market segment, where there was no chance of commercial viability. Ironically, this is precisely the argument that Boeing used in the 1980s against Airbus's move to launch the A320 and A330/340. The difference was that Airbus had correctly gauged the market's requirements.

Returning to the case of the 1970s' wide body competition Lockheed's L1011 launch was delayed because the development of the engines for the L1011 fell foul of Rolls-Royce's bankruptcy. Meanwhile, the American company's own bankruptcy was only averted in 1971 by a federal loan guarantee of $250mn. Concurrently, MDC's DC10 suffered a number of catastrophic accidents and arguably was an aircraft which the FAA should never have certificated, due to faults in the locking system of the cargo doors and the vulnerability of all three hydraulic control systems to buckling of the cabin floor because of depressurization. In other words the B747 came out on top in the US because of errors made by Boeing's competitors, not because Boeing was less involved in defence work. Boeing courageously pursued a new and radical concept which itself restructured the market by offering genuine mass air transportation and gave the company a monopoly product. But regarding Mr Woodard's recent comments many in Europe wonder why the acquisition of MDC is a good idea if defence provides no spin-off? Former MDC executives could certainly have provided an answer. At the end of the life of the DC10 the company was helped through to the launch of the MD11 by orders for the military version of the tri-jet, the KC-10 tanker. Although, in the interim, it has become clear that the MD11 has also not succeeded commercially, perhaps because it has failed to meet its predicted performance parameters for range and payload. If Boeing continues the MD11 line it will be as a cargo aircraft.

The Fruits of Consolidation and Public Support

Turning to the present day the US aerospace industry is highly integrated and consolidated with economies of scale and scope being attained. In the 1990s in excess of $100bn of merger activity has created three giant aerospace conglomerates with Boeing at the apex.[69] This consolidation reveals mercantilist motives and has not resulted from market forces. As Dowdy notes, 'This rapid consolidation of the American ... industry can be partially attributed to conscious policy decisions of the Department of Defense'. [70] The same point is made in a US General Accounting Office document: 'DoD has encouraged the defense industry to consolidate and eliminate excess capacity to remain competitive and financially viable'.[71] Included in the planning was a DoD incentive to create mergers by reimbursing a portion of the cost. In consequence, Secretary of Defense Les Aspin's instruction in 1993 for the major players to consolidate (the so called 'Last Supper') has resulted in an unprecedented degree of integration with the three major corporations now having combined turnover approaching £110bn. These corporations dwarf their European equivalents, (See Table 2 below).

In the commercial market the major consequence of the American consolidation is that the largest manufacturer (Boeing) now has an enormous defence business portfolio. But as we have seen Boeing itself claims that defence/commercial synergies have declined. However, this can be contested. Oliver Sutton notes, 'Boeing's ... merger with McDonnell Douglas will further facilitate access to dual use technology R&D, largely funded by the US defence department and NASA'. [72] This should come as no surprise. In its role as a sub-contractor for the B2 Boeing developed new machinery for the manufacture and testing of composites which were used for the B777. Some of the funding for this came from the MANTECH programme (now the Defense Manufacturing Science and Technology Programme). Previous MANTECH projects assisted in fuselage and wing development for MDC and Boeing. Additional funds are also available through the Pentagon's Independent R&D Recovery Programme, which allows non-product specific research to be partly recouped through contractors making an additional overhead on military orders.[73]

Table 2 - Total Turnover of US Companies vs European Companies

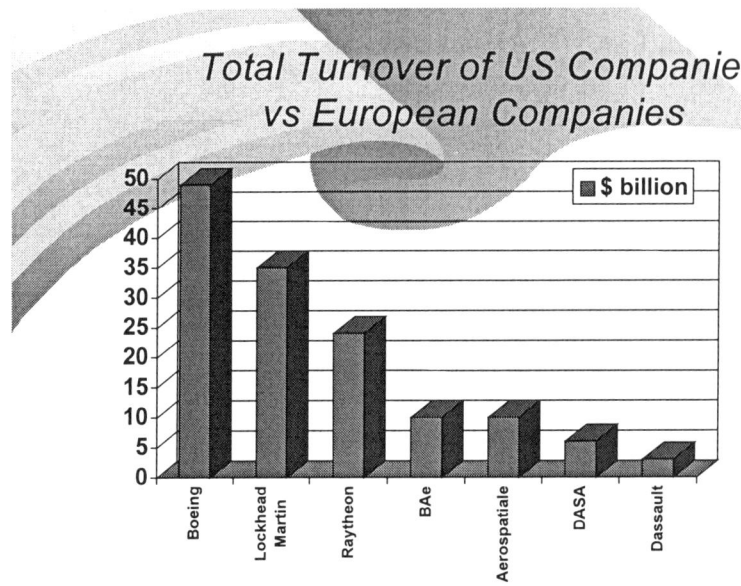

Source: *Aerospace International,* (February, 1998, p. 14).

In seeking to emphasize the role that military funded programmes have played in the development of US civilian industry one encounters another prejudice which militates against a serious analysis of American high technology industries. The doctrines of laissez faire economics have generally downplayed the significance of the military in the US economy. However, I support the following contention of David Noble:

> I would like to suggest that this conventional view of the role of the military in technological development is problematic on both counts. First, because the military role has not been the "externality" that it appears to be when viewed through the lens of the neo-classical economist. Rather it has been central to industrial development in the United States since the dawn of the industrial revolution.... Second, the influence of the military on technologies is not temporary, something removed when the technologies enter the civilian economy. The influence spills over in the specific shape of the

technologies themselves and in the way they are put together and used.[74]

As Noble argues in order to understand the nature of DoD industrial policy it is essential to see the role that the US military has played in driving and proving new technologies. However, in the 1990s this has been given a new twist. The competitive trade threat posed to the EU by Boeing's new defence arm is underscored by the US government's heavy investment in a new Dual-Use Programme. In order to get better value for money from its huge procurement budget the Pentagon has encouraged its contractors to seek cheaper commercial technologies to input into military systems and, as we have seen, the defence and civil sectors have been encouraged to merge together. In some circles this has led to the false assertion that commercial/defence spin-on means that the civil side is now subsidizing defence. But this misses the point of the Dual-Use Programme. The dual-use philosophy recognizes that the technological superiority of the US military will now depend on the strength of American civilian high technology industries. Thus, instead of a defence R&D spin-off, which produced a makeshift industrial policy in the aerospace sector, the commercial industry will now be supported more directly in order that the Pentagon can leverage the critical technologies for defence. A key element in the new Dual-Use programme was the Technology Reinvestment Project (TRP), which by 1995 had awarded $800mn to firms seeking DoD funds for dual-use applications.[75] Government statements make transparent the benefits that will accrue to the civil sector: 'As an additional benefit, a dual-use strategy will allow DoD's continuing investments in technology to contribute more to our nations commercial performance and economic growth'.[76] Thus industrial strength and military might are now linked together more tightly than ever. With regard to the commercial aircraft industry a key TRP project was the Advanced Composites for Propulsion Programme (ACP). Aiming to reduce the production costs of composites by 30% the programme secured $130mn public funding and was geared to improving commercial competitiveness.[77] Another TRP project which illustrates the benefits of the Dual-Use Programme for the commercial industry was the Fly-by-Light Advanced System Hardware project (FLASH).

The main contractor on FLASH was McDonnell Douglas and the programme enabled MDC to accelerate its development of fly-by-light avionics for defence and commercial use. FLASH, which took a significant share of the 1993 TRP budget of $464mn, will assist in competitiveness by lowering aircraft weight and reducing the overall amount of electrical wiring.[78]

In 1996 TRP was replaced by the Defence Dual-Use Technology Initiative (DDUTI) which funded TRP projects begun before October 1995. In tandem with the successor to MANTECH (the Defense Manufacturing Science and Technology Programme) these programmes have put substantial funds into projects aimed to increase the competitiveness of the US aircraft industry. Overall the DoD was appropriated $1.965bn for Dual-Use in FY1996. The successor to MANTECH (DMSTP) was allocated $185mn.[79] The following programmes are supported by DoD funding:

- Design and Manufacture of Low Cost Composites Wing and Fuselage Initiatives;
- Manufacturing Technology for Welded Titanium Aircraft Structures;
- Active Matrix Liquid Crystal Displays (these offer superior visibility for flightdeck crews when instrumentation is viewed in sunlight. They are also smaller, lighter and use less power);
- Metal Forming Simulation to improve product quality and reliability;
- Large Aircraft Robotic Paint Stripping;
- National Flat Panel Display Initiative.

As we have seen the Department of Defense funds a large number of research and development programmes. While some have military only applications, other have direct relevance for the commercial aircraft industry in areas such as manufacturing technology, avionics and airframe development programmes. However, the stated policy is to bring the two closer together. A US National Science and Technology Council paper on aeronautics illustrates the point perfectly:

> The significant basic technological commonality between military and civil aviation products and services must be exploited to increase the productivity and efficiency of our R&T development activities. This requires government and industry, working together, to actively seek technological goals that are common to both civil and military applications... [80]

The Role of NASA

In the section above I have given an overview of some of the supports available to the civil aircraft industry from the DoD, as well as indicate the broad policy implications of the Dual-Use initiative. The second major locus of institutional support for the large commercial aircraft industry is the National Aeronautics and Space Administration (NASA). In focusing on NASA we should remember that its official aim is to promote the supremacy of the US commercial aeronautics industry. Moreover, during the Clinton administration NASA's Aeronautical Research and Technology Programme has had a central role in the new Presidential policy for the promotion of advanced technology. The new focus on NASA was made clear in 1994 by US Transportation Secretary, Frederico Pena:

> While eschewing any return to regulation, we have defined a new role for government as an active player in aviation. One example of this philosophy in the Administration's initiative is the proposal to increase NASA's budget by 18%, so that the agency can *subsidize* [my emphasis] launches for private-sector projects. The programmes to receive the bulk of this funding are the Advanced Subsonic Technology programme and the High Speed Research Programme[81]

In order to fulfil its mission NASA provides research facilities for US firms, it institutes invaluable demonstrator programmes, it pays US firms to do research and it increasingly seeks the optimum routes to commercial applications of new research. However, in the sensitive climate of renewed concern over political support to the US aerospace industry corporate executives are keen to distance themselves from the public support provided by NASA. At the Paris airshow in 1997 Boeing's Phil Condit offered the following reassurance: 'Since 1993 when we have submitted reports to the US government on this issue, there have been no benefits accruing to US commercial airplane programmes from currently funded Department of Defense or NASA programmes'.[82] But interestingly, in a political climate where Congress is seeking better value for money, NASA is more frank than previously concerning its ultimate aims:

> Future U.S. competitiveness in aeronautics... is dependent on sustained NASA advances in aeronautics research and technology. The aeronautics Enterprise will pioneer the identification, development, verification, transfer, application and commercialization of high-payoff aeronautics technologies.

Activities pursued as a part of this enterprise emphasize customer involvement, encompassing U.S. industry, the Department of Defense and the Federal Aviation Administration.[83]

Thus, rather paradoxically from the industry's point of view, sensitivity in the US about government expenditure is increasing the openness of the industrial policy in aerospace. NASA now explicitly links its R&D to the issue of US national interests and commercial competitiveness. As pressure on budgets increases, so too does the need to have a clear and logical rationale for public support of commercial aeronautics. In the US Congress there is a keen understanding of the implications of NASA's programmes for strategic trade:

> NASA undertook these efforts [HSR and HST] largely in response to fears that the U.S. aircraft industry was falling behind Airbus in its technological capabilities, as well as to help the industry address the gap that had emerged in its commercialization of new technologies... In addition, NASA is trying to make its own research efforts more responsive to the commercial manufacturing cycle by timing the development of new technologies to coincide with the onset of new U.S. commercial programs.[84]

The overall picture of state support to the US aerospace industry is complex and difficult to disentangle. But NASA's own statements give the lie to the claim that the commercial industry does not receive substantial government supports. In its 'Spin-off 97' document NASA Langley recalls its own contribution to the B777:

In May 1996, the first Boeing 777 stopped by Langley Research Centre as a salute to NASA's involvement in its creation. Several Langley innovations were instrumental in the development of the aircraft, such as:

- fundamental mathematical procedures for computer-generated airflow images which allowed advanced computer-based aerodynamic analysis;
- wind tunnel tests, confirming the structural integrity of 777 wing airframe integration;
- knowledge of how to reduce engine and other noise;
- radial tyres that are used on the aircraft underwent strength and durability testing;

- increased use of lightweight aerospace composite structures for increased fuel efficiency and range. The 777's floor beams, flaps and tail make use of lightweight composites.[85]

The NASA document also details other aspects of the extensive contribution the agency made to the B777's development. Research at the Marshall Space Centre contributed to the development of the Pratt and Whitney engines, while NASA Ames assisted with new inlet, hinge and strut blankets to make the aircraft more resistant to fire.[86] Perhaps most important of all NASA (and DoD) assisted Boeing in the development of radical new fly-by-wire and fly-by-light technologies for the new automated flight management system on the B777.[87] This is critical in terms of competitiveness as previously Airbus had pioneered new, automated flight management systems for the A320, A330 and A340. The NASA document concludes: 'Together, industry and government skills melded, jointly contributing to the airplanes operating efficiency, passenger service, environmental compatibility and safety'. [88]

With regard to the trade issues raised by the 1992 Bilateral Agreement NASA programmes highlight the problems posed for the EU in monitoring US compliance. The only projects which the US side reports to the World Trade Organization as indirect subsidies are the Advanced Subsonic Technology and High Speed Research programmes. But in the six years since 1992 NASA has spent approximately $400mn annually on its Research and Technology Base programme which aims to develop new technologies for subsequent commercial aeronautics' applications. Since 1992 this represents a total spend of $2,428bn which has not come under WTO scrutiny.[89]

The US refusal to recognize the R&T Base programme as a subsidy to the commercial aircraft industry goes to the heart of the problems analyzed in this chapter. R&T Base represents public investment in R&D designed to develop new technologies. Some of these technologies contribute to innovations which can be seen to contribute to public welfare in areas such as safety or environmental protection. However, many lead to the emergence of new technologies which directly benefit private companies. Basic research is expensive and often cannot quickly be applied to any commercially viable technology. NASA funding of this research thus significantly reduces the two key areas of technological and financial risk for commercial companies such as Boeing. In the area relevant to airframe manufacture R&T Base focuses on aerodynamics, materials, controls-guidance-human factors, flight systems,

systems analysis and hypersonics. These are critical in airframe manufacture.

In its 1996 fiscal year budget report the NASA Office of Aeronautics indicated that the following applications could be traced back to earlier R&T Base projects:

- supercritical wing for the B757 and B767;
- winglets for the MD-11 and B747- 400;
- acoustic nacelles for the MD-11, B757, B767 and B747
- composite structures and advanced alloys for the B757, B767, B747 and the MD-11;
- advanced displays for the B757, B767, B747 and B777.

As the factual evidence and arguments presented above indicate the NASA R&T Base programme has contributed much to technologies used in the design and manufacture of highly successful commercial aircraft. This should be clearly recognized in Europe, but even in the US critical questions have been asked about the programme. In the FY 1996 House of Representatives hearings of the committee responsible for NASA appropriations, the chairman, J. Lewis, put forward the following written question, 'Most of the efforts being funded are for the direct benefit of civil aviation.... What is the rationale for these government expenditures which benefit private businesses'.[90] This is precisely the question Europe should be asking at future trade negotiations on the funding of large commercial aircraft manufacturing.

Conclusions

The qualitative analysis and evidence outlined above shows clearly that it is meaningful to speak of a US industrial policy for the aerospace sector. But the fact that NASA and DoD programmes clearly involve an industrial policy for commercial aircraft manufacturing does not obviate the problem that the precise benefit of such activities cannot be ascertained. An urgent need in this area is for a model which can act as a test of the commercial value of the large DoD and NASA inputs. In the meantime a clearer understanding of the history of the US industry and an appreciation of the neo-mercantilist strategy of the Clinton Administration points to more meaningful conclusions than the traditional assessment offered. In the past firms producing aircraft for the commercial sector benefited from synergies and cross-subsidization between defence and civil. Major risks could be taken on the commercial side because the defence contracts strengthened the capital base of the companies.[91] In the 1990s the defence and commercial sectors have moved to integrate and synergies now go both ways. Further, the new giant aerospace units can now receive more focused political support, precisely because the competition is overseas and not domestic. With the Cold War long over, competition with allies in high technology sectors can be more aggressive and aims, in my view, at recouping some of the vast investment in defence that the US previously made on behalf of the Western Alliance.[92]

Mergers in US aerospace cannot simply be seen as the play of market forces; they represent strategic calculations and include Pentagon and executive input. In the Clinton administration economic strength is recognized as the foundation of national security and pre-eminence in high technology is regarded as the bedrock of economic strength. In order to secure effective defence procurement the Dual-Use programme now explicity focuses on commercial industry and, in itself, is a form of industrial policy. Neo-mercantilist support for Boeing and other aerospace giants is an attempt to protect high technology sectors, regarded as critical to US military and economic security. It is a classical example of strategic trade investment policy (STIP).

Regarding export advocacy the US government now has a coherent and effective policy directed from the Department of Commerce Advocacy Centre in Washington. This center supports export sales worth in excess of $20bn a year and secures several hundred thousand US jobs. As Jeffrey Garten has recently asserted business is at the heart of US state policy: 'Throughout most of American history, commercial interests have played a central role in foreign policy, and vice versa'.[93] Today aerospace is the prime example of linking commerce and foreign affairs. What's good for aerospace is good for America.

Notes and References

1   See Judith Goldstein, 'Ideas, Institutions and American Trade Policy', in G. John Ikenberry, David A. Lake and Michael Mastanduno, (eds), *The State and American Foreign Economic Policy*, (Cornell University Press, Ithaca, New York, 1988), p. 216.

2   Ibid, p. 216.

3   Jens Van Scherpenberg, 'International Competition and European Defence Industries', *International Affairs*, Vol. 75, No. 3, (1997), p. 107.

4   Steven Gill and David Law, *The Global Political Economy,* (Harvester Wheatsheaf, Brighton, 1988), p. 28.

5   Quoted, David Balaam and Michael Veseth, *Introduction to International Political Economy,* (Prentice Hall, New York, 1996), p. 23.

6   Arthur A. Stein, 'The Hegemon's Dilemma, Great Britain and the International Economic Order', *International Organization,* Vol. 38, No. 2. (Spring, 1984) pp. 361-362.

7   Ibid, p. 362.

8   Ibid, p. 362.

9   Paul Kennedy, *The Rise and Fall of the Great Powers,* (Unwin Hyman, London, 1988), p. 368.

10 Balaam and Veseth, *Introduction to International Political Economy,* p. 28.

11 Ernest May, 'The U.S. Government: a Legacy of the Cold War', in Michael J. Hogan, (ed), *The End of the Cold War: its Meaning and Implications*, (Cambridge University Press, Cambridge, 1992), p. 218.

12 Gregory Hooks, *Forging the Military Industrial Complex*, (University of Illinois Press, Urbana, 1991), p. 235.

13 Michael A. Sherry, *The Rise of American Airpower: the Creation of Armageddon*, (Yale University Press, New Haven, 1988), p. 91.

14 Wayne Biddle, *Barons of the Sky*, (Henry Holt, New York, 1991), p. 270.

15 Ibid, p. 270.

16 Bruce Franklin, *War Stars*, (Oxford University Press, 1988), p. 113.

17 Biddle, *Barons of the Sky*, p. 271.

18 Ibid, p. 273.

19 David Weldon Thornton, *Airbus Industrie: the Politics of an International Industrial Collaboration* (Macmillan, London, 1995), p. 25.

20 David Mowery and Nathan Rosenberg, 'The Commercial Aircraft Industry' in Richard R. Nelson (ed), *Government and Technical Progress*, (Pergammon Press, New York, 1982), p. 140.

21 Clive Irving, *Widebody: the Triumph of the 747*, (William Morrow, New York, 1993), p. 83.

22 Quoted, *Wall St Journal*, (July, 30, 1991), p. 1.

23 Laura D'Andrea Tyson, *Who's Bashing Whom? Trade Conflict in High Technology Industries*, (International Institute for International Economics, Washington D.C. 1992), p. 169.

24   Quoted, Vicki Golich, 'From competition to co-operation: the challenge of commercial-class aircraft manufacturing', *International Organization*, 46, 4, 1992, p. 912.

25   Ibid, p. 912.

26   Anthony Sampson, *The Arms Bazaar*, (Viking Press, New York, 1977), p. 269.

27   Thornton, *Airbus Industrie*, p. 63.

28   Golich, *From competition to co-operation*, p. 918.

29   Thornton, *Airbus Industrie*, p. 29

30   Ibid, p. 94.

31   Ibid, p. 80.

32   Ibid, p. 80.

33   Tyson, *Who's Bashing Whom?*, p. 157.

34   Jean Picq, *Les Ailes de l'Europe*, (Fayard, Paris, 1990), pp. 116-117.

35   Thornton, *Airbus Industrie*, p. 104.

36   Mike Bagshaw, '*Human Factors in Aviation Safety: the Strongest or Weakest Link*', paper delivered at Aerospace Research Group, UWE, Bristol, (19/3/97).

37   Ian McIntyre, *Dog Fight: the Trans-Atlantic Battle over Airbus,* (Praeger, Westport, Conn. 1992), p. 162.

38   Ibid, p. 162.

39   Quoted, ibid, p. 167.

40   Quoted, ibid, p. 167.

41   Ibid, p. 173.

42   Ibid, p. 176.

43   Letter from Boeing to Dept of Commerce, quoted ibid, p. 176.

44   Tyson, *Who's Bashing Whom*, p. 155.

45   Quoted, Thornton, *Airbus Industrie*, p. 138.

46   Ibid, p. 138.

47   This is even apparent in the work of those advocating so called 'new trade theory'. For an implicit critique of the impact of Airbus subsidies on the USA's aircraft industry see Paul R. Krugman and Maurice Obstfeld, *International Economics,* (Harper Collins, New York, 1994), pp. 278-286.

48   See, Arnold and Porter, '*U.S. Government Support of the U.S. Commercial Aircraft Industry*', (Washington, DC. Nov, 1991).

49   Quoted, Wolfgang Piller, 'The Airbus Issue from the European Point of View', Presentation to the American Advisory Board, (DASA, Oct 25, 1993), p. 9.

50   See Van Scherpenberg, *International Competition*, p. 108.

51   Ibid, p. 108.
52   Matthew Lynn, *Birds of Prey, Boeing v. Airbus*, (Four Walls Eight Windows, New York, 1997), p. 1.
53   *Manchester Guardian*, (March, 26, 1997), p. 3.
54   This has been characteristic of the studies commissioned by the EU. Regrettably many do not enter the public domain.
55   Quoted Tyson, *Who's Bashing Whom*, p. 155.
56   See George Eberstadt, *'Government Support of the Large Commercial Aircraft Industries of Japan, Europe and the United States'*, report prepared for the Office of Technology Assessment of the Congress of the United States, (May, 1991), p. 95.
57   Ibid, p. 12.
58   Ibid, p. 32.
59   Ibid, p. 39.
60   Eugene Rodgers, *Flying High: the Story of Boeing and the Rise of the Jetliner Industry,* (The Atlantic Monthly Press, New York, 1996), p. 162.
61   Eberstadt, *Government Support,* p. 39.
62   M. J. Hardy, *Boeing*, (Beaufort, New York, 1982), p. 66.
63   John Newhouse, *The Sporty Game*, (Alfred Knopf, New York, 1982), p. 113.
64   Wolfgang Demisch, cited in Eberstadt, *Government Support*, p. 56.
65   *Financial Times*, (December, 16, 1996), p. 19.
66   Tyson, *Who's Bashing Whom*, p. 165.
67   Ibid, p. 187.
68   Ibid, p. 187.
69   John Dowdy, 'Winners and Losers in the Arms Industry Downturn', *Foreign Policy*, (Summer, 1997), p. 90.
70   Ibid, pp. 101-102.
71   United States General Accounting Office: National Security and International Affairs Division, B-279557, (April 1 1998), p. 2.
72   Oliver Sutton, 'Who Cares About the WTO', *Interavia*, (May, 1997), p. 19.
73   Eberstadt, *Government Support*, p. 59.
74   David F. Noble, 'Military Technology and Technical Change', in Merritt Roe Smith (ed), *Military Enterprise and Technological Change*, (MIT Press, Cambridge, Mass, 1987), pp. 330-331.
75   'Second to None: Preserving America's Military Advantage Through Dual-Use Technology', *National Security Council Office of Science and Technology Policy*, (Washington, D.C. 1995), p. 35.
76   Ibid, p. 2.

77   Hearing on Perspectives on the Dual-Use before the Subcommittee on Acquisition and Technology of the Senate Committee on Armed Services, 104th Congress, 1st Session, (1995).

78   Department of Defense, (1993).

79   Budget of the United States Government, Fiscal Year 1996.

80   National Science and Technology Council, 'Goals for a National Partnership in Aeronautics Research and Technology', (Washington, 1995), p. 5.

81   Statement of US Secretary of Transportation, Frederico Pena, (Washington, D.C. January 6, 1994).

82   *Financial Times*, (June 24, 1997), p. 5.

83   NASA FY 1997, Congressional Budget Agency Summary: High Speed Research Program Goals, p. 11.

84   United States Congressional Budget Office, Council on Competitiveness, (February, 1995), p. 152.

85   'Spin Off 1997' NASA Langley Research Centre, (1997), p. 54.

86   Ibid, p. 54.

87   Ibid, p. 54.

88   Ibid, p. 54.

89   Figures from NASA FY 1996 Budget Estimates and 1997 Budget Estimates, NASA electronic publication at http:/www.hq.nasa. gov/office/codeb/budget/r-narl.htm.

90   Hearing on FY 1996 Appropriations, Before the Subcommittee on Departments of Veterans Affairs and Housing and Urban Development and Independent Agencies of the House Committee on Appropriations, 104th Congress, 1st Session, (1995), Written Question of Subcommittee Chairman, J. Lewis.

91   Van Scherpenberg, *International Co-operation*, p. 101.

92   Ibid, p. 107.

93   Jeffrey E. Garten, 'Business and Foreign Policy', *Foreign Affairs*, Vol. 76. No. 3, (1997), p. 67.

4 The US Drive for Aeronautical Supremacy

DAVID W THORNTON
Campbell University North Carolina

"The US Drive to Aeronautical Supremacy", perhaps implies a greater degree of purpose and foresight on the part of the American aeronautical industry and the American government than is justified. Yet throughout the history of the sector's development in the US, there has been a palpable sense that aeronautics is simply too important for the US to be anywhere but in the first rank, and that somehow the US had the right to (or even maybe was destined to) dominate the industry. And throughout its history, there has been the sense on the American side of rivalry with the nations of Europe, and that, more than in any other industry, the stakes of the competition have been so high that no quarter could be given, even among friends and allies, and that all involved on both sides have always understood the situation this way.

So you can see that my perspective on the history of aeronautics in general and on the development of the US industry in particular is a thoroughly mercantilist one, meaning that I view the relationship between the companies that build and operate aircraft for commercial purposes and their respective national governments as cooperative, complementary, and indeed symbiotic. Designers and builders of aircraft have always sought the financial support of governments, most typically but not only in the form of military contracts, just as operators of commercial air services have relied upon governments to provide the physical and legal infrastructure that have made air travel economically viable. For their part, governments have always taken an active interest in the fortunes of at least some inventors and builders, and of course have insisted on the right to regulate access to and activity in national airspace, commercial or otherwise.

These mercantilist partnerships have assumed different forms at various times and in various places, yet in my view have been essentially similar in function and purpose; to assure that the aeronautical capabilities (technological, industrial, and commercial) of the respective countries are nurtured and protected and given every advantage over their rivals; goals that have proven expensive and elusive but none the less vital. This chapter traces the evolution of the American aeronautics industry from this mercantilist perspective, emphasizing throughout the interaction among the three main elements that make up the industry: the companies that design, build and market aircraft for commercial purposes, the companies that buy, lease and operate them, and the national government that has played such a major role in shaping the economic environment of them both.

Given the space constraints and this cannot be a comprehensive treatment of the subject, but instead a thematic one using examples to illustrate key points, namely: 1) Despite the prominence of laissez-faire ideology in the US, the government has always played and continues to play a direct and pervasive role in the development of the American aeronautical industry, 2) that government involvement has been undertaken in large measure as a response to a perceived challenge from the European nations, individually and collectively, 3) that aeronautical capabilities both military and commercial have been and are today the single most important element of US political and commercial influence in the global arena, and 4) that the US fully intends to remain the world's dominant power in aeronautics.

Today, at least in the popular imagination, Americans attribute the achievement of powered flight to the skills of and risks taken by mostly American inventors and entrepreneurs - the Wright Brothers, Glenn Martin, Donald Douglas, Charles Lindbergh, John Northrop, William Boeing. While I do not wish to detract from the contributions made by these and many other pioneers of flight, the part of the story that is much less appreciated is the extent to which the priorities and resources of the national government have shaped the structure and dynamics of the industry, and that government policies have played such a large role in determining the success or failure of these individuals and firms.

Americans are particularly loath to admit that government and industry might coexist in such a complementary rather than antagonistic fashion, and tend to view any such examples that might be admitted as merely episodic or coincidental. Perhaps if our public and our politicians understood the history as it has actually happened, they might be less prone to hysterics about the character of international competition in aeronautics today. But instead the widely held view is that any overt partnerships of government and industry are inherently unnatural and illegitimate, bastard progeny of an unholy union, and thus the targets of opprobrium and even a kind of revulsion. But the facts of economic history show that, at least when it comes to aeronautics, the Americans have never shunned the very same mercantilist practices they have condemned in Europeans, they have merely sought and found mechanisms that can be rationalized if reconciled with a laissez-faire, neo-liberal ideology.

Indeed, Americans drew a great many lessons in this regard from Europeans during the period leading up to WWI, and were especially impressed by the practical results stemming from direct governmental support of aeronautical research, development and production so impressed in fact that delegations were sent from the States who returned home convinced that the US government could no longer sit idly by while the Europeans forged ahead. One particularly significant result of the American concern was the creation in 1915 of the National Advisory Committee for Aeronautics (NACA), whose mission it was to conduct basic research on topics with both civil and military application.

Few results were achieved from this overt government support of aeronautics in these early days, and the case made by those in the US who argued for even greater governmental attention to and support of the sector was not helped by the undistinguished performance of the American industry and its products in the Great War. Indeed, the early 1920s were dark days for an industry almost completely lacking in public acclaim and political support, and advocates of military air power such as General Billy Mitchell were really almost lone voices in the wilderness.

But two pieces of legislation in the mid-1920s were to prove the salvation of the industry - the Air Mail Act of 1925, and the Air Commerce Act of 1926. The latter law gave the federal government the power to license pilots and aircraft, and to regulate air traffic, and also included five-year aircraft procurement plans for the Army and Navy. For its part, the Air Mail legislation not only allowed the government to contract private concerns to carry the mails, but also committed the government to build and maintain a network of lighted airways across the country. As Heppenheimer has observed: "In developing its airmail routes, the Post Office, though operating as an arm of the government, was playing the classic role of entrepreneur". Under the direction of the Aeronautics Branch, the federal government was also the driving force behind the creation and maintenance of a network of radio communications and weather information that served as the foundation for subsequent commercial development in aviation. Anthony Sampson (p.41) sums it up this way: "However resourceful the local pioneers, it was the federal government which laid the basis for the serious airlines".

Despite the onset of the Depression, the 1930s were better times for US aeronautics, and in fact were a period of very substantial technological innovation and industrial restructuring. Yet again the impetus for this change came at least as much from governmental policies as it did from engineers and entrepreneurs. By the late 1920s, NACA research was actually yielding some practical results in the form of wind-tunnel testing the aerodynamic effects of "cowling" engines by installing them within the wing structure of an all metal monoplane. And in the early 1930s, the Postmaster General Walter Folger Brown used his contracting power to reconfigure the industry around a few conglomerates that both built and operated aircraft for mail and commercial services. Although his work was largely dismantled under FDR's New Deal, and the airlines separated from the builders of aircraft and engines in 1934, most of the major US airlines still around today got their start under Brown's corporatist tutelage. Moreover, the aircraft manufacturers managed to survive the Depression mainly on the basis of military contracts, which accounted for the lion's share of their sales and profits.

So it is really impossible to understand much at all of the history of the US aeronautics industry up until WWII without accounting for the role of the national government in shaping its economic and regulatory environment, and thus influencing directly (through NACA research), and indirectly (through Air Mail contracts and the provision of physical and legal infrastructure) the most salient technological characteristics and structural features of the sector. And it should be recalled that the government encouraged US airlines of this period to emulate more effectively their imperial European counterparts in carrying the American flag to not only to Europe, but Latin America, Asia and indeed around the world, with Pan Am acting as the main "chosen instrument" of FDR and his State Department.

Despite the scale of its industrial base and the relatively large size of its internal market for air transport services, the US on the eve of WWII remained only one among many aeronautical powers, and indeed was not in the technological forefront, as German, British, French and even Italian and Japanese capabilities were at least equal to the Americans. But the ensuing dozen years or so would alter the global aeronautical balance dramatically. Although increases in exports to Europe and Asia due to rising international tensions had made an important contribution to the sales and profits of the major American aeronautics manufacturers in the late 1930s, it would again be US government demand that would transform the organizational, geographic and technological shape of the industry in the 1940s. Attempting to responding to the French call after the Nazi invasion in the Spring of 1940 for "clouds of warplanes", President Roosevelt demanded that the US industry be able to turn out at least 50,000 planes a year. Any lingering hesitancy on the part of politicians or industrialists to expand production was dispelled for good on 7 December 1941.

Developments in military aeronautics associated with WWII, the Korean War, and the intensification and geographic spread of the Cold War (including Vietnam) were extensive, rapid and radical in their cumulative effects on the nature of war and international power balances. The relative positions of the Europeans and Americans underwent a drastic shift with regard to the scale of aeronautical capabilities (as was the case in military, economic and political relations more generally) as the US government poured enormous resources into procurement of the wherewithal to fight an extraterrestrial Cold War with the USSR. As a result of this massive and sustained stream of funding, and coupled with US hegemony in the transatlantic alliance, the US came to dominate aeronautical design and manufacturing across the board as its firms produced for the material means for the defense of NATO and beyond.

Airpower assumed a crucial new role in World War II by giving U.S. and Allied military leaders the means to fight a two-front war. At home, tremendous increases in productive capacity were attained; an aviation industry workforce of fewer than 49,000 in 1939 grew to over 2.1 million in 1943. Branch plants, licensee and subcontractor arrangements all were used to create the necessary production and assembly space; the major airframers became primarily designers and assemblers of parts and sections built elsewhere. Labour and capital were combined effectively; from January 1940 to the Japanese surrender in August 1945, US manufacturers produced some 300,317 military aircraft.

But unit numbers alone mask the importance of the continual increases in aircraft size and weight, and much of the new productive capacity, in terms of tools, skills and organization, literally had to be invented on the shop floor. Flexibility and coordination were the watchwords in ascending steep production learning curves. Output per employee increased from 21 pounds in January 1941 to 96 pounds in August 1944, while the cost of producing a four-engine, long-range bomber fell from $15.18 to $4.82 per pound.

The cessation of hostilities in 1945 brought a drastic, if predictable, drop in the level of government orders that had so dramatically expanded and transformed the US aviation industry. But fears of repeating the disorderly and damaging contraction after World War I were not to be realized, because both international politics and the conduct of warfare had been changed irrevocably in the interim. Most among the military leadership in the United States recognized what their German and Japanese counterparts knew all too well: that American air power had been decisive in defeating the Axis. Therefore, among the many important provisions of the NSA of 26 July 1947 was the creation of the United States Air Force (USAF) as a separate military service - Billy Mitchell's long-standing dream was finally a reality.

The enhancement of the status of the US military air power was reinforced by the December 1947 report of the Finletter Commission entitled "Survival in the Air Age", which concluded that United States military strategy should be based primarily on air power. Events only confirmed the validity of these views; indeed, the situation in Berlin 1948-1949 provided a challenge that seemingly could be met only through the effective application of air power, and the Berlin Airlift went a long way in establishing the importance and credibility of the USAF.

The new reliance on air power in assuring national security meant that the newest of the armed services would take the lead in issuing massive, long-term contracts to firms for the development and manufacture of what had now become expensive and complex weapons systems. Through the procurement practices of the USAF, the political and military leadership of the United States exerted dramatic influence on both sides of the market, providing not only final demand for the products but also insuring it a steady stream of research and development (R&D) financing. The Korean conflict provided an especially dramatic fillip to the industry: "the Pentagon's spending on the aerospace industry shot up from $2.6 billion in 1950 to $10.6 billion in 1954". In fact, for the 1945 to 1969 period, "the defense portion of total R&D expenditures never fell below 65%", and during that period the Air Force spent over 70% of its funds on product development.

The intensity of Cold War conflict was decisive in transforming the technological and organizational features of the US aviation industry, not least because it "marked the watershed between piston and jet production". Yet for all of its advantages in simplicity of design and the accompanying savings in power to weight ratios and aerodynamic efficiency, the development of the jet engine was perhaps the single most important factor behind the rapid increases in the complexity and cost of developing new aircraft.

Taken together, the rapid changes in the nature of the post-war threat and the technological responses to that challenge meant that US military planners became enmeshed in a procurement process involving the research, design and development of highly complex industrial products. It was the symbiotic relationship between the imperatives of the international situation, as perceived by the US political and military leadership, and the technological and organizational characteristics of the aeronautical industry, that provided the impetus for eventual American dominance of this crucial economic sector. Indeed, the economic and organizational impact of these policies was so great that the US government had in effect a de facto industrial policy toward the aerospace sector. Under the intense geopolitical pressures of the Cold War, as Gregory Hooks has noted, "the air force could not rely on market forces to maintain the world's largest and most technologically advanced aircraft industry. National security had become equated with industrial planning".

But the impact of these procurement policies was necessarily to be felt far beyond the core of the emerging military-industrial complex. The nature of the technologies and manufacturing processes in aeronautics insured that the effects of government research and procurement policies would be felt in related sectors on both the military and commercial sides of the industry. Since, as Mowery and Rosenberg have observed, "the history of technical development in commercial aircraft consists largely of the utilization for commercial purposes of technical knowledge developed for military purposes at government expense", the effects of the massive government R&D effort were transmitted rapidly into the civilian arena as well. Defence contractors doubled as commercial manufacturers and incorporated airframes, propulsion and flight-control systems developed for military use into civilian products, while selling both types of goods into the vast and uncontested US market.

Firms quick to capitalize on the translation of capital, technology and production process knowledge into commercial ventures positioned themselves and their products at the crucial nexus connecting the military and economic domains of national security. Exemplifying this trend, Boeing Aircraft Co. gained substantial advantage over its domestic and international rivals alike by converting its Dash-80 prototype into both the KC-135 tanker (developed for in-flight refueling of B-52 bombers) and the B707 commercial airliner that was to dominate the passenger traffic market for 10 years. The pattern was repeated in engine development later in the 1960s, as "military supported research on power plants for the giant C-5A transport led to the development of the high by-pass ratio engines that now power the wide-body commercial transports".

So, by converting funding and expertise gained on military contracts to civilian applications, certain US firms were able to derive products that would effectively create entirely new markets as their use was adopted. But not only was the US market the target - as Europe rebuilt with the help of American aid money and transatlantic traffic levels jumped, "before long the Europeans were buying Douglas, Lockheed and Boeing airliners under the Marshall Plan". Neither were American aircraft and engine builders prepared to rely solely on the emerging market for mass civilian air travel made possible by the new technology; profitable military sales remained crucial sources of capital and innovation for future product development. And neither did these firms intend to confine themselves to the US domestic defence market; pressure on their European competitors were intensified as the US government stepped up its efforts to sell to NATO countries weapons developed for its own use, both as a means of extending political influence in the Cold War contest and to lower the unit cost of increasingly complex and expensive systems.

It should also be mentioned briefly that US airlines were also the beneficiaries of US policy during WWII and the Cold War: "When at last the United States went to war, all the airlines went to war". Throughout WWII, US military airlift capacity was powerfully augmented by the fleet of commercial airliners, and their activities were coordinated under the Air Transport Command (ATC) of the Army Air Forces created by General Hap Arnold. The major domestic carriers were given regional responsibilities for ferrying supplies within the US and overseas, some of which would be turned into profitable business opportunities after the war.

And the scope and configuration of US government regulatory power over civilian aviation also underwent changes during this period of vital importance to the development of US commercial aeronautics. The most notable prewar accomplishment of the new CAA (created in 1938) had been the systematic evaluation of and improvement in the nation's airports and ground-based infrastructure, especially the management of the construction of Washington National Airport, which opened for business in June 1941 as the world's most modern. Wartime exigencies meant that "the CAA inevitably came under the influence of the military and the increased security consciousness". Narrowly avoiding direct takeover by the Army, the CAA benefited from a wartime expansion of its budget, oversaw a big spurt in airport construction, took an increasingly direct responsibility for air traffic control, and trained thousands of civilian pilots.

The CAA was hard pressed to handle the new demands on regulatory capabilities by the proliferation of pilots, aircraft and air travel services created in the immediate postwar period. Cold War imperatives, therefore, meant that federal oversight of civil aviation through the CAA would have to make do with growing yet still inadequate funding and rapidly obsolescing equipment in the post-war period. Yet despite these limitations, the CAA did important if relatively unappreciated work in determining the source of and solutions to aircraft design and construction flaws that continued to plague flight safety and thus limit its commercial appeal.

During the second Eisenhower administration, the federal government sought novel political and administrative solutions to the evident growing pains of a booming industry. Most pressing was the advent of jet aircraft for commercial purposes, as both Boeing and Douglas sought to capitalize on the misfortunes of the British de Havilland Comet by introducing the B707 and DC-8, respectively. The increased speed and range offered by the new technology promised to inaugurate a new age of travel for both the airlines and their customers, however, the new technology relied heavily upon government to realize its full commercial potential. As a historian of the FAA, Stuart Rochester, has noted: "The operational efficiency of the jets would depend in the long run on the CAA's success in modernizing the airways and the traffic control system".

Pressure grew to create an independent agency responsible for making and enforcing all regulations relevant to commercial air safety, including the development and operation of air traffic control systems, and the promulgation of rules and regulations concerning the certification of pilots and the maintenance of aircraft. Legislation creating the Federal Aviation Agency (FAA) was signed into law by President Eisenhower on the 23 August 1958, with the new agency given "sole responsibility for the control of US airspace and the development of a common civil-military system of air traffic control".

Among the most controversial of the projects undertaken by the FAA concerned the possible development of an supersonic transport (SST) aircraft in the United States, with the federal government and the FAA playing a major role in the project. As the US military and NASA (the successor to the NACA) began to redirect its research and development efforts from winged aircraft to ballistic missiles, many in the industry feared for the future of American leadership in commercial aeronautics. Sharing this concern, FAA head Najeeb Halaby was successful in having an appropriation of $12 million included in JFK's supplemental 1962 budget for the FAA to initiate a feasibility study of a commercial SST. It is clear that the pressures of "international rivalry played an important role in race to the SST". Not only had the British and French governments joined forces to support the efforts of their respective national firms to develop Concorde, but the premier US overseas airline, Pan Am, had agreed to purchase six of the new aircraft.

Faced with the real prospect of additional U.S. airlines ordering the European plane, the American SST program remained of central concern to the new Johnson administration. Characteristic of its ambiguous dual role of both promoting and regulating the aeronautics sector, the FAA was also involved in the complex process of determining the characteristics and implications of the "sonic boom" associated with SST technology. Tests conducted at Edwards Air Force base during 1966 revealed that "sonic boom would preclude the flight of all SSTs, including the Concorde, on overland routes". Clearly, such restrictions would appear to seriously compromise the commercial viability of the technology. However, after evaluating the potential damage that might be done to the US aircraft manufacturing industry if leadership in SST technology were conceded to the Europeans, and considering the further erosion in the balance of trade that would be caused by the purchase of European aircraft by US airlines, it was decided on the 22 December 1966 to accept anyway the most recent FAA findings and recommend to President Johnson that Phase III of the SST project should begin.

Even as the SST continued to clear technological, economic and financial hurdles, during 1969 nagging concerns surrounding its potential environmental impact were being transformed into opposition potent enough to eventually kill the programme. Although the project staggered on, by the end of March 1971 both houses of Congress had voted the programme down, and the American version of the supersonic transport aircraft was officially deceased. But this death should be understood as a casualty of the just-dawning awareness in the US of the political salience of environmental issues in the US and it was certainly not for a lack of effort that the FAA's pet project to maintain US leadership in a crucial new aeronautical technology failed to bear fruit.

The aeronautics industry in 1970, including both the military and commercial sides of the business, embodied and powerfully reinforced American political and economic hegemony in the Cold War era. In responding to the geopolitical imperatives of the Cold War, the United States government had financed the creation of awesome industrial and technological capabilities. US firms had, by virtue of their participation in large military contracts, developed the technology and expertise necessary to make commercial jet airliners viable, and they aggressively pursued the opportunities created by their early lead.

Although owned and controlled by private capitalists, the US aeronautics firms of the 1960s (and the commercial product line they were able to offer to the world, through which they created and then dominated an entire new industry) owed much of their impressive industrial capabilities and dominant market position to government funding. Moreover, at that time the huge US market was controlled regarding pricing and fare structures and therefore, "the regulated, large domestic market provided a strong base of demand for technological innovation by the aircraft producers".

Once established, mainly because of economies of scale that raised further barriers to entry, the market power of American firms in the world civil aviation market continued to grow well into the 1970s. Taking substantial commercial risks to capitalize on its capabilities, and outmaneuvering both its European and American rivals, by the mid-1960s Boeing had become the dominant firm in a new and rapidly expanding market.

Given the extent of American control of the world civil airframe market, the aeronautics firms and national governments of the major European states had to engage in a calculated gamble. In order to resurrect their capability in the production of commercial airliners, and thus regain the right to engage the Americans in a battle for current and future market share in a high-cost, high-risk, oligopolistic industry, the Europeans would have to devise and implement a strategy capable eventually of changing the very rules of the game.

In a market in which design, production and marketing constituted the operational level of a larger strategic contest, therefore making the aircraft themselves the point of contact in an economic and industrial rivalry of much broader scope, each and every decision concerning product development would be of crucial significance. At stake was more than the benefits of high value-added employment or technological spin-offs, or even the prestige of building aircraft. Due to its strategic character and oligopolistic structure, the very configuration, and thus the future evolution of the commercial aviation sector, would be affected by the fortunes of the European effort.

Therefore, arguably the most important development in commercial aeronautics during the 1970s and 1980s was the re-emergence of a European capability in large airframe manufacturing in the form of Airbus Industrie, a consortium of national firms supported by their respective governments. In order to be successful, not only would the Europeans have to accommodate the distinctive interests and capabilities of the respective national firms and governments, they also would have to do so in a way that translated commercial imperatives into a business strategy capable of first regaining a foothold in the global market for commercial airliners, and then wresting the technological and industrial initiative from the Americans.

The products of the American manufacturers (McDonnell Douglas and especially Boeing) were the concrete representation of US leadership in the aeronautics industry and thus also a manifestation of American political and economic dominance in the Cold War era. The characteristics of the American commercial aircraft lines (range, payload, fuel consumption) defined the very terms in which any prospective European response to the American challenge would have to be expressed. In order to be effective, European political and economic aspirations would have to be translated into the same currency as used by the Americans: a line of aircraft with performance characteristics comparable to existing products, yet able to attract demand in a market in which the terms of competition already had been set by the leading firms.

For the US civil airframe manufacturers, AI's persistence in building, marketing and even designing new aircraft despite any apparent prospects of programme profitability were an anomaly. At first it had seemed safe ignoring the upstart: As Yoshino notes, "Until the late 1970s, the US manufacturers had dismissed Airbus as just another feeble and disappointing effort of the European commercial aerospace industry". But with AI's sale to Eastern Airlines in 1978, attitudes in the US industrial and political circles changed rapidly, as Americans recognized that the consortium was "committed to a fundamental goal that was different from their own". From this point forward, both US aerospace executives and government officials began to perceive the Airbus consortium for what it was: a means to much larger ends in a strategy calculated to reestablish a permanent European presence in global civil airframe manufacturing.

In a "zero-sum" contest such as the emerging transatlantic struggle in civil airframe manufacturing, success for one player in garnering outside resources also would deny their use to the other. In the late 1970s, therefore, British capital, technology and expertise represented an important prize for both the Airbus partners and the American manufacturers. Seen in light of the strategic engagement, BAe's decision to join AI from 1 January 1979, even paying an entry fee for the privilege, was a major victory for the consortium. By solidifying the financial, commercial and political prospects of the collective European effort, the official British return to the Airbus programme also allowed the consortium to consider more daring options regarding its next move.

In relation to the consortium's long-term objectives, the early 1980s were especially important. The market leader, Boeing, had just introduced two new products, the single-aisle B757 and the wide-bodied, twin-engine B767, with the latter a direct competitor of the A300/A310. The launch by Airbus in 1984 of the single-aisle A320 involved not just the penetration of a new market segment but also a major technological leap. By introducing a fully computerized flight control system and redesigning the cockpit around the new technology, AI sought to take a major step in differentiating its products from those of its competitors.

The wisdom of the European move was vindicated as the order book for the new aircraft grew rapidly, including major purchases from important airlines in the United States. So, with the A320, AI confronted the American manufacturers not only with competition in an additional market segment but also with a product that promised to set new industry standards. This wresting of the technological initiative from the industry's dominant players was thus a very significant element in consortium's the overall strategy. After it introduced the A320, AI was no longer merely responding to conditions established by its competitors; now it was influencing directly the very rules under which the competition would take place.

With the commercial success of the A320, the technological prowess of the partners had been combined with the financial support and political will of the national governments in implementing a game plan that had begun to pay real dividends. Airbus Industrie wasted no time in following the A320 with the launch of not one but two new products in 1987. The A330/A340 program was a prudent and calculated extension of the product line into the last remaining US-monopolized segment: a move with which "Airbus Industrie sought above all to consolidate its position by imposing the technological breakthroughs of the A320 as new standards".

Now able, like its major competitor Boeing, to offer airlines a range of aircraft across the major market segments, AI has attained the stature of the world's second largest civil airframe manufacturer. But concomitant with this stature, and from the perspective of our topic today, more important than the achievements in technology and marketing themselves, is the fact that AI has thoroughly and permanently altered the very structure of the industry in which it now competes. Even as Boeing remains the market leader and is the single most significant force in the industry, American hegemony in the civil airliner market has been thoroughly challenged if not broken decisively.

This success has generated an intense transatlantic political debate concerning the legitimate role of government in supporting industry, as Airbus and its product line depended heavily on financing from the French, German, and British governments. The Americans firms and the US government viewed such state funding as distorting the market for commercial aircraft and intentionally damaging one of the few remaining American industrial strongholds. For their part the Europeans argued that their government monies could not begin to match what had been provided to American aeronautics firms through US defence contracts and other forms of support and protection. Although the high-temperature dispute was supposedly resolved in the 1992 accords, today neither side is truly satisfied, and the potential for open transatlantic confrontation on the issue of subsidies remains real.

What of the most recent developments? What is the direction of US policy in this key sector, and how will this affect the European aeronautics industry? A great deal of ink continues to be spilled concerning the nature of the changes in the structure of international politics wrought by the collapse of the USSR and the end (if not resolution) of the East-West conflict. To summarize this discourse is beyond the scope of this chapter, but it is appropriate to draw some conclusions about the impact of these seismic shifts in the security realm on the character of the international economic relations, with specific reference to the European-American rivalry in commercial aeronautics.

First of all, it is clear that since the implosion of its primary military and political threat, the United States enjoys a measure of supremacy in the realms of security and diplomacy unrivaled in its past history. Both the fact and impression of this primacy was greatly enhanced as result of the Gulf War, in which a US-led coalition dispatched the formidable (at least on paper) forces of Saddam in a sort of high-tech blitzkrieg. The operations involved the orchestration of impressive "lift" capabilities (which involved quite a lot of commercial air transport capacity pressed into the service of national security) to build up an enormous storehouse of assets in the region, the delivery of ordnance from a combination of air and sea "platforms", and coordinated movement of multinational ground forces, adding up to an overwhelming combination of logistical and technical capabilities. Despite the fact that Saddam still clings to power, the unmistakable impression left by the Gulf War is that the US wields an unrivaled force projection capacity built on industrial and technological capabilities that leave it with no "peer" competitor.

This striking degree of US preeminence in the military realm has been reinforced by a concomitant but probably coincidental resurgence in the performance of the American economy. Despite the 1992 Clinton campaign's incessant emphasis on the failures of the Bush administration ("its the economy, stupid"), nearly all indicators of macroeconomic health had already begun to point upward in 1992. Perhaps a bit like the cock taking credit for the dawn, the Clinton administration was able to claim the creation of 10 million jobs and preside over a falling budget deficit, record low unemployment combined with almost no inflation and low interest rates, a booming stock market, and thus in the elections of 1996 ride the wave of an economy seemingly going from strength to strength. While the deficit in visible trade has remained wide, that gap can also be construed as a further indication of economic strength, as the US continues to serve as a magnet sucking in from abroad raw materials, goods and labour (documented and otherwise) at a stunning pace.

Although the Clinton administrations cannot take credit for this fortuitous convergence of circumstances, they most assuredly deserve recognition for their determined and concerted efforts to marry these developments in the realms of security and economics into a coherent "geoeconomic" strategy designed to extend US commercial and political influence abroad. Despite a perceived lack of interest and expertise in foreign affairs (reinforced by his own proclamations concerning the priority of domestic concerns such as health care reform), as Van Scherpenberg has argued, Bill Clinton arguably is distinguished from his post-WWII predecessors by a "more active industrial, technology and export promotion policy emphasizing economic security in defining national security". To an unprecedented extent, the Clinton era has been characterized by the coordination of the efforts and abilities of the various parts of the administrative bureaucracy relating to the active pursuit of US economic interests overseas, which have been explicitly linked through the Trade Promotion Coordination Committee (TPCC).

Much of the impetus to coordinate the ability of the US government to promote the export of American commercial goods and services can be found in pressures emanating from post-Cold War developments in the defence industrial base. In hopes of realizing the promised but still elusive "peace dividend", the Pentagon has used declining procurement budgets as a lever to encourage the rationalization of its contractor base through a combination of acquisitions, mergers and even the elimination among suppliers of military equipment. Especially significant in its connection to the commercial realm is the fact that this ongoing consolidation is occurring in a technological and industrial context in which the lines between the civilian and military sectors are becoming increasingly blurred. As military strategy, tactics, operations and equipment come to rely more and more heavily on so-called information technologies (IT, especially data processing and microelectronics), the "defence industry is gradually dissolving into civilian high-technology industries".

As the defence and civilian industrial base are more tightly fused, the economies of scope and scale that might be realized by raising output and lengthening production runs through overseas sales of high-technology products, whether civil, military or "dual-use", become increasingly important to government and industry alike. As the military and economic dimensions of national security have become so tightly linked at the technological and industrial levels, "the defence industry thus has become part of a pattern of intensifying economic and trade competition, especially in high-technology industries, that is being fought out by commercial as well as political means". In this competition, the Europeans find themselves at a marked disadvantage relative to the sole superpower that has demonstrated the willingness and ability to use its enhanced leverage in the security realm to affect the outcome of commercial contests, such as the 1994 sale to Saudia Airlines.

These post-Cold War developments of course have direct relevance to the US-European rivalry in commercial aeronautics and civil aviation, as the competition for global market share, especially in the manufacture of aircraft but also in the provision of air services, assumes an increasingly strategic dimension. Under pressures to consolidate at least as severe as their American counterparts, European aerospace firms continue to shed workers as their respective governments wield the budget axe. With the US aerospace industry much further along in the process of post-Cold War rationalization, as one analyst has noted, "the broader technology base of emerging US industry giants on what probably will be lower-cost base will put European aerospace companies, as a class, at a major competitive disadvantage". The ominous implications for the European industry are not lost on its leadership-consolidate quickly and effectively, or risk elimination from the arena.

An even sharper edge has been applied to the transatlantic rivalry in commercial aeronautics by the merger of Boeing and McDonnell Douglas. The new company should generate $48 billion in projected annual revenue, employ 200,000 workers and offer a product line including the world's premier fighter aircraft (F-15, F/A-18), military transport (C-17), missiles, space vehicles, electronic products and systems, and, of course, the most comprehensive line of commercial aircraft. For many observers, the national political and strategic rationale behind the merger is clear. As one astute observer has noted: "You have one national aircraft company now. It says that our policy is based on a definition of markets on a global basis. I believe that's very realistic. Ultimately, the marketplace would have demanded it, but the Clinton administration really saw the need and responded".

For the Europeans in general and for Airbus Industrie in particular, the implications of the proposed merger are worrisome at best and indeed potentially disastrous, because the new American entity promises to wield a degree of market power unprecedented in the history of the industry. First, the new Boeing would have cash reserves of around $6 billion, and the additional revenue generated by McDonnell Douglas's defence products would be available to the new entity. Not only will defence sales cushion the eventual and inevitable downturn in commercial orders, they "also will enable Boeing to use the cash flow to fund growth of new commercial aircraft products".

Second, the combined commercial product line of the merged company would account for over 90% of the world's existing fleet of aircraft, meaning a steady stream of revenue for decades to come from the lucrative sale of spare parts and product support services. Also, it can be safely assumed that at least some McDonnell Douglas customers would retain some loyalty to the company and its product line, giving the merged company an advantage in future sales competitions with Airbus. The expansion of the commercial product line that would be offered by the new Boeing could also provide opportunities for cross-subsidization of revenues among aircraft types, perhaps with the MD-95 line serving as a sort of loss-leader to sell customers on a package deal including a variety of more profitable aircraft. Even before the merger proposal, Boeing had moved to sign "exclusivity" supply agreements with both Delta and American airlines, even though Boeing has agreed to revoke these under pressure by the European Union. Finally, the new, single American firm would exert a great deal of influence over the global network of suppliers, who may be pressured to make a short-term business decision or even a long-term contractual choice between the European and American manufacturers.

Clearly, the creation of a single and much-strengthened American competitor has increased the pressure for and raised the stakes of a thoroughgoing consolidation of the European aerospace sector, perhaps with Airbus Industrie serving as the focal point. But serious obstacles to this process remain, as European firms remain reliant on the priorities and decisions of their respective national governments for the funding of future projects, while those governments remain loath to relinquish control over assets so vital to national security. In view of the dramatic and indeed ominous developments on the other side of the Atlantic, Airbus Industrie is pressing forward with renewed urgency in a multifaceted effort to remain competitive. One of the more controversial elements of the strategy is to have AI play a new role as designer and manufacturer of military equipment in the form of the Future Large Aircraft (FLA), proposed to replace European and world fleets of Lockheed C-130 Hercules transports. To manage the project AI has created a subsidiary, Airbus Military Co. (AMC), which would collaborate in the production phase with aerospace companies of the countries having made firm commitments to purchase the aircraft. Yet the status of the entire project remains uncertain, with European governments reluctant to make firm budgetary commitments.

Airbus Industrie also continues to take steps toward its oft-stated goal of reorganization into a "single corporate entity". Under the new plan agreed in January 1997, the consortium's members would abandon the GIE structure and transfer ownership and control of industrial facilities and engineering staffs to a unified company scheduled to come into being in 1999. But certainly the devil will be in the details, as the members must first agree to valuations for the assets to be transferred to the new entity, some of which are state owned in part or whole, and the plan also raises thorny issues of partial foreign ownership of industrial assets crucial to each country. And if the unified company is formed as planned, the new entity will also include an Italian member for the first time, as Alenia has agreed to become a full partner in the European group.

Certainly, the European competition, however it organizes itself, has a formidable task at hand in the new Boeing now sitting atop a consolidated and streamlined American defence industrial base, with the active support of the U.S. government in overseas commercial sales contests.

5 Civil/Defence Linkage in Aerospace: The Political Significance of a Strategic Industry

Dr DEREK BRADDON
Director, Research Unit in Defence Economics
University of the West of England, Bristol

Introduction

Following the end of the Cold War, defence and aerospace industries are gradually transmuting into a range of high-technology industries where global competitiveness is the over-riding goal. In the United States, the unifying of civil and military interests is taking place with remarkable speed, illustrated most clearly by the proposed $25bn merger of Lockheed Martin and Northrop Grumman and the $18bn merger of Boeing and McDonnell Douglas. The United States has recently supported this unification process through a much more active industrial and trade strategy designed to mobilise, strengthen and integrate the full spectrum of advanced technologies in civil and military aerospace. This 'new mercantilist' strategy involves focusing all available political, security and economic leverage on key strategic markets while supporting specific strategic industries from which maximum positive economic benefits for the Unites States can be extracted.

This chapter explores the implications of this 'new mercantilist' strategy in terms of the growing political significance of the aerospace industry, the civil/defence linkages that lie at the heart of the strategy and the kinds of response required of the European aerospace industry, if it is to remain a major player in the intensely competitive global aerospace market.

Civil/Military Aerospace Symbiosis and US Competitiveness Strategy

Historically, it can be argued that the US has gained enhanced global competitive advantage in aerospace (and in critical supporting industries such as avionics and electronics) from a stated commitment to a free trade/free market philosophy which has masked a covert strategy of government-financed indirect industrial support. Over several decades, and particularly more recently, massive government funding of research and development in the military aerospace sector has been implemented through the procurement decisions of the Department of Defense (through, for example, the Defense Advanced Research Projects Agency), the Department of Commerce (through, for example, the Advanced Technology Programme) and NASA (through, for example, the Aeronautical Research and Development Programme).

The US aerospace industry has gained much from these military/civil technology synergies where, often, whole systems developed for the military were 'spun-off' to civil applications, reducing costs and risks for commercial users. Again, in many instances, products and technologies designed for commercial application have also been able to achieve 'spin-on', that is, higher and longer production runs due to the procurement of large military orders, reducing commercial costs and enhancing competitiveness. Commercial gains here have frequently been at the sub-systems level in materials or in manufacturing process technology, broadening the relevance of, and benefits to be derived from, military-funded research and development expenditure.

The symbiosis between military and civil aircraft development in the US has been crucial in both fuelling and sustaining its leading edge in technology development. In avionics, for example, military technology continues to migrate to civil aircraft design and production including, for example, data and signal processors, data buses, software elements such as operating systems, and sensors such as infra-red and millimetre wave imagers. All of these, arguably, had their origins in the military technology developed in the 1970s; for example, digital avionics systems for the F15 and F16 aircraft, reinforced in the 1980s and 1990s by Joint Service initiatives to upgrade avionics for the A12, F22 Tactical Aircraft and the RAH-66 Light Helicopter. More recently, and of perhaps the greatest potential strategic and commercial significance, has been the development of satellite technology in the form of the US NAVSTAR Global Positioning System (GPS). From the US perspective, the commercial impact of GPS has been described by the Office of Technology Assessment as 'exceeding anything envisioned by the US military' with 'civil applications moving forward at breakneck speed'.

It is important to note that, increasingly, the technology flow has become not only two-way between military and civil sectors but that the flow from civil to military in the US has also increased sharply in recent years, strengthening the synergies between the two sectors. In the US, following the end of the Cold War, the defence industry has gradually dissolved into a range of high technology industries where global competitiveness is the over-riding goal. As a result, the most promising route to commercial success in the aerospace industry now resides in the greater integration of civil and defence sectors. New over-arching systems integration skills and new integrated production technologies allow civil users enhanced access to leading edge defence research and development while providing the military sector with access to path-breaking civil advances in information technology and microelectronics to drive forward the trend towards 'information-based warfare'.

In the US, as nowhere else, this unification of civil and military aerospace interests, under-pinned by extensive and deep-rooted government research and development programmes, is taking place with remarkable speed. This process has been driven by the sharp and prolonged reduction in military expenditure, both in the US and globally, that has been a consequence of the ending of the Cold War. Recent estimates suggest that global defence expenditure in 1996 amounted to some $811bn, the lowest level since 1966 and about 40% below its 1987 peak. In the US, defence expenditure has declined by about one-third since 1987 and US weapons procurement by about two-thirds. In addition, recent estimates for future US defence budgets suggest a further reduction in expenditure of 10% up to 2002.

While the downturn in US defence expenditure is clearly an important factor in hastening the consolidation of the US defence and aerospace industries, that expenditure still remains significant at around 80% of the Cold War average. Furthermore, the high profile conversion strategy launched by the Clinton administration in 1993 under the Technology Reinvestment Programme now appears to be operating primarily in the interests of the military sector. The demise of this programme in 1996 and its replacement by the Dual Use Applications Programme appears to have strengthened further the leaching of civil technology developments for military use, rather than the reverse.[1]

As part of the consolidation and restructuring process, many US prime defence contractors have had little choice but to pursue a range of corporate strategies.

These strategies include:

- pursuing market consolidation by focusing on core business to increase their share of a smaller defence market by down-sizing, cost reduction and enhanced efficiency;

- pursuing collaborative strategies to share costs and risks and secure greater economies of scale and scope;
- rationalising supply chains in order to enhance the overall efficiency of the production process; and
- pursuing diversification and conversion strategies to enter or expand civil business, harnessing and transferring technologies as appropriate and, in some cases, complete divestment of defence divisions.

Examples of such strategic adjustment since 1990 are abundant and, between 1992 and 1997, 32 defence companies were concentrated into nine, with the loss of 1mn jobs with the most intensive consolidation taking place after the so-called 'Last Supper' in 1993 when the US authorities signalled their desire to see major restructuring in the industry and made clear that such consolidation would be unimpeded by government intervention.

Among companies attempting to sharpen their defence market focus while also pursuing corporate rationalisation to enhance their competitive position in what has been termed 'the fourth and final phase' of restructuring are Boeing, McDonnell Douglas, Lockheed, Martin Marietta and Northrop Grumman. Lockheed Martin was formed from the merger of Lockheed with Martin Marietta and Loral. The merger represented a strategy of vertical integration and, in common with some other recent mergers within the US defence industrial base, brought together defence-electronics business and information systems to target one of the few parts of the defence market that is currently expanding. Further examples include Northrop's purchase of Westinghouse's defence-electronics business and Raytheon's acquisition of E-Systems.

Furthermore, the proposed merger of Boeing and McDonnell Douglas, announced in 1996, sharply raises the profile of defence activities within the Boeing organisation. Having already acquired the defence and space business of Rockwell International for $3.2bn, the merger with McDonnell Douglas should increase the share of defence to about 40% of Boeing's projected $48bn revenue for 1997. The proposed merger is an example of horizontal integration within the industry. McDonnell Douglas, for example, manufactures the F15 and F/A18 fighter aircraft, the C17 transporter, the Apache gunship, and (with British Aerospace), the Harrier jump-jet and Goshawk trainer. Boeing, on the other hand, contributes parts to the advanced F22 fighter aircraft and, with Lockheed Martin, won the contract to build the prototype Joint Strike Fighter, the AWACS early-warning aircraft, the Chinook and Comanche helicopters and the Osprey helicopter/aircraft.

The case of McDonnell Douglas also provides an illustration of the degree to which corporate adaptation to the difficult business climate for defence companies can go badly wrong. The corporation began the 1990s as the top defence contractor in the world. It was damaged by cost over-runs and shrinking defence budgets and, in an attempt to sharpen its market focus on defence supply, underwent major rationalisation halving its employment to 63,000 and succeeding in winning a contract with the Department of Defense to supply 80 C17 planes. During this period, McDonnell Douglas became involved in discussions on possible mergers and/or alliances with Boeing, Rockwell and Raytheon but no deals materialised until the 1996 formal merger proposal with Boeing. More recently, the merger proposal announced by Lockheed Martin and Northrop Grumman will create the world's largest defence company.

US Trade Strategy and 'New Mercantilism' - the Political Dimension

Over the last few years, the US appears to have been implementing a much more active industrial policy which links economic security directly with national security. As Nau comments:

> The new US government policy...is almost entirely orientated towards business and export salesmanship.[2]

This strategy has involved:

- within the US, the mobilising, strengthening and integrating of US advanced civil and military technologies in a targeted and comprehensive dual-use approach, as outlined above;
- the co-ordination of government departments (particularly, the Departments of Defense, State and Commerce) to pursue joint strategic initiatives;
- globally, the targeting of all available political, security and economic leverage on key strategic markets, offering a blend of high-technology market leader defence and aerospace products, together with the provision of security made possible by the unique 'global reach' of the US military. This translates into a double-edged technological and commercial superiority for the United States

aerospace industry in both civil and military markets, achieved at modest budgetary and political cost.[3]

The European Response

It is the absence of a similar major restructuring in the European defence industrial base that now puts the European aerospace industry at greatest risk. For, in Europe, the process has scarcely begun.

Since the 1960s, Europe has had experience of a number of trans-national collaborative ventures in the defence/aerospace sector, including 22 in aircraft production, seven in aero-engines and 12 in missiles. Only 15% of procurement expenditure in France and the UK has been deployed on collaborative ventures and 25% in Germany. The experience of collaborative projects in the defence/aerospace sector across Europe suggests that, for an important reason, significant costs have to be borne by the partners. These include higher administration and organisation costs; costs associated with the allocation of high-technology development work between partners sometimes at a sub-optimal level; the tendency to duplicate research and development and, in some cases, production work; costs associated with national modifications to a trans-national product; consultation and partner agreement delays; and collaborative project management costs.

Nevertheless, over the last few years, Europe has begun to recognise the need for countervailing power in the defence/aerospace market to that of the giant American corporations and the 'new mercantilist' strategy of the US government. Most notably, in 1988, the IEPG instituted an action plan to create a more unified European arms market based on competition, joint ventures and multinational consortia across the European nations. The urgent need for greater integration of European civil and military technologies was emphasised by Lionel Jospin, the new French Prime Minister, at the Paris Air Show in 1997 in commenting that

> I consider essential rapprochement between civil and military technology in the aeronautic sector.

The problem for Europe relates to the apparent desire in some countries, particularly France, to retrain a 'national champion' approach to the defence/aerospace sector for reasons partly to do with security and national prestige. Only tentative steps towards a genuine merging of resources in these critical sectors across Europe has thus far been considered,[4] perhaps the best example being the establishment in February 1996 of an Anglo-Franco-

German forum to consider the future of the aerospace industry (involving Rolls-Royce, MTU and Snecma).

Mergers at the national level within Europe simply do not deliver companies with the market power necessary to compete adequately with the US giant corporations. For example, against defence turnover estimates of $25bn for Lockheed Northrop and $18bn for Boeing McDonnell Douglas, an Aérospatiale/Dassault merger in France would achieve turnover of only around $5bn.

Another proposal which moves beyond the national champion approach and which has received considerable discussion is the Weston Plan to create a European trans-national giant corporation, Eurospace, from a merging of appropriate divisions of British Aerospace, GEC Marconi, Daimler-Benz Aerospace and Aérospatiale/Dassault. This would create a company with a turnover in excess of $20bn, capable of competing effectively with the Boeing/McDonnell Douglas and Lockheed Martin giants.

The strategy behind the US drive towards fewer, larger and more powerful defence/aerospace corporations is to seek enhanced civil/military synergies, while reducing central organisation and research and development costs and enabling the new organisation to spread the risk of potential project cancellation or cutback over a greater range of systems. In addition, the formation of strategic alliances, technology partnerships and further consolidation in the supply and sub-contract network of the US defence/aerospace industry, has accentuated the industrial revolution taking place in this sector.

For defence/aerospace contractors, these organisational, managerial and production-related changes have accelerated their evolution into what is known as M-form, multi-divisional organisations. As a result, sharper market focus and enhanced production flexibility have enabled such companies, especially the large prime contractors in the US defence/aerospace sector, to implement wide-ranging and accelerating corporate rationalisation decisions. With little real progress in European restructuring, the vigorous US rationalisation and restructuring process has succeeded in keeping key US manufacturing industries ahead of their most advanced overseas competitors in terms of industrial productivity and commercial competitiveness.

Since it is unarguably the case that the unmatched military power of the US also allows it to offer a unique package of security-for-trade deals with overseas customers, the leverage available to the United States through its trade-security linkage puts it in a league of its own in this competitive environment. The implications for the European aerospace/defence sector is all too clear. The need for determined and substantial intervention by European governments both to accelerate the restructuring of these critical sectors and to provide adequate trade support measures to enhance their global competitiveness, in line with US strategic policy, has never been more urgent.

Notes and References

1   G Bischak, *US Conversion after the Cold War, 1990-1997, Lessons for Forging a New Conversion Policy,*   Bonn International Centre for Conversion, Brief 9, (July 1997), p 5-8.

2   H Nau, *International Affairs,* (Summer 1994).

3   For further discussion, see Scherpenberg JV, *Transatlantic Competition and European Defence Industries: a new look at the trade-defence linkage, International Affairs,* (73, 1, 1997), pp 99 - 122.

4   Enter McBoeing, *The Economist,* (21 December 1996), pp 101-107.

Part II

The European Challenge

6 The European Response to Globalisation

ADOLFO REVUELTA
Vice-President, Strategic Planing
CASA

Introduction

"Globalisation" describes a scenario where multi-sectorial aerospace companies compete in a worldwide market. The companies that operate in this scenario must therefore have the necessary capacities and capabilities to maintain a simultaneous presence in the different sectors of the aerospace business, and means to access a market of worldwide dimension. The alternative for the companies without such prerequisites is to become "niche" players.

Globalisation is not a new issue for aerospace. In fact, the aerospace business has been, to a certain extent, globalised for many years. This is demonstrated, for instance, by the export figures of aerospace companies which in general have maintained a simultaneous presence in different niches of the market.

Europe has been exporting for many years, on average, up to 30% of its total annual turnover for aerospace (*Figure 1*), and the companies, as a result of the industrial restructuring processes carried out in the past at national levels, have, in general, an active presence in defence, space and civil markets. If globalisation is not new for the aerospace industry, what is it that's changing?

The changes are the rules which drive the behaviour of the globalised market and the nature of the companies which operate in this scenario.

This change is a consequence of several factors. The most important ones are the deregulation in the civil market, the reduction of the military budgets after the end of the Cold War and the increased complexity of the products demanded by the market. These factors together are driving the changes taking place in the aerospace industry.

Deregulation in the civil market, almost finished in the US and under process in Europe, is developing two serious consequences, with one single result.

On the one side, the concentration of the demand side of the market promoting the creation of very big companies or alliances between airlines with a tremendous buying power which will press the margins of the aircraft manufacturers. On the other side, the fierce competition between the airlines that have survived the deregulation process has made the cost of aircraft a key issue for sales success.

At a recent conference, Phil Condit, Chairman and CEO of the Boeing Company, was referring to this issue with the following words:

> Our history (in civil aviation) basically shows that the first part of our modern aviation development was focused on technical performances. Then, came deregulation and now cost to our customers has become the critical part of the equation. Under deregulation, a new set of rules developed. Today cost is very important.

I would say more important than ever before.

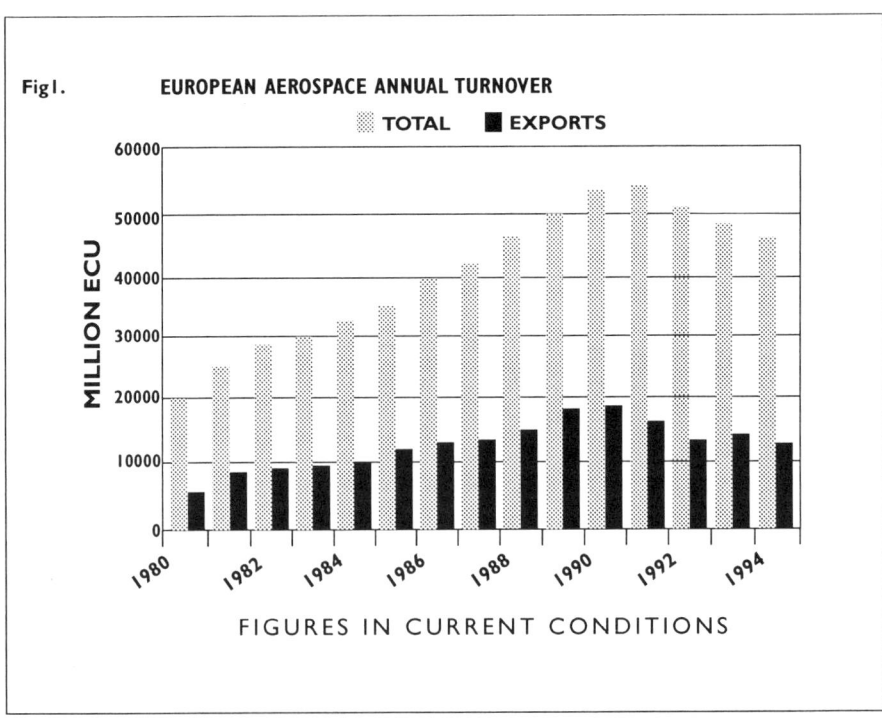

In conclusion, the tendency is for the civil market to be dominated by a demand configured around very big customers to whom the aircraft manufacturers have to offer a full range of products at more and more competitive prices, as well as an outstanding maintenance service to support their fleets in operation.

This pressure on the margins of the manufacturers will be maintained in the future in spite of the robust market demand increase, forecast for the next 20 years for civil aviation.

In fact, part of the expansion of the civil market is because the reduction in margins of the aircraft manufacturers and also of the airlines, has been transferred to the end users who pay less and less to travel on aeroplanes.

Let us talk now about the defence market. The budgets for defence applications are suffering a substantial reduction as a consequence of the end of the Cold War and the collapse of the former Soviet countries. This reduction has drastic consequences for the aerospace industry in terms of reduction of turnover and associated margins, substantially bigger than the margins in the civil market.

The combination of deregulation in the civil market and reduction of the defence budgets, have changed drastically the market in which aerospace manufacturers used to operate.

The scenario is evolving from a situation where a healthy military business representing more than 50% of total activity for the sector tallies with a civil business with lower but acceptable margins, to a new situation where the military business has decreased substantially and where the potential growth of the business is going to be based on a civil market where very powerful customers are going to push down the margins to limits never achieved before.

Regarding the third mentioned factor, the evolution in the technical complexity of the products, it is evident that future aerospace and defence systems will be much more than single platforms. They will be more a set of different systems coupled together, requiring a variety of technologies and skills for their development.

This tendency will demand from the aerospace manufacturers a massive effort in research and development of the necessary technology, and increase pressure to explore the synergies associated with their simultaneous presence in the different aerospace markets.

To sum up, the global competition scenario can be characterised by a worldwide market dominated by powerful customers which demand more technically complex products at more competitive prices. The current forecast is that these characteristics will be intensified in the future.

These changes in the market are necessitating drastic changes on the manufacturers' side. They need to develop their structures and behaviours to survive and remain competitive in this new environment.

The new conditions demand new conglomerates with enough power to operate simultaneously in the different sectors of aerospace business; enough capacity of innovation to properly respond to the increased technological complexity of the new products, and enough dimension to operate in a worldwide market where negotiating local alliances and joint ventures is becoming a key issue in accessing such markets.

The trend in the global market is that the number of companies and products in competition will be reduced. The main competitor of the European aerospace industry is the US industry. It has already reacted to the new scenario through a process of mergers between different companies, creating new enterprises with a dimension far bigger than the European companies, and with a capability to operate simultaneously in the civil, defence and space markets. These conglomerates can be considered as global enterprises.

So far, Europe, with a fragmented market and an industrial structure based on national champions, has been at least up to now, unable to progress in the consolidation of its industry and has based its competition with the Americans on European collaborative programmes.

In the new global scenario with a restructured US industry stronger than ever, and the fragmentation of the European aerospace market, we must develop a series of actions if we want to become a global player and survive in the next century. In my opinion, the following steps must be taken by the Europeans.

European Product Policy

In a global market competition the European aerospace industry must compete in all the niches of the market. It makes strategic sense for our industry to break any monopoly position of our competitors.

The priorities for our industry should be to launch and develop those products which break the monopolistic position of the US industry in the market place.

In the civil aircraft business, Airbus has no presence in the 350+ seater segment nor in the 100-seater niche. It means that the Airbus A340-500/600, the A3XX and the A3IX have to be identified as the European priorities for this market.

As far as the military products are concerned, the FLA (Future Large Aircraft), the European response to the US monopolistic position in the heavy military transport market and the consolidation of the series production of the Eurofighter 2000, where four out of the six European countries with significant aerospace industries are involved, have to be considered as key programmes in the European military products priority list.

In a longer timescale, our industry must set up a pan-European research program to develop a technological demonstrator of what will be the next generation of the European fighter aircraft, and to develop the technologies to be applied to an eventual supersonic civil aircraft to be developed, either under the leadership of the European industry, or in collaboration with the Americans.

Even in this last case, if we do not make the necessary technological effort in this field, we will not be able to collaborate with the US industry in terms of parity.

European Restructuring Process

Some of the mentioned programmes will have to be developed within a European restructured industry. The restructuring process in Europe is extremely difficult to go through, but we must.

It cannot be avoided because our industry needs to gain size in the new global competitive environment and to set up a more stable co-operation scheme, covering the whole range of aerospace products. The creation of ad-hoc consortiums or alliances in specific products or market niches, as it was the case in the past, is no longer effective in the new situation.

The restructuring process, based on the creation of a single European aerospace entity, will enhance the competitiveness of our industry and will avoid in the future the competition between similar European products benefiting from economies of scale, and optimising the effort of our industry in the competition for the global market. I would like to take the opportunity to make some comments on matters which I consider critical for the future viability of our industry.

The integration process which could take place in stages, the restructuring of the Airbus consortium being the first one, should envisage a final entity which includes not only the civil business but the defence and space activities as well. Only a European entity with a simultaneous presence in all these markets will have the necessary dimension and strength to be able to compete with the new enterprises created by US industry.

In my view, the final entity should be the result of a pan-European process of horizontal integration of the seven European airframe companies, by merging the current capacities of Aérospatiale, Alenia, British Aerospace, CASA, DASA, Dassault and SAAB. An alternative model based on a vertical integration of aerospace companies will add no value to the final company and will complicate the process by introducing non-aerospace activities and new companies which would need to be accommodated.

The restructuring process also has to resolve (overcapacity and the level of industrial redundancies) which currently exist between these companies, and has to be balanced in terms of distribution of the restructuring effort and the allocation of responsibilities and activities to be developed in all of the companies involved.

Only if this is acceptable to everybody will we be able to set up a pan-European aerospace enterprise, where individual companies could create centres of excellence at a European level. As I have already said, the task is very complex and difficult.

There are national interests involved in the process which have to be properly accommodated into the final scheme, taking into account that the aerospace industry is perceived in our countries as a strategic issue.

Also, we have to find a solution to prevent any potential power imbalance in the ownership of the integrated entity as well as design a company structure and managerial organisation which will improve the efficiency and competitiveness of the new entity, compared with what we have today.

And all these problems, and some more, have to be resolved at the same time as the European aerospace industry maintains competition with an already restructured US industry.

Finally, the restructured European aerospace industry has to set up long term strategic links with the aerospace industries of other countries (predominantly in Asia). Access to these rapidly growing markets requires the creation of alliances and joint ventures which permit it to produce where sold. This new approach will demand from the European aerospace industry the resources required to enter new markets and to participate in their growth. At the same time such alliances will allow the aggregation around our industry of complementary strengths to participate in future European programmes.

Europe as an Integrated Market

The two actions to be carried out by the industry already discussed - the launch of new strategic products and the restructuring process of our aerospace industry - are not enough to compete in the global scenario if they are not complemented by other key actions which have to be primarily developed by the European institutions and the national European governments.

The European domestic market is a fragmented market for suppliers but also for institutional purchasers. In this latter case, fragmentation affects the European defence market and makes it difficult to coordinate among European governments.

As a consequence, in the past, we faced so often two or more European products competing with each other in the global markets, without the necessary political support for export sales, or the economies of scale of the competing US products.

There is no doubt that the progress towards the coordination of military requirements at European level will avoid such competition among European projects, enhancing the competitiveness of our industry and its future products.

The accessibility of the European defence market to US companies is also a consequence of the previous lack of coordination. Up to 75% of all European defence imports are accounted for by US firms, and the trade balance for defence products between US and Europe is 6 to 1. Such unbalanced trade situation endangers the future of our defence industry, including aerospace.

Our governments have to realise that investment in European products is a way of optimising the benefit defence expenditure gives our industry, at a time when budget constraints of European countries are bringing defence expenditure to minimum levels.

Europe also has to coordinate its effort in R&D technology for our aerospace industry as it is a key element for success in this business.

The aerospace industry is of strategic importance to Europe and investment in research and technology for this industry must be seen as a strategic issue as well. This position is reinforced by the fact that the US industry relies on a long tradition of public/industry partnership and public investment in industry's research and technology which is currently running at about four times the level of European investment. Today's research and technology investments provides the basis for tomorrow's products. Although European industry is investing heavily, using its own resources, it cannot hope to stay in the technology race with the US, unless there is a strong financial support from European governments similar to the one enjoyed by US industry from its government.

Additionally, the increase in technological complexity of future aerospace products, together with the required investment in new projects, does not allow aerospace activities to be confined to the national level of member states. The European aerospace industry must progress and develop its research and technological activities at a European level. A combined effort between its central institutions and its member states must exist in order to prevent duplication at European level of what it is already being done at the level of different member states.

In conclusion, the global market with its new rules has became too big a business for single European countries. In the new scenario, Europe has to operate as a single unit at both the industrial level and at the institutional level as well. The sooner we achieve such unity, the better.

7 The Role of the EU as a Catalyser for the Integration of the Aerospace Industry in Europe

HELMUT SCHMITT von SYDOW
EU Commission DGIII

The European Commission believes strongly in the vital role aerospace will play in the future prosperity of the Continent. The Commission is ready to contribute within its means and competencies to help improve the industry's competitiveness and its long-term viability.

In the civil sector, the Commission wants Airbus Industrie to be a tough, but fair competitor to Boeing/McDonnell Douglas. The Commission fought during the Uruguay Round to ensure that the final outcome produced a balanced Europe/US trade compromise. The Commission is absolutely determined that Europe's civil aircraft manufacturers are not going to be hounded from the market by unfair subsidies.

The Commission is more and more concerned by the increasing level of indirect subsidies for the US aerospace industry through NASA, and by the funnelling of money from vast United States military research programmes toward the civil sector. This is being monitored carefully, and the Commission may consider reorienting some of its own strategic approaches in the future if this trend continues.

The US government's direct interference in favour of civil and military export sales is another practice that can severely distort the global aerospace marketplace, and is contrary to World Trade Organisation rules. There have regularly been charges that the US has resorted to this sort of practice. The Commission will continue to counteract this, and in the longer term, try to persuade the US to forego such government pressures altogether.

But ultimately, we will only be able to defend our interests if we act as one. Too often, in many political and foreign policy issues, I am afraid to say, that is not the case. So let me be frank about the future: if we are not cohesive, acting together, there is a good chance that the European aerospace industry will be severely weakened in the global marketplace.

The Need for a Rational European Production and Distribution System

The impetus for restructuring must come from industry itself. This should not only involve partners in industry groupings such as Airbus Industrie, but other civil and military producers as well. While the European Commission does not have direct influence in this domain, it can nevertheless facilitate this change.

An example of how Commission action can help is the special Aeronautics Task Force. The European Commission has developed an ambitious research policy in the Fourth Framework of the Treaty of Maastricht, with more than 400mn ECU earmarked for the aeronautics sector through different programmes (Brite-Euram, Esprit, etc.). The Aeronautics Task Force was created to promote downstream research and to improve co-operation with industry. The next research and development research framework programme, FP V, will amplify this effort. It is vital that industry continues to work closely with the Commission to define the optimum European project-based proposals to improve long-term competitiveness.

The aerospace industry plays also a major role as an irreplaceable asset to underpin a European Defence Identity. The aerospace industry accounts for approximately 50% of the defence-related industries (including electronics for aerospace). Without the ability to develop and produce the necessary aerospace products, autonomy in the formulation of an independent defence policy would be significantly diminished. There are thus important foreign and security policy considerations in the maintenance of a healthy and competitive aerospace industry.

It is evident that Europe must pursue its own defence identity, the root of which is a strong industrial, scientific and technological component. The importance of this is evident in alarming economic figures. Since 1984, European defence industry employment has dropped by 37%, and 600,000 skilled defence jobs have been lost. While some of this is inevitable due to failing defence budgets, the reduction in spending cannot explain all of the losses.

Worse still, intra-European defence trade amounts to only 3-4% of total national European procurement. And while US companies have a significant share of European defence business, Europe has virtually none of the American marketplace.

Another difficulty that must be addressed is the unnecessary proliferation of programmes. Some 10 European companies are producing helicopters and military aircraft, while 11 companies build missiles. There are only five in each sector producing the same hardware in the US, enabling those companies to benefit from the larger American market and from economies of scale.

Industrial logic can accelerate the advancement toward a true European defence identity through steps such as: demonstrating to politicians the wisdom of trans-frontier defence cooperation and procurement, merging overlapping military/civil activities, rationalising the production process, making real success of co-operative armaments programmes designed to satisfy specific European defence needs, and by encouraging the European Union and Western European Union to develop European armament programmes through a European Armaments Agency.

Defence procurement issues should be addressed as a matter of priority. With escalating costs and budget restrictions, ever fewer new programmes will be launched but the programmes will be of such importance and last so long that they will effectively structure the industry for the next 30 years or so. The Commission proposed the establishment of a European defence procurement regime which could lead to the creation of a European domestic defence market and harmonisation of procurement requirements, schedules and procedures in its 1996 communication on the defence-related industries.

Political progress towards a European defence identity will take time. At each step, the Union, through its institutions, will have to show capability, capacity and the ability to act in a timely way. But to those who argue that such matters are the essential domain of national sovereignty - and inappropriate for the European Union, I say the following: the world has changed, forever. Solitary national action in almost all foreign and defence domains is over. We live in the world of burden-sharing and consensus-building. In fact, what we are really talking about is sharing sovereignty - which in many cases is the only way of regaining sovereignty that we have all but lost.

Aerospace Includes also Space Activities of Significant Importance

The space sector plays a key role in the development of information technology, which in Europe alone is a market of well over 300bn ECU and growing at nearly 10% per year.

Huge potential markets are opening up in satellite communications, satellite positioning and remote sensing with values of hundreds of billions of ECU. Whilst Europe is strong in space-launch services as a result of Ariane and the Arianespace commercial management/marketing organisation, it is weak in other growing segments. As a result, a concerted effort is needed to translate Europe's investment and ideas into winning, innovative products for the 21st century. As with Airbus and the commercial air transport sector, there is fierce space sector competition from the US whose industry receives heavy government funding through military procurement and research.

There are many emerging space issues of prime importance for the European Union: the World Trade Telecom negotiations, access to new frequencies for non-geostationary satellite systems, implementation and design of the second-generation Global Navigation Satellite System, and fair competition rules for space launch service providers, to name a few.

To sum up, my impression is that, in the aerospace industries, we need more Europe, not less.

The European Commission has issued a detailed communication on these issues: *"The European Aerospace Industry: Meeting the Global Challenge",* European Commission, COM(97) 466 fin., (Brussels, 24 September 1997).

8 Consolidation in European Aerospace: A UK Perspective

ROBERT WHITFIELD
Director Strategy & External Affairs
British Aerospace Airbus

Introduction

My role as Director of Strategy and External Affairs for British Aerospace Airbus is very much focused on the strategic evaluation, direction and management of our business as a full partner within the Airbus consortium. My aim is to ensure that Airbus' success in the world market continues to thrive and that it is equipped for, and grows into the next millennium. With that in mind, my chapter covers the broad and extensive issues affecting the consolidation of the European aerospace industry as a whole and British Aerospace's view on this. I have outlined the drivers, the barriers and challenges we face and some of our views on possible structures for a consolidated industry. Inevitably, of course, I have concentrated on Airbus, not least because, in our view, it is the way forward and the first step to the ultimate goal of total consolidation within Europe.

Concentrating first on the civil side of our industry, our goal is to form the Airbus Industrie consortium into a single company - the SCE or Single Corporate Entity by 1999. This element in isolation cannot address the whole picture, but achieving the SCE will create a benchmark company forming a bridge for the rest of the industry to follow.

Timing

I will return to the SCE later in the presentation but at this stage it is important to highlight that the single most important factor in the whole process, is that of speed and timing. It is imperative, as we see it, to the future of European aerospace that we act now and do not delay; indeed in my view this action is well overdue.

We are already trailing behind our main competitors in the US and delaying the inevitable will make it increasingly difficult for us to retain

103

our current position in the world market, let alone realise the benefits of consolidation and improve our position overall. When we talk about 'consolidation', many see this in simple terms as 'combining' the companies, but the second meaning 'to solidify or strengthen' is what we must focus on. We must ensure that we move in time to achieve the strengthened European aerospace industry that consolidation will bring.

The Drivers

So why do we need to do anything at all? Well, let us look at what drives us.

US Defence Restructuring (fig1)

1996 and 1997 have witnessed considerable change in our industry globally, and in the US in particular. We believe that Europe would benefit from a position of collective strength in any future collaborations with the US rather than one of individual weakness.

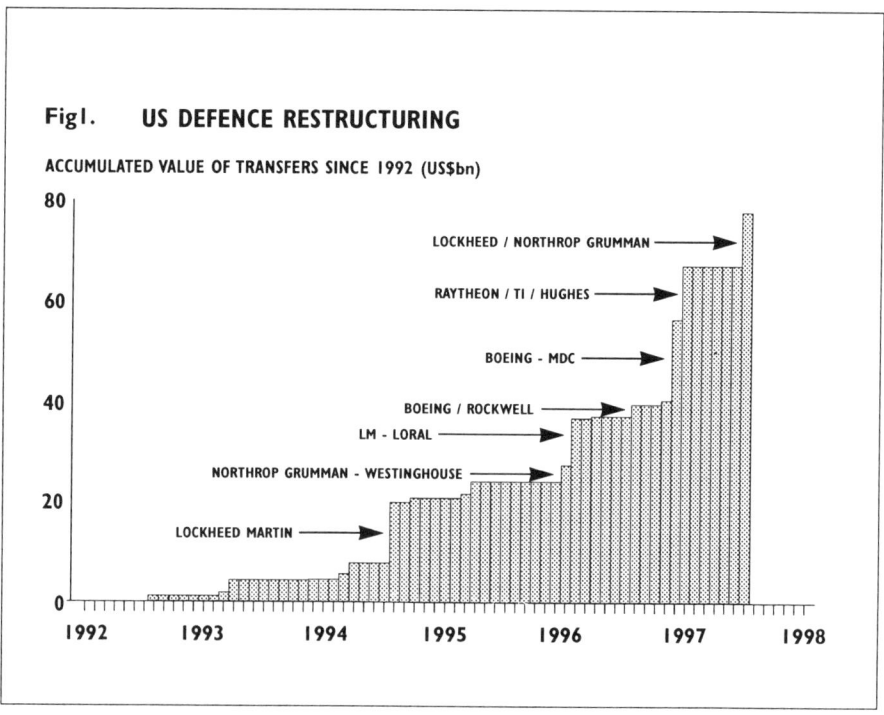

Fig1. **US DEFENCE RESTRUCTURING**

ACCUMULATED VALUE OF TRANSFERS SINCE 1992 (US$bn)

Economies of Scale

The process of consolidation has moved on apace in the States - with the combined strengths of Raytheon Hughes, Lockheed Martin and Boeing - the latter having first absorbed Rockwell Aerospace and Defense and now recently McDonnell Douglas. As a result we now see a US aerospace and defence industry dominated by just three companies.

The average size of US companies in this sector has grown by 300% in the last few years. They have annual sales volumes of between $30bn, $40bn and beyond compared to the largest European aerospace companies such as British Aerospace and DASA with sales around $12bn.

US/European Defence Industrial Base (fig 2)

In the defence sector, the many contractors in the UK, Germany, France, Sweden, Italy and Spain together have a combined defence budget of some $120bn. This compares to just one third of the number of contractors in the US with a US defence budget of $270bn. In Europe we are trying to support three times the number of contractors on less than half the budget.

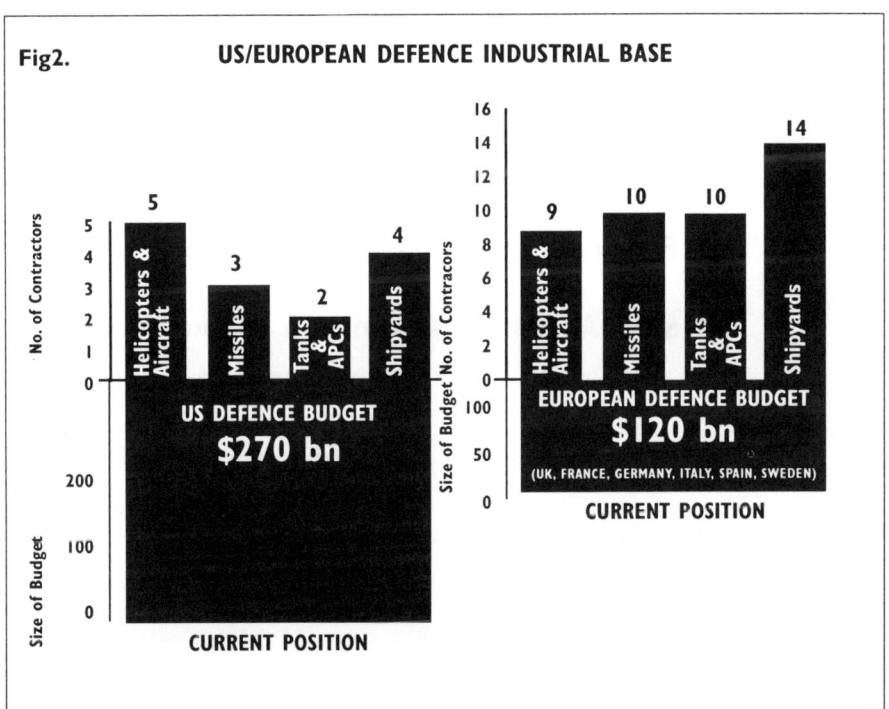

105

There is only one customer in the US with one set of requirements. In Europe there are many customers. So, not only the supply but, also the demand is divided and weakened by too many parts.

US Aerospace Scene (fig 3)

Although still dependent on companies being well run and efficient, the opportunity in the States to affect substantial advantage through economies of scale is enormous. We expect to see their costs reduced through rationalisation and the removal of duplication. The resulting US companies - which are already formidable competitors in the world market - are becoming even more powerful adversaries who, in time, could well seek further acquisitions outside of the US.

Market Share

The United States already dominates the world defence, space and civil aircraft markets. With the size of the US defence budget, together with a significant level of defence exports, the US accounts for well over half of the defence market worldwide.

Fig3.   **THE US AEROSPACE SCENE**

● **Production Advantage**

● **Sales Advantage - dominant market share**
                       - export strength

● **R&T and Development Advantage**

● **High levels of Government support**

In the civil aircraft sector Boeing's already dominant position has been further strengthened with its recent acquisition of McDonnell Douglas. It now has over 70% of the world civil aircraft market by value. In terms of market penetration, 84% share of fleets of aircraft are Boeing's, including military conversions, a total 87% share of all jet aircraft with civil origins are Boeing - and in terms of seats the figure is around 93%. The statistics here speak for themselves. There were very strong arguments for forming the Airbus SCE before the US merger but this has become even more fundamental and urgent now.

Investment in Research and Technology

Not only is the US investing far more in Research and Technology applicable to civil aircraft than the European Governments combined - over $1.5bn (£1bn) per annum, compared to less than quarter that figure for Europe - there is also wasteful duplication in Europe which has to stop.

Export Markets

The fourth and final driver is the view of the export market - especially the Asia Pacific and China. Individual European countries have little chance of exerting influence in the marketplace in comparison to one remaining world super power. Experience shows that senior people in the developing countries in the Asia Pacific region recognise the need to collaborate with the West, but they want a straight choice between the US and a combined Europe.

Challenges and Barriers

There are many barriers and challenges to be overcome in the defence sector. And, although not insurmountable, we have to be realistic about them and recognise the effort that will be required to succeed and to move beyond current arrangements. There are issues of national sovereignty and a desire for self-dependency in defence. But ultimately surplus capacity and too many companies will lead down the path to greater interdepenency. Governments will face a choice, either to relinquish some control or watch their defence industries slowly wither and die in the face of superior US competition.

Every country must be prepared to compromise in order to make consolidation work, for example for some there will inevitably be some loss of employment as rationalisation takes place. Establishing Centres of

Excellence and ensuring each country benefits from wealth generation is the key. There will at least for the foreseeable future be a need for Governments to invest in Research and Technology and major future projects such as A3XX and FLA and they must be able to see returns on this investment - jobs and returns to the balance of payments for example.

A consolidated European aerospace and defence industry should not produce winners and losers. There can be no place for expectations of gaining power and control: countries cannot seek to hold a leading share or position. However, the possibility of each national government holding a golden share to preserve its essential interests in an emergency situation may well prove necessary.

The fourth major challenge will be the valuation. That will not be easy, especially with a number of what are today State owned companies. But we should not be deterred by such problems.

The Ultimate Goal

For us, the answer is a determined effort on the part of all the major European players to negotiate the establishment of a single European aerospace and defence company. The ultimate goal is a company which operates its business across national borders and is managed by a single unified structure. Such a company should embrace Aérospatiale-Dassault, DASA and BAe with a minimum business base covering civil and military aircraft, guided weapons, defence systems and systems integration, with potential for including space and helicopters too. The industries of Sweden, Italy and Spain should also find a place. This company will have directors and a headquarters in each country with responsibility for compliance with national security and export regulations, for acting as a senior interface with national governments, and for helping balance the respective national interests with those of the multinational company.

In consultation with governments, the company management will rationalise the business across national boundaries so the company retains on an equitable and profitable basis, production facilities and centres of excellence in each country.

Airbus SCE

The barriers to achieving this are much higher in the defence sector. Although desirable, achieving such consolidation in one step is not realistic. Consequently we may have to accept transitional steps to reach the ultimate goal. The first is achieving the Airbus SCE (figs 4 & 5). With

Airbus we have a head start, less barriers to overcome and, a way of moving forward in the urgent time scales needed to combat the threat - hastened particularly by the speed our competition is able to move at in the civil market.

The Airbus Industrie partners, Aérospatiale of France, DASA of Germany, CASA of Spain and ourselves, British Aerospace, have already taken the first step towards the goal, with the signing of a Memorandum of Understanding at the start of this year in which we agreed to work towards achieving the single company by 1999.

Airbus benefits from 25 years of collaboration. We work well together and have a mutual respect for our national and cultural differences which have worked over the years to the benefit of Airbus in establishing optimum solutions. We have no internal or external competitive problems - the consortium is built on established centres of excellence. We do of course retain certain rivalries in capability but not in the market or in our products.

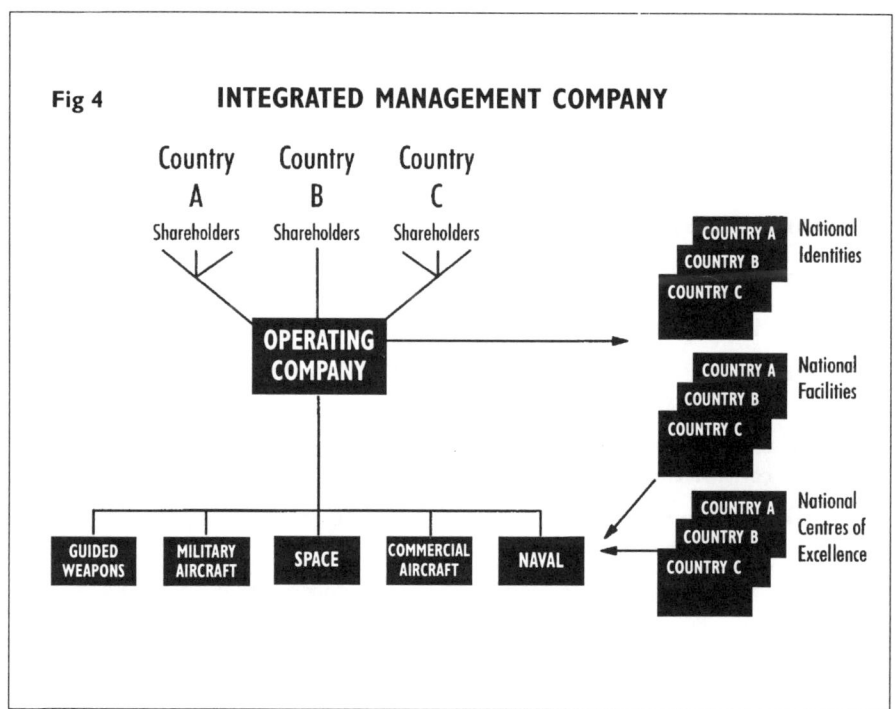

Fig 4   INTEGRATED MANAGEMENT COMPANY

Employment and returns on investment in Airbus are already established and proven. Neither do we have the sovereignty complications of the defence business. Given the threat from the competition and the advanced position we already find ourselves in, we must proceed now.

Both the partner companies and their governments have some hurdles to overcome of course, particularly for industry the valuation agreement. However, ground work on this goes on as I speak and we will all be well placed for negotiations when the time comes. The Airbus Memorandum of Understanding confirms the partners' joint commitment to the goal of European consolidation. All the partners have agreed the SCE is the way forward.

We also have the support of our governments. In June when the Ministers representing the Airbus partner countries met during the Paris Air Show, they discussed the SCE and issued a statement confirming they '..shared the determination of the industry to reach a satisfactory agreement within the lines and timing laid down in the Memorandum of Understanding signed in January 1997...'

Fig 5

AIRBUS RESTRUCTURING

- In January 1997 Supervisory Board signed MOU to change SCE

- MOU sets out timetable and actions to establish SCE by 1999

- Major change involving transfer of engineering and manufacturing assets

- Single Airbus management with authority and accountability to control the business

- Continuation of the partners' change to maximise opportunities for process improvement

  To make Airbus Industrie even more competitive and provide commercial rate of return on investment

In spite of Boeing's clearly dominant position today, we are confident that if Airbus can establish a fully integrated entity quickly and launch aircraft to compete at the top and bottom ends of the market (the Jumbo and 100-seater sectors), a genuine duopoly can be established. Of course, everything isn't quite as clear cut as we see it in the UK - and you may have seen some press comments in recent months.

Some people argue that total consolidation - that is military as well as civil - is the only real step. They believe the peaks and troughs of the aerospace industry will make the business vulnerable if its core activity only comprises the civil sector of the market. They believe that other elements must be incorporated from the outset to add diversity to the business and reduce its dependency on one sector. The formation of the SCE would initially have the same share holders as today however - each of those shareholders would have the same balance of exposure to the civil and military sectors as before. The defence elements of the Airbus partner companies can therefore be combined as and when it is practical, without any delay in the formation of Airbus SCE.

Another area of differing opinion is the benefits to the partners through the cross fertilisation of Research and Technology work gained through both civil and defence interests. At British Aerospace we do not see this as a problem. There is no competition between the defence and civil sides of the businesses. Therefore we see the mutual benefits gained from sharing research and technology continuing. In our view there is no reason why this co-operation should disappear with the formation of the SCE.

Finally, the issue of national identity is perhaps regarded with a higher level of significance by some of the Airbus partner countries than others. An agreement cannot be reached without all the partners and we are all committed to ensure none of the partner countries lose out in the negotiations.

The aim of the SCE is to build an even better, stronger Airbus and ensure it continues to thrive for the benefit of all. Without the SCE its future could be jeopardised. With the time pressures upon us we must take the first step soon to operate Airbus as an SCE; this will help us secure our current position until the rest of the industry can overcome the other barriers and eventually join us in what we sometimes refer to as 'EUROCO'.

Looking back to the birth of Airbus Industrie in the 1960s - the European response to the growing lead and strength of the US in civil aircraft manufacture - many sceptics did not believe it would work. Yet time has proved them wrong as Europe has recovered to develop an extensive range of large civil aircraft and won around 40% of the large commercial aircraft market in which it now competes.

Now is the time for a strong drive to sort out Europe to ensure we can work with the rest of the world from a position of strength - both in civil and ultimately, in defence markets. If not, we will be reduced to a niche player with an increasingly limited technology base.

Europe must get its act together to compete with the US and negotiate as equals not as junior partners. It is imperative we get on with the first step - the formation of the Airbus SCE. Substantial progress has already been made under the Airbus Memorandum of Understanding and we must now keep up the momentum and act quickly to meet the agreed timescales.

9 The European Response to the Challenge of American Consolidation in Civil Aeronautics

MICHEL BIELER
Director of International Affairs
Airbus Industrie

Introduction

Airbus was created 25 years ago from the vision of some European industrialists with the support of a number of politicians. These individuals realised three things:

- That the large civil aircraft industry was strategically important for Europe's economic future;
- That the only way to survive in a world market dominated by the US industry since World War II was for Europe's aerospace companies to join together instead of developing money-losing national programmes that competed against each other in the European market;
- That financial government support in the form of reimbursable launch aid was required to help spread the risks and the long payback period specific to this industry which private funding cannot afford at an initial stage of industry development.

Nobody among the 'founding fathers' could have imagined that in less than 20 years Airbus, starting from a unique niche product, would become the world number two in a market where US competitors were so solidly entrenched. In such a short time span relative to this industry cycle, Airbus has:

- developed a full range of products (which has to be further extended as I will explain later) and established its credibility in terms of customer support in the market place;
- captured more than 30% of the world market overcoming the new entrant commercial handicap. That means today sales of more than 2300 aircraft to 140 customers worldwide;
- turned its business into a profitable one (despite the price war instigated by Boeing) while reimbursing the initial government loans at a rate of $1bn a year (at the current rate).

The commercial success of Airbus has infuriated the Americans who consider the domination of the LCA market by US industry as the norm. In fact, despite the neo-liberal dogma that the US preaches around the world, the US Government does not like competition insofar as it challenges what it considers as pertaining to its strategic interests.

The Americans have been quick to forget that their own industry's dominance has been built up thanks to relentless government funding and support over the last 30 years which is still continuing today. However since the early 1980s, when Airbus' market penetration was still limited, they have continuously stigmatised European industrial policy and Airbus' reimbursable launch aid which they have simplistically qualified for the purpose of their argument as a subsidy.

To prevent the launch of the A330/A340 programme, the US government escalated the issue in the late 1980s into a quasi-trade war using the complete repertoire of retaliatory threats. They succeeded in imposing on Europe - which is unfortunately sometimes weak when it has to withstand US pressure - the 1992 bilateral agreement.

This agreement has since brought relative 'Peace in the Valley'. But this is at the price of a major - and undoubtedly premature - European concession to accept tough ceilings on reimbursable launch aid while conversely US indirect (and not recoupable) support remains uncontrolled. Since 1992, billions of dollars have been poured by NASA and the DoD into the US industry, which according to them generate no 'identifiable benefits' to LCA programmes.

In this overall trade context, there is no doubt that the Boeing/MDC merger is the last concerted and finely engineered move to create in the wake of US defence consolidation, a globally dominant national champion in the civil aircraft sector. Even if it is at the price of some compromise with antitrust law, this newly created champion has, in the US view, the muscles needed for restoring US dominance in the LCA market by marginalising Airbus, the only remaining challenger.

The politicisation by the US administration with threats of a trade war and the personal intervention of President Clinton against the EU when speaking in opposition to the merger, is proof of the USG's commitment to get the merger through according to its strategic views.

What are the Relative Strengths and Weaknesses of Boeing and Airbus After the Merger?

One can summarise the competitive advantages granted by the merger to Boeing in four major areas.

The first is its size and financial power (Table 1 below):

Table 1

Turnover:
1997	Estimat $39bn	Airbus $\cong$ $10bn
1998	$54bn	
1999	$57bn	

Pretax profit:
1997	Estimat $2,6bn
1998	$4,9bn
1999	$6,1bn

Cash in hand:
1997	Estimat $6,6bn
1998	10,3bn
1999	14,8bn

- Direct employment in the US = 220.000 jobs;
- 1996 combined market share = 70% in aircraft > 100 seats ;
- Combined Boeing-MDC fleet in service = 84% of aircraft operated in the world in 1996.

The second area relates to Boeing's complete family of LCA products from 100 to 400+ seats with a monopoly on the two extremes of the range (100 seats and 400+ seats) further reinforced by the MDC acquisition; moreover

115

it has complete freedom to decide what it will keep from MDC's product range and how it will tactically use them.

The third area of competitive advantage results from the dual nature of the business with military/space representing 40% of turnover. This offers significant leverage to Boeing's civil activity in four main fields:

1. The military business gives Boeing a huge capacity of generating cash and profits from the US military procurement machine which is still, post-Cold War, twice the size of the European defence market and provides significant competitive advantage for export sales. Specifically Boeing enjoys now a US monopoly of military versions derived from civil aircraft (tankers, AWACS, military transport aircraft, etc.) as well as the potential for sale of civil derivatives from military funded aircraft such as the MD 17 and Osprey 22.
2. It provides Boeing with the capacity to mitigate civil cycles with the more stable military business.
3. The new Boeing will benefit from the concentration of the Boeing and MDC DoD funding for R&D and procurement contracts providing huge technological spill-over potential for civil products.
4. In the case of government backed export drives the new Boeing will have unbeatable ability to 'bundle' civil/military deals with USG support and to provide combined offsets.

The fourth area of competitive advantage offered to Boeing by the merger is enormous influence in two fields.

The first field is in political lobbying. Boeing's strong presence throughout the US territory (direct jobs in 30 states and suppliers in all the states) and the fact that it is today by far the largest US export-earning generator will increase its capacity to mobilise and influence an already highly motivated US administration (cf. Ron Brown 'advocacy' policy) in support of Boeing's commercial interests.

The second field where the merger increases Boeing's influence is in the business/procurement field at the level of 'rapports de force' with its suppliers.

Its worldwide buying power increases its capacity to exert pressure on the supply chain and lock-out Airbus' access to suppliers, subcontractors' partners or countries. This is not a theory but a fact of life proven by several recent instances of such behaviour.

Boeing has offered a number of undertakings to the EU MTF to win European Union authorisation for the merger. These limit to a certain extent Boeing's ability to abuse its dominant position in competition.

However, these so-called merger remedies do not cover the full range of potential abuse, particularly the advantages gaining from its civil/military combination. Moreover, and as already illustrated by some post-merger instances, Boeing's undertakings concerning its corporate behaviour will require relentless monitoring if they are simply not to be ignored in the heat of competition. Notwithstanding the undeniable competitive advantages granted by the merger, one must also wonder if 'big is always and necessarily beautiful'.

Practically speaking, a lot of Boeing's management attention will be distracted during months and years to come in digesting the merger. They will have to arbitrate many important issues related to organisation, industrial and social matters.

This might divert their focus from fundamental business priorities in the civil aircraft field like matching delivery commitments with keeping on track on the cost cutting exercise announced to Wall Street. As recognised by Phil Condit the new size of Boeing is not necessary compatible with the speed of reaction expected by the market.

On the other hand, and I am thinking here of IBM, such a giant risks arrogance, excessive ambition and self confidence which might be rejected by a market place which will become highly sensitive to the monopolist syndrome: for instance, Boeing's new diversification policy, particularly in the maintenance and training field is already hurting several of its own customer-airlines.

Let me turn now to Airbus Industrie: the European David weighs five times less in terms of turnover. You can expect this David to remain slim, fast and aggressive. Without falling into the trap of over-confidence or undue self-satisfaction, the Airbus success story so far does give some confidence in its future ability to successfully compete with the new US Goliath.

This confidence is based on two trump cards, which in my opinion are the key factors explaining Airbus' performance to date.

Firstly, Airbus - I believe - has quite simply a better product range 'setting the standard' in two main aspects:

- the product range is based on a family/cockpit commonality concept, not available to Boeing (thanks to Airbus' FBW technology). This commonality gives the Airbus family a significant advantage in terms of crew cost and operational flexibility which means lower costs for airlines;

117

- the current Airbus product range is well positioned in terms of design, cabin concept and technology to meet the current and future market expectations.

In the meantime, Boeing with its steady - and financially fully understandable - derivative policy can only promise 'yesterday's aircraft for tomorrow'. That is the case for its 737 NG, for which market acceptance appears lukewarm despite the huge existing market base of the popular 737 'classic'.

Boeing also tried its 'yesterday's aircraft policy' with the 747-500 and 600-X which were quickly rejected by airlines, with severe criticism from British Airways. The difficult decision on cockpit layout between the B747/B777 demonstrate Boeing's weakness in the commonality field. The same problem arose over the choice of a B777-like cockpit for the 767-400, which has ended its commonality with other B767 models. One cannot make new products by systematically upgrading old ones and expect to fully meet market expectations.

Secondly, the Airbus system has achieved a noticeable improvement in industrial efficiency in terms of cycles/inventory/production cost reduction, despite the limits imposed by the existing GIE structure. It has 'made virtue' of its structural handicaps vis-à-vis the American industry among which are:

- low $;
- difficult social employment conditions in Europe;
- smaller production volume;
- cross subsidisation by the B747's high margins to other competing Boeing products.

Nevertheless these productivity efforts which have to be pursued by a restructured SCE have permitted Airbus to withstand the Boeing price war so far while maintaining profitability.

These achievements were analysed and highlighted in the report on Airbus Industrie by Mr Joe Campbell from Lehman Brothers which came as a great shock to the financial sector used to listening to the usual Boeing propaganda which invariably refers to Airbus as the 'loose, inefficient and highly subsidised European consortium'.

What will be the European Answer to the US Civil Aircraft Consolidation?

I have tried to prove in part II that a significant part of the answer was prepared even before the US consolidation occurred.

Now that we face the Boeing/MDC challenge, the Airbus strategy will in no way be a defensive one, which inevitably would marginalise Airbus sooner or later as a niche player "à la MDC".

Instead it has to be an aggressive strategy, targeting a 50% market share. This is the only long term sustainable position in a duopoly situation with a competitor like the new Boeing. This strategy has five requirements:

1. Airbus must extend the range of its products to the 100, and more importantly, the 400+ seater segment where Boeing currently enjoys a monopoly; this will enable us to 'kill' Boeing's cross subsidisation capabilities. This action is already underway with two new programmes being studied in parallel:
    The A3XX targeting the 500 to 800 seat market. Stretched derivatives of the A340 (-500 and -600) are currently on offer to launch customers. These new models together with the A3XX will attack the B747-400 in a pincer movement and at the same time address the replacement market for OG 747s.
    The AE31X programme, under discussion with China, Singapore and Alenia in addition to current Airbus partners, will target the 100-seater market to challenge the B737-600 and the MD-95.
2. Airbus' long term strategy requires that it keeps up with the latest technology through increased levels of government funded R&D comparable to those enjoyed by Boeing. Airbus has to maintain its technology leading edge and continue setting the standards with its new programmes while maintaining the highly valued commonality concept.
3. Airbus has to further improve its industrial competitiveness to achieve profit objectives despite price pressure and increase reactivity to market demand by quick resolution of in-service and customer support problems.
4. Airbus must become a global player in developing significant risk-sharing partnerships and cooperating with other players in the world, opening new markets and improving its cost base. For the A3XX programme the objective is to have at least 40% of the airframe produced outside the existing Airbus consortium. In the AE31X the specific Airbus share is currently planned not to exceed

25% of the total programme. Discussions on cooperation are currently taking place all around the world.

5.   Airbus has to access the financial markets to raise the funds necessary for development of new programmes.

It is obvious that all the substrategies to be implemented for supporting Airbus' ambitions to increase its market share depend on a quick implementation of the Airbus GIE restructuring into a Single Corporate Entity. This restructuring is not a goal in itself but necessary to achieve additional efficiency.

This restructuring will remedy what Jean Pierson calls the 'genetic limits' of the GIE structure in two areas which are fundamental for the implementation of the 'Airbus answer' to Boeing:

1: The decision making process

The restructuring will empower the SCE management with full authority and accountability in all fields of decisions on Airbus' business including those which were previously spread among partners and not accessible to the GIE for decision making.

The streamlining of the chain of commands is a prerequisite to increase Airbus' operational efficiency in the new competitive situation allowing the SCE to address three key issues namely:

- maximisation of cost efficiency and profitability including procurement optimisation;
- increased reactivity to the customer base in solving quickly in-service problems and product support issues;
- capability to make quick and fully informed decisions on product opportunities and commercial challenges.

2: Access to the financial markets and Airbus' strategy of globalisation

The Airbus strategy requires financial and industrial partners prepared to make significant commitments for funding or cooperation. It is obvious that these partners will need to deal with a company that speaks with one voice and is capable of showing a robust balance sheet and a profitable bottom line.

With the recently announced move of the French government, it appears that the restructuring of Airbus is now under way. The process can therefore be expected to accelerate and the target for completion appears to remain on track.

Considering that Airbus will soon be a 30 years-old partnership dealing solely with one market, it seems totally logical from an Airbus perspective to delink its restructuring from the much more complex issue of European defence and space restructuring. This exercise will involve more participants, competing products and national interests and will obviously require much more time to solve, when time is of the essence.

With hope and good management, the Airbus example will pave the way and might be the reference standard for the next step of consolidation in defence which is as sorely needed as the civil one, if the Europeans are to withstand the industrial giants who have emerged from the recent US consolidation.

Conclusion

The Boeing-McDonnell Douglas merger creates a new challenge for Airbus. However, this is less challenging than the one Airbus has successfully faced in capturing 30% of a market starting from scratch.

I have expressed my strong conviction that Airbus in 1997 holds significant trump cards. I believe that Boeing despite its increased fire power - mainly derived from the MDC military aircraft division - might have some structural weaknesses which will be revealed in the long-run. At least, I do hope so!

Airbus has a clear objective of what it needs to achieve and a vision of the strategies to go there. Without any shadow of doubt, all these strategies require a quick and complete implementation of a new SCE, which is essential to compete head on head with Boeing 'à armes égales'.

I believe that in addition to the industry's efforts, the governments of Europe have an important role to play in the challenge. I am confident that through the Boeing/MDC merger process they have realised the US government's determination and the high stakes of the contest.

Airbus expects from them that they play their role of government 'à la US' in three fields:

- encourage, accelerate and facilitate the civil restructuring without any linkage with the military process;
- grant the necessary finance for a specific and significant effort on Research & Development programmes to match the US level of funding;

- give us, without fear of the usual US protests, a level playing field for business and police with determination any unfair behaviour or violation to the rules.

10 Meeting the Challenge: The Emergence of Airbus as a Single Company

PETER BRUCE
External Affairs and Business Development Manager
BAe Airbus Ltd.

In introduction I would like to point out, that as a British Aerospace employee and as an individual my views should not be taken as the agreed position of the Airbus partnership as a whole. The need to state this is inextricably linked to the structure of Airbus today and will become plain during my chapter.

This chapter can only provide the framework for understanding the way forward on Airbus SCE with much of the detail still to be worked out. The first part of my chapter will look at aspects of the GIE from the formation of Airbus and the second half will address the need for change and the position in forming the new SCE.

According to a McKinsey survey, 70% of all joint ventures break up within a fairly short period of time. A Columbia University study gives strategic alliances an average life span of three and a half years and a survey conducted by Coopers & Lybrand and Yankelovich, Skelly and White found that fewer than a third of collaborative ventures studied met or exceeded partners' expectations. So Airbus has been an exceptional example with its 27 years of success.

The civil aircraft business is worth 1Trillion US dollars over the next 20 years. The battle for this potential revenue, exports, high added value jobs and technology spin-off to other industries is why the structure and effectiveness of Airbus is so important not just to Europe but to global consumers as a whole.

In 1949 the first flight of a jet airliner, the Comet, took place and orders flowed in from around the world. This marked a high point in potential for European aviation, being almost 10 years ahead of the US B707 first flight. However little more than 20 years later Europe had dropped to under 5% market share against a dominant US industry position. How did this come about?

The US and particularly Boeing's dominance was based on both the huge single market of the US and deep military and national strategic funding by government. The US promoted and still promotes today synergies between military and civil aircraft. For example the B707 came from the KC135 military tanker/transport with on-developments using the fuselage design for the B727 and B737. The B747 originated in the C5 Galaxy transport and engine studies paid for by the Defense Department. The US has always seen this money as a good long term investment for the nation but in contraposition has been quick to point the subsidy finger at Europe when it does a quarter as much.

Returning to Europe's early presence, numerous factors contributed to the ultimate failure in the market but key was the adherence to national programmes for far too long. The problem of achieving international collaboration in an acceptable and simple commercial way in this strategic industry was not solvable at the time. Even the later Concorde collaboration showed up the failure of managing by government committee. However behind what many observers saw as the falling curtain on the European large aircraft industry, the Airbus partners were left to quietly get on with piecing together one of the only possible solutions in the 1960s' political environment.

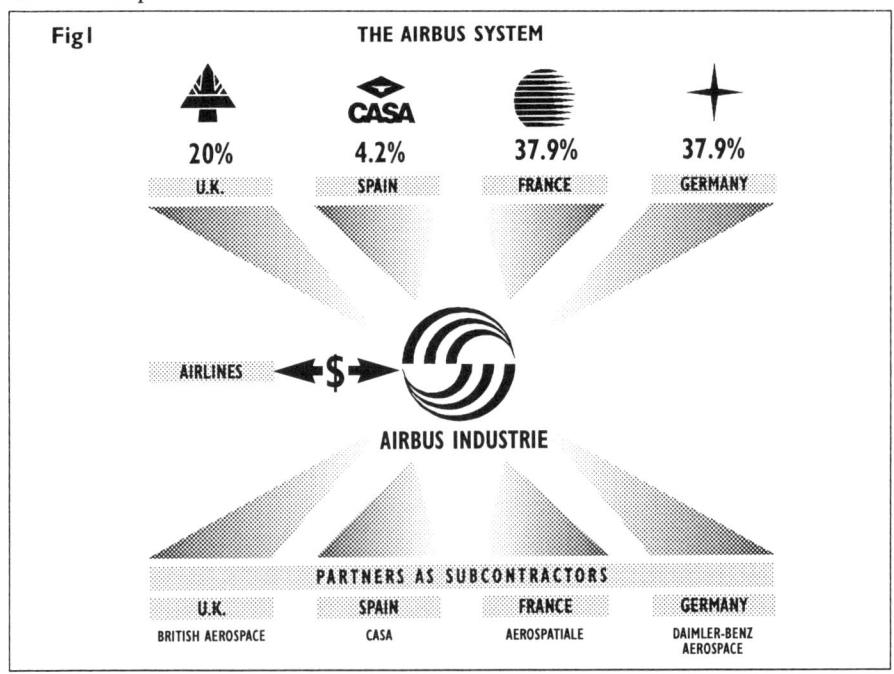

Fig 1 — THE AIRBUS SYSTEM

The Airbus System (fig 1)

The Airbus business was formed in 1970 around a GIE. This is a French legal partnership structure which is used generally for much smaller business ventures to combine together the partners' resource capabilities but to leave control of those resources with the individual partners. This solution allowed the Airbus business to have a central identity and single point of customer interface for sales and long-term support while maintaining national control. Ownership percentages reflected national strengths, investment and some historical quirks about entry which I have insufficient space to explain here. Business decisions are taken by the partners with the work also subcontracted to them in workshare percentages broadly reflecting ownership.

The structure means all major decisions in the partnership need to be by consensus and almost all investment funding and risk is borne by the partners. All receipts by Airbus from the global market are in US dollars, a hangover from post World War Two reconstruction. However, all costs to the partners are in local currencies with often large fluctuations in exchange rate over aircraft project timescales. This currency risk is all passed through the Airbus partnership to the partner businesses to deal with.

The nature of politics inside a partnership is often colourful and Airbus is no exception. The different partner business situations and views mean there is never total agreement on the long term although there is intense scrutiny of product and other key investment decisions that are agreed at a particular time. Thus there was never any formal long term strategy or objectives agreed, although partner positions have grown closer over time.

The following list of four objectives constitutes what might have been a coalescence of opinion in the minds of the Airbus pioneers:

- Launch product range
- Develop customer base
- Achieve 30% market share
- Achieve profitability

Although the A300B was the only official product at formation, the GIE was able to accommodate changes in the scope of the business as success led to more product launches.

Civil airliners are 30 year products with large ongoing support and training needs. To change from one aircraft type to another is expensive so the need to ensure a wide customer base was paramount for future success.

With the US companies Boeing and McDonnell Douglas dominant in the 1970s, a 30% share seemed a pretty visionary target at the time, but one that if achieved would help to deliver the necessary long term profitability as a fourth objective.

Creating an Industry (This should perhaps really read the Re-creation of a European industry) (fig 2)

The story of Airbus's epic road to success is fascinating and not well known but I have no time to tell you much here. I shall constrain myself to the major steps illustrated by this order history.

The long early tail for the A300B at low order levels is indicative of the difficulty of entering the civil airliner business even if you have four major European partners with numerous product successes behind them. The A300B had to be innovative to succeed and was so, creating a new market segment for transatlantic range, widebody comfort, twin engined aircraft, later copied by Boeing with its B767.

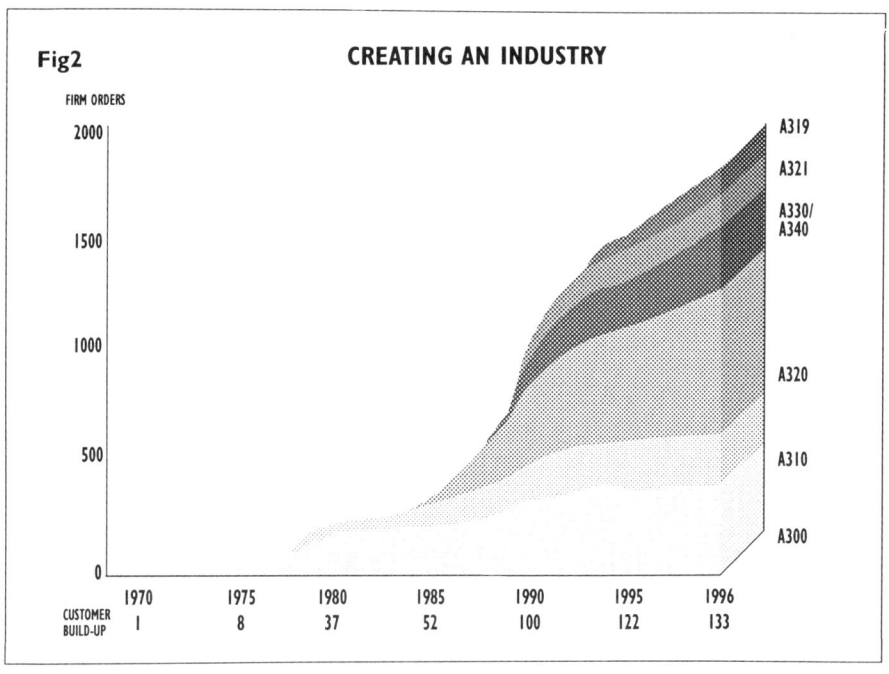

126

Airbus' credibility grew after the 1978 Eastern Airlines order and the confidence helped the A310 launch with a longer range than the A300B but a slightly lower capacity. Product enhancements continued with extensive use of carbon composites and an all new "glass" cockpit operated by only two flight crew.

A big leap of faith was taken with the next all new aircraft. The smaller 150 seat Single Aisle A320 was the choice with its fly by wire, sidestick control. However Airbus' philosophy is that all technology must benefit the customer and they came in droves for this aircraft which has been the fastest selling aircraft in history to 1000 sales including the variants of the stretched A321 and the shorter A319.

The other major investment to date that really risked the whole viability of Airbus was the A330/A340 series developed as a 5000 nautical mile, two engine aircraft and an 8000 nautical mile four engine aircraft variant on a common airframe. Effectively two aircraft for the price of one. This aircraft series is large (up to 400 seats in dense configuration) and expensive at $90-120mn a piece so despite the small aircraft numbers in the chart, it represents half of Airbus' turnover.

The GIE structure has coped with the launch of all these products and fleet growth past 1000 aircraft.

The Future

So what of the future for Airbus? It might sound like success is assured. All the four objectives stated earlier have been achieved. Almost 60% of Airbus is commercially owned not state owned and profitability is strong and necessarily improving. Sales are booming currently so, some would say, why change an Airbus structure that has stood the test of time?

The devil lies in the detail as usual which in such a long term industry will make the difference between success or failure. Despite a 30% market share, Airbus still only has 13% of the fleet of civil airliners flying and less than 10% of the seats, making it effectively a market entrant still for decades to come. The recently approved merger of Boeing and McDonnell Douglas illustrates the competitive threat:

- Airbus has half the throughput to recover its costs against;
- it also has more investments to make than Boeing to extend its product range;
- aircraft prices are currently 30% lower than five years ago;

- Airbus gets far less funding from governments than the US gives its industry and Airbus has to pay most of it back!

It all sounds both very unfair and a tough hill to climb, but Airbus is used to challenges. It has to and will adapt to succeed.

The recent changes in market prices and competition are not small or cyclical; they are profound and lasting. They set the tone for competing in the 21st century marketplace. Airbus must ensure it improves cost competitiveness from internal continuous improvement and more competitive sourcing and partnership policies.

In order to improve its cost structure and economies of scale, Airbus must strive for a 50% market share to match the new strengthened Boeing. To achieve this market share in sectors it has existing products in, Airbus will have to continue to enhance these and launch derivative developments to maximise benefit from current investment.

Also, Airbus does not currently compete in the '100-seater' or 400+ seat sectors which are Boeing monopoly segments. Customers want to be able to buy a full product range from a manufacturer for operational cost effectiveness reasons. Also the large aircraft sector alone is estimated at 25% by value of the market overall. Airbus must therefore launch new products to fill these gaps in its product range and have the technology to deliver much lower DOCs for airlines. Providing competition in these sectors will also remove Boeing's monopoly profits. Both these factors will benefit consumers appreciably but the manufacturer, Airbus, cannot capture these benefits to reinvest.

The market development reference in the last line reflects the fact that this is not a US or European business but a global one. Key strategic partnerships will be needed for the largest and highest growth markets such as China which has signed an MOU to be the major partner on the A31X, in the <100-seater sector. This product will break Boeing's monopoly with the B737-600 and MD95.

Airbus Restructuring

The Benefits

By bringing Airbus under a single management, it will be possible to have a single co-ordinated strategy throughout the business to maximise value as a whole. Decisions can be taken more quickly and actioned inside a cohesive strategic framework.

The single corporate entity will be able to rationalise business activities, removing duplications of scope such as long bed machining facilities or composite technology programmes. This will also achieve greater economies of scale in production.

Airbus in the 21st century will need much more commercial investment finance and global strategic partners as stated in the previous Figure. A Single Corporate Entity will have the business strength to attract the commercial money needed; and the SCE structure will enable new partners to come on board much more easily by providing a single negotiating interface and decision making structure.

The potentially biggest threat of the Boeing/McDonnell Douglas merger is the leverage gained though bringing together the massive civil and defence businesses of Boeing and MDC with a turnover greater than most small countries' GDP such as New Zealand. Airbus will also need improved access to the strengths of a combined European military aerospace business, rather belatedly as this is where the US started with its national strategy. The success of Airbus' restructuring would bring this wider restructuring a step closer to reality without impairing the ability to exchange technology, skills resource or finance with the military arms of the partners.

Current Airbus Restructuring Position

There has been much scaremongering and controversy in the press about the SCE partner positions over the last six months, much of it unhelpful in marketing the competitiveness and business focus of our industry to the wider public. This is regretful but it does mean you know more of the issues and I can be more brief with you.

The Airbus partners signed at the beginning of this year an MOU agreeing to form an Airbus Single Corporate Entity by 1999. Various working groups have been set up as illustrated in this list to work out how to achieve the SCE in the most effective manner to ensure growing Airbus business success. It is a highly complicated task because the constituent nationally based elements are not separately listed on the stock markets, which would give a publicly assessed long term valuation. They are not even separate businesses in their own right but are enmeshed within wider businesses covering military and other products. Other examples of the difficulties are:

- the fact that there is no European company status or common tax regime in Europe;

- the difficulty of achieving a coordinated Government position on the future competitive framework such as for R&T programmes;
- reaching agreement on the most effective new management structure and appointments to key positions;
- reaching valuation decisions on cash flow and other measures (when the industry is in such a rapid state of change to make forecasting performance particularly difficult for some);
- deciding who will have authority over what resources and at what ultimate price

The French policy line has been most pawed over since the election but is now looking much more positive again and compatible with various French merger and privatisation plans. At this time we cannot say exactly what the SCE will look like and there is a large amount of haggling still to be done 'in darkened rooms' before any agreement is finally reached. Lastly on timescales, the MOU stated date to reach full agreement on the Single Corporate Entity was to be end of 1997 and this still appears possible. Full implementation is planned for 1999.

Building on Current Airbus Industrial Success

It is essential that the new SCE structure improves the ability of Airbus to compete successfully from the industrial standpoint. The new management authority vested will lead to a much more coordinated and efficient operating company over time. However the changes will be progressive with many needing to wait for appropriate product introduction decisions before they can be commercially viable.

Of prime importance to unlocking the potential for the new organisation will be a respected and impartial leadership approach that can gel the diverse resources spread across European facilities and culture into a single team.

Another key aspect will be developing the people skills of the company through sharing of best practice and developing cross-functional teams for improving areas of core competence across Europe.

We must not forget our past though, and Airbus's current success rests on some key strengths that must not be lost. Internal competitions have been run on cost and performance at key project stages to extract best value for money and have kept the partners lean and competitive to win the work. Innovation has been a hallmark of Airbus success to date and this must continue if we are to win more market share from Boeing. Customer focus and the personal touch has ensured Airbus success in the face of incumbent US supplied fleets. The new consolidated Airbus company must maintain its small and personal feel, well captured in the epithet 'think global, act local'.

Finally I will just mention one of the peripheral business areas that is nevertheless important for the future success of the SCE, but will be dealt with separately. Airbus Military Company or AMC will be formed later this year to run the FLA military transport project and is planned to cover military variants of Airbus products. AMC is planned to be a subsidiary of Airbus SCE in due course with minority shareholders that reflect the wider partnership of the FLA project membership. In this way broader global partners can be incorporated into launching strategic new Airbus based projects, both military and civil.

Providing a Competitive Business Framework

As well as the industrial setup and actions in the new SCE, the right business environment and a more level playing field is essential for a successfully competitive Airbus.

European Governments must take action to create a more level playing field for Airbus to compete on against a US supported industry. This means funding coordinated pre-competitive R&T programmes (particularly demonstrators), defending European interests on new environmental regulations, strong defence in the arena of trade regulation disputes being proactive where appropriate, or controlling global air transport policy evolution.

Europe must also set up strong European institutions such as the European Joint Aviation Authority to counter any undue pressure from the US FAA (with its objective to help US industry dominate the world). Another need is to ensure European interests are upheld in determining new Air Traffic Control rules and regulations to operate globally.

European governments will also need to ensure they are supportive to European aerospace companies doing business around the world. This means supporting key partnership relationships politically.

Conclusion

- After 1000 years of history characterised by warfare, Europe is now politically coming of age with a new understanding about coordinated international action in a global trading environment. Airbus also needs to evolve its structure and to do so immediately to meet the new strategic competitive threats.

- Following the Boeing/McDonnell Douglas merger, Airbus is the only means of achieving real competitive forces for consumer benefit in a market worth $30bn today and doubling in the next 10 years. Evidence shows that effective Airbus competition in a market segment means a 15 to 30% price reduction delivering huge consumer benefit. Thus Airbus must be as competitive as possible against Boeing for all our sakes.

- Coordinated government and industrial action on the aerospace defence markets is even more difficult to achieve than on the civil side of the business. An Airbus Single Corporate Entity can show what is possible in efficiency, allay some of the fears of losing control by individual nations and act as an example to facilitate wider European aerospace restructuring at the earliest time. The Airbus Single corporate entity is an important stepping stone to achieving this wider objective.

- Aerospace is such a vital strategic and economically important industrial sector in Europe that governments and industry must make haste to achieve the necessary strategic changes. Industry is doing all it can to bring about the restructuring changes needed for a competitive industry.

However, it is essential that European governments also show vision in working together to deliver a business framework that can encourage and achieve a competitive and successful European aerospace industry from which we can all benefit.

11 Integration and Consolidation in European Military and Civil Aerospace: An Urgent Task

HORST PREM
Chief Scientist
Ludwig-Bölkow-Stiftung

The Situation in Europe

Europe has to move from a common market for agricultural products and also establish a common market for high-tech products. If you analyse the EU budget[1] for 1999, 44% of the money is invested in agriculture, 37% in structural funds, and only 3% in pre-competitive and generic research. If we want to become a Europe with a valuable share of high-tech products on the world market, we have to inverse this ratio between agricultural and structural funds to a research and technology investment, which would then provide a serious basis for a common security and foreign affairs policy. Compared to other industries, aerospace plays a dominant role due to its widely developed European structures and its strategic significance. Procedures and methodologies of research and development in the aerospace field have always penetrated other industrial sectors. Finite element methods, aerodynamics, thermodynamics, or microelectronics and last but not least energy-technologies like the fuel-cell-technology have been applied in aerospace first. The stringent requirements in respect of weight/energy criticality and micro-dimensions force the aerospace industry to move ahead earlier than other industries.

But the European aerospace industry has not yet adapted to the post-Cold War scenario due to the absence of a European Security and Foreign Affairs Policy. The conflict in former Yugoslavia clearly demonstrates this European weakness. Whereas the USA redefined its security policy in this situation as a policy of technological superiority and therefore restructured its industrial base in the aerospace sector, Europe is divided with negative consequences on employment. To overcome this situation and remain competitive in the world market, the national governments responsible for security policy and therefore also for an aerospace industry in Europe, should harmonise their policies and pave the way to a Europe of high-tech products. There is no increase of the EU budget necessary, as long as structural-funds are not only used as funds for social programmes and infrastructure, but also for common European programmes to improve Europe's technology competitiveness, because this is an element of structural policy, too.

European Aerospace within the Triad

A comparison of exports and patents in different sectors of industry (figs 1 to 3)[2] clearly illustrates the relative strengths and weaknesses of the main players in the Triad of America, Europe, and Japan.

By way of explaining the next three charts: on the outside, various business fields are listed from business machines through aerospace to electronics. The white line illustrates the relative number of patents registered in each business field, while the black line represents the volume of exports. Patent activity, of course, is an indicator of R&D investment from the private sector.

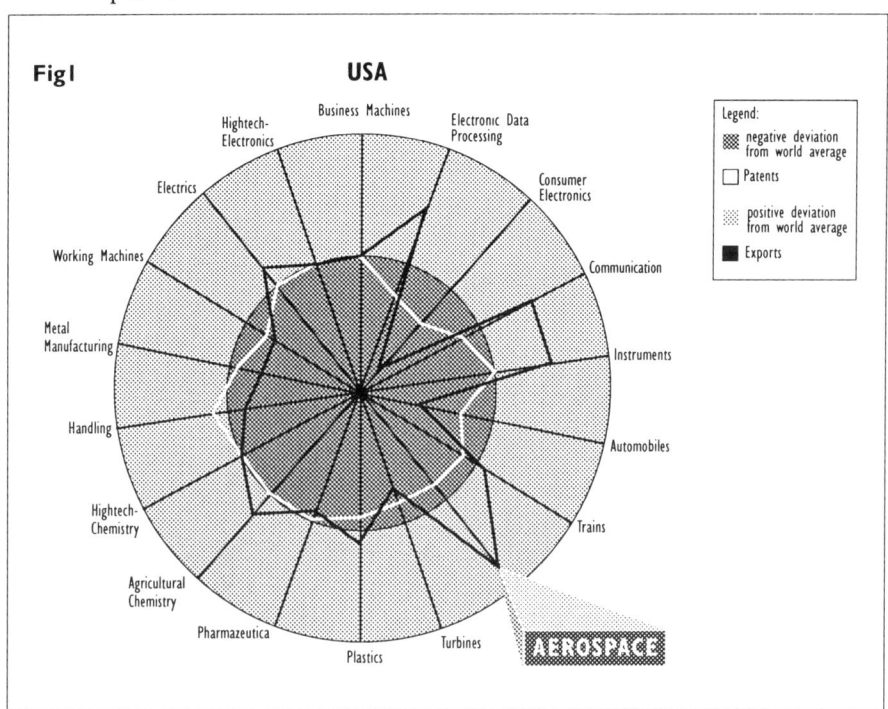

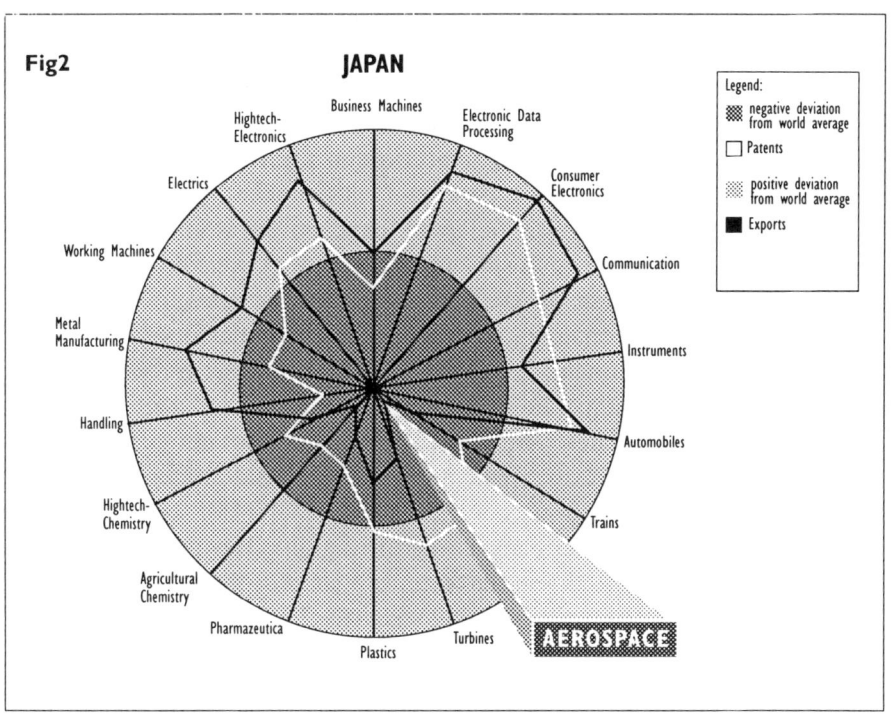

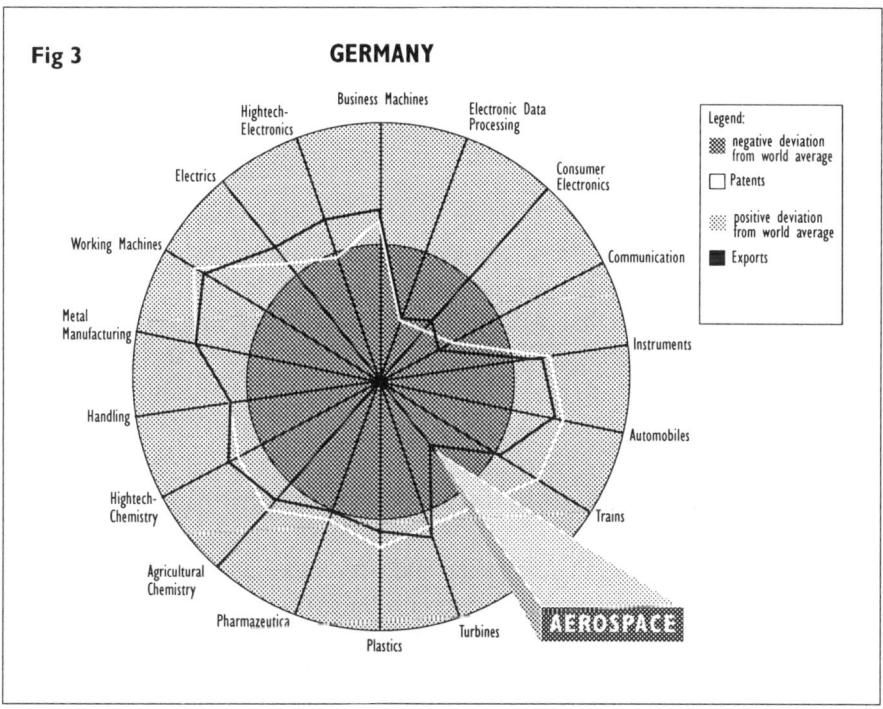

Finally, the outer edge of the circle in the centre indicates average activity in patents and exports.

The US has registered a relatively low number of patents, even in those fields in which American export levels are high. In the fields of electronic data processing, communication, instruments, and especially aerospace, American exports are very high without a commensurate rise in patent activity. This suggests fields of business in which government funding has enabled US industry to achieve a powerful international position, however adequate private investment (that is, patents).

Japan shows concentrations of exports and patents in its main fields of interest. Namely, in high-tech electronics, electronic data processing, and communications, but most of all in areas of consumer electronics and automobiles. The aerospace industry does not yet contribute to Japan's trade surplus, but its patent efforts indicate a strategic approach to the world market.

The picture for Germany is also revealing. We have to use the German one, because we do not have consolidated data for all of Europe. But I think it summarises, to a certain extent, the European scene. It shows a high correlation between patents and exports in medium-tech fields of machinery, metal manufacturing, chemistry, and turbines. In aerospace, however, the Europeans have registered an above average number of patents (that is to say, have privately invested in the aerospace industry), but have achieved below average export levels.

The conclusions from this analysis are:

Both Europe and Japan have made above average investments in their aerospace industries, but have achieved significantly lower than average exports in this industry. The US has a relatively low level of patents in the aerospace industry, but has achieved an extraordinary high export level. This suggests a high level of support from US government and leads us to the crucial element of the European aerospace industry in global competition:

Direct and Indirect Support in the US versus Europe

Historically, the European aerospace industry has had to rely on direct governmental financial support for certain large programmes, because the European nations have not yet established a common industrial, foreign, security and technology policy. There does not yet exist in Europe a single market comparable to the US. Europe is not a single nation, but is rather dominated by conflicting interests, industries, and nations. Consequently, Europe does not have anything comparable to the American common research establishment and contracting basis.

Integration and Consolidation in European Military and Civil Aerospace

It is not sufficient for Europe to complain about the dominant US position with respect to indirect support. The question for Europe is how to achieve a similar position in indirect support for its aerospace industry. Figure 4 summarises examples of US Defence Projects commercially used:

- the development funding for the Boeing 707 came from previous work Boeing had done to develop and build the US Air Force KC 135. Furthermore four years after ending production of KC 135 the civil version B707 exceeded the number of military versions produced. This is production aid Airbus Industrie never received;

Fig 4 EXAMPLES OF US DEFENCE PROJECTS COMMERCIALLY USED

MILITARY	TRANSFER TO	CIVIL	BENEFIT
KC135 (TANKER)	→	BOEING 707	90% OF TECHNOLOGY
C-5A (LARGE TRANSPORT)	→	BOEING 747 DC10	STRUCTURAL & AERODYN. CONFIGURATION EG. WING DESIGN & NACELLES
TF-39 (LARGE ENGINE)	→	CF6 (DC10/AIRBUS ENGINE)	SAME TECHNOLOGIES AS FOR THE TF-39
NASP (NAT. AEROSPACE PLANE)	→	HSCT (HIGH SPEED CLV. TRANSP.)	SIMILAR TECHNICAL REQUIREMENTS
INTERNET FOR RESEARCH CENTRE	→	INTERNET FOR PUBLIC DOMAINE	PRIORITY OF US-SW-INDUSTRY WORLDWIDE; USE OF EUROPEAN DEVELOPMENT WWW
GPS	→	GPS	US-ONBOARD EQUIPMENT WORLDWIDE; FULL USE OF TECHNOLOGIES

- the Boeing 747 and the McDonnell Douglas DC 10 both rely heavily on wing and nacelle design from the US Air Force C5A transport prototype design;
- next step in this race is the conversion of the C-17 to a MD-17;
- the CF6 engine used for the DC 10 and for Airbus shares the same technologies used for the US Air Force TF 39 engine;
- the NASP design represents the future HSCT aircraft;
- the Internet for connecting military research centres paved the way for the overwhelming position of the US software industry in the world today;
- the Global Positioning System (GPS), now opened for civil use with the perspective of providing precision navigation in civil areas, is also used to prolong the dominance of the US onboard equipment industry worldwide.

No new generation of large US civil aircraft, engine or onboard equipment will be developed without substantial government support.

Fig 5 summarises the US governmental backing by NASA demonstrator programmes.

Fig 5   **NASA DEMONSTRATION PROGRAMS COMPARED WITH EUROPE**

Experimental Demonstrators USA (1993)		*Experimental Demonstrators Europe (1993)*	
B-757	Hybrid laminar flow testbed (subsonic)	F-100	Technology Demonstrator for laminar flow research
B-737	High lift flap technology		
F-18	High angle-of-attack research vehicle		
SR-71	Flight research testbed for high-speed civil transport		
UH 60	RASCAL Helicopter, nap of the earth fight guidance, GPS precision navigation flight system	**?**	
XV-15	Certification profiles for noise abatement, failure modes and handling qualities	*National Demonstrators,*	
F-15	Highly integrated digital electronics control	*which are not comparable*	
2F16-XL	Hybrid laminar flow control (supersonic), for civil transport	*with US Experimental Demonstrators*	
X-30	National Aero-Space Plane		
X-31 Strike fighter technology demonstrator			

The mere quantity of US programs shows a further distortion in competitiveness

Whereas only the first two American programmes are clearly in the civil area, the remainders have clear applications for civil aircraft. It is almost inevitable that this technology developed under military auspices will flow down into the civil aircraft sector and profit the American civil aircraft industry. These are prime examples of indirect support.

If Europe wants to avoid being accused again in front of a GATT/WTO panel and avoid subsidies with negative consequences for its aerospace industry like the 1992 Bilateral Agreement, we have to adopt the American method of funding. The only way ahead is to establish a level playing field for the aerospace industries on both sides of the Atlantic. My suggestion is to use a top-down approach based on the EDIG definition of demonstrators (see Fig 6). To encourage the integration and consolidation in European military and civil aerospace, the Departments of Defence of the nations involved, together with the Commissioner of External Affairs of the EU should define Technology Demonstrators, System Concept Demonstrators, and Operational Demonstrators for the technological support of an European Security and External Affairs Policy.

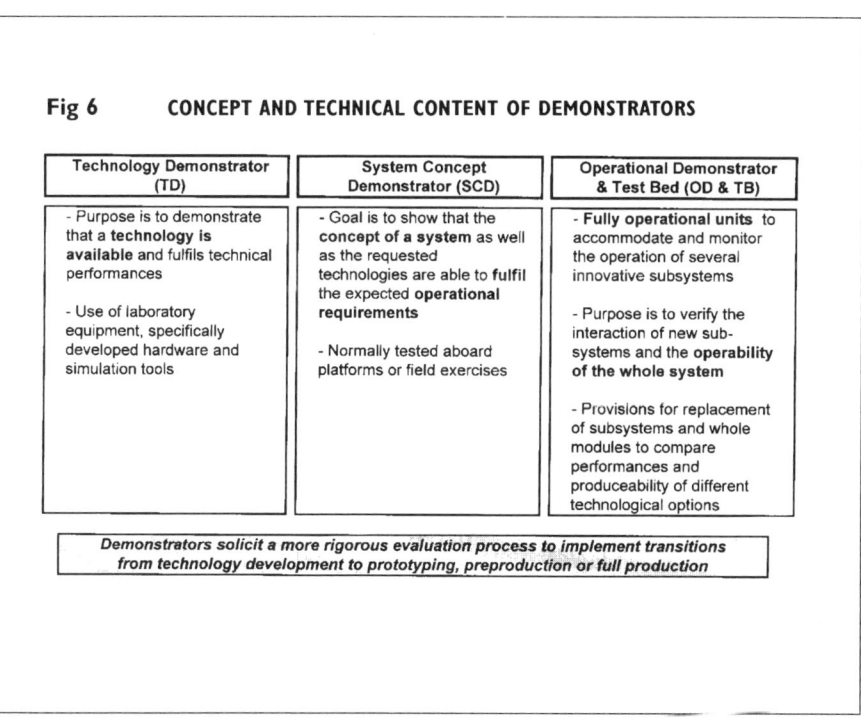

Fig 6   CONCEPT AND TECHNICAL CONTENT OF DEMONSTRATORS

Technology Demonstrator (TD)	System Concept Demonstrator (SCD)	Operational Demonstrator & Test Bed (OD & TB)
- Purpose is to demonstrate that a **technology is available** and fulfils technical performances - Use of laboratory equipment, specifically developed hardware and simulation tools	- Goal is to show that the **concept of a system** as well as the requested technologies are able to fulfil the expected **operational requirements** - Normally tested aboard platforms or field exercises	- **Fully operational units** to accommodate and monitor the operation of several innovative subsystems - Purpose is to verify the interaction of new subsystems and the **operability of the whole system** - Provisions for replacement of subsystems and whole modules to compare performances and produceability of different technological options

Demonstrators solicit a more rigorous evaluation process to implement transitions from technology development to prototyping, preproduction or full production

If necessary a team of wise men should make definitive proposals for this European Demonstrator Philosophy, which has to cover the civil aerospace aspects also.

Yugoslavia is an example of where Europe failed and endangered its democratic values, because we are not able to counterbalance the information war. This is a technological problem. So my suggestion is to define European demonstrators of different levels of technology not only for better energy efficiency, like laminar-flow-technology for sub and supersonic flight or reduction of pollution due to noise and emission, but also to use the space-based communication and navigation technologies[3] to defeat technologically the upcoming crises around the globe and within Europe.

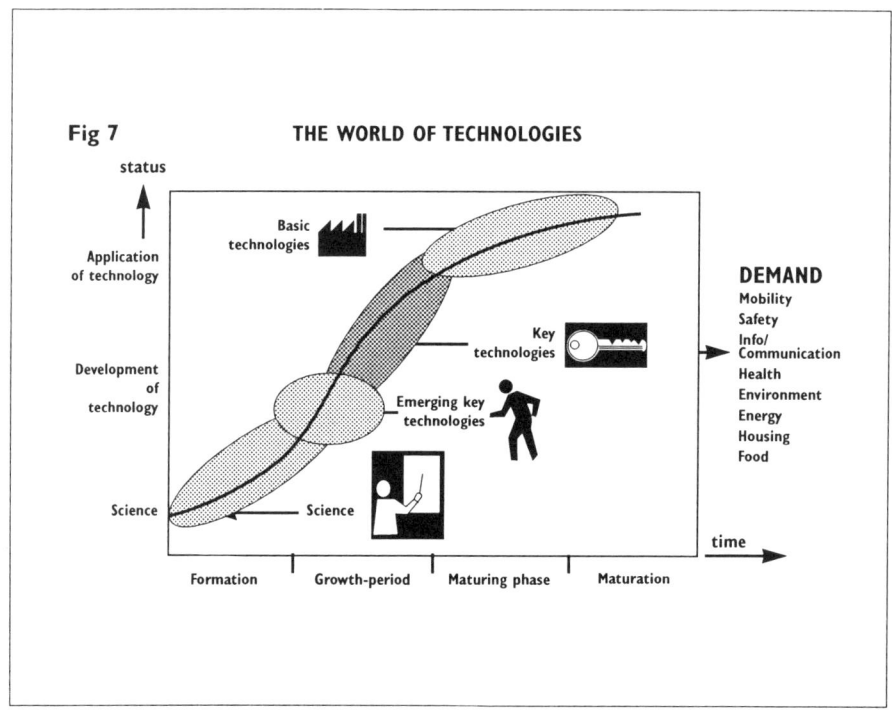

Fig 7 — THE WORLD OF TECHNOLOGIES

Conclusion

The following principles seem to be essential to gain equal conditions for the European Aerospace industry:

- Integration and consolidation can only be achieved in technology projects which do not divide into military and civil aspects.
- European guide concepts with respect to key technologies technology demonstrators are essential for this integration and consolidation. Typical examples are: reduction of drag, reduction of emission, use of robotics in non cooperative environments, knowledge-based systems for navigation aids, adaptive and smart structures for aeroplanes, transportation systems and energy conversion systems without pollution, etc.
- The complex world of technologies is summarised in fig 7. To encourage greater competitiveness:

  1. National governments liable for the aerospace industry should establish a common European security and foreign affairs policy together with the EU Commission and decide on that basis the technology demonstrators necessary
  2. Governments should establish a framework for a common market on competitive high-tech products including military products
  3. No single nation will be in a position to achieve global competitiveness in high-tech products without a cooperation strategy
  4. Within this overall cooperation scenario, industries have to form financially and technologically strong companies.

Therefore, there is no alternative to a vertically integrated European aerospace industry for supplying the world market with competitive aerospace products on a profitable basis. Due to the strategic importance of the aerospace industry, competitiveness of this industry is essential for the overall competitiveness of the EU, as long as Europe wants to overcome its employment problems and gain a greater market share in the export of high-tech products.

    This is the only way in the long run to keep standards of living in Europe at today's level and play a major role in defending democratic values through a serious security and external affairs policy. The key-industries of today at the moment are completely dominated by the USA.

Notes and References

1   V*orentwurf des Gesamthaushaltsplans der Europäischen Gemeinschaften für das Haushaltsjahr 1998*, (SEC (97) 600 - DE, Europäische Kommission, Brüssel, May 1997).

2   Legler H et al, *Zur technologischen Leistungsfähigkeit Deutschlands,* Bericht an das Bundesministerium für Forschung und Technologie, (April 1993 und erweiterte Fassung vom Dezember 1995).

3   Patronage Wiesheu O, *First European Symposium on Global Navigation Satellite Systems*, (GNSS 97 German Institute of Navigation, Bonn, 1997).

Part III

Project Case Studies

12 Can FLA Bring About a New Approach to Defence Procurement in Europe

IAIN G GRAY
Head of FLA
British Aerospace Airbus

Introduction

Debate about the need for FLA has never had greater exposure in the UK than in the last 18 months. Much work has already been done within the industry and hence we welcome the recent news that the UK has joined the other European nations in being ready to issue the Request for Proposals. I strongly believe FLA is the right military transport aircraft for Europe in the next century. However, the principal objective of this chapter is not to discuss the product or the advantages that I believe the product will bring to our European Rapid Reaction support in the future, but to describe how I believe the commercial approach being applied to FLA can bring about a new approach to defence procurement in Europe, helping us, in turn, to realise a competitive position against the giants in the US.

Elsewhere in this book you will have read about Airbus and its approach to competing against Boeing in the commercial aircraft market. Before discussing the large military aircraft market, I would like to remind you of how Airbus has developed over the last 25 years to break the US monopoly in the commercial aircraft market and how this Airbus system will be used in an effective manner to allow development of the FLA and other Airbus derivatives in the large military aircraft sector.

Some 35 years ago there were no Airbus aircraft - to coin a phrase the first Airbus only existed on paper.

A look at the products of the time and their sales indicated that the balance was firmly tilted in favour of the US (fig 1). Europe with a variety of different products needed to respond or they would either go out of business or at best act in the role of subcontractor supporting the profits of the major US manufacturers.

But respond it did - through the establishment of Airbus Industrie (fig 2) - a partnership collaboration initially between France and Germany

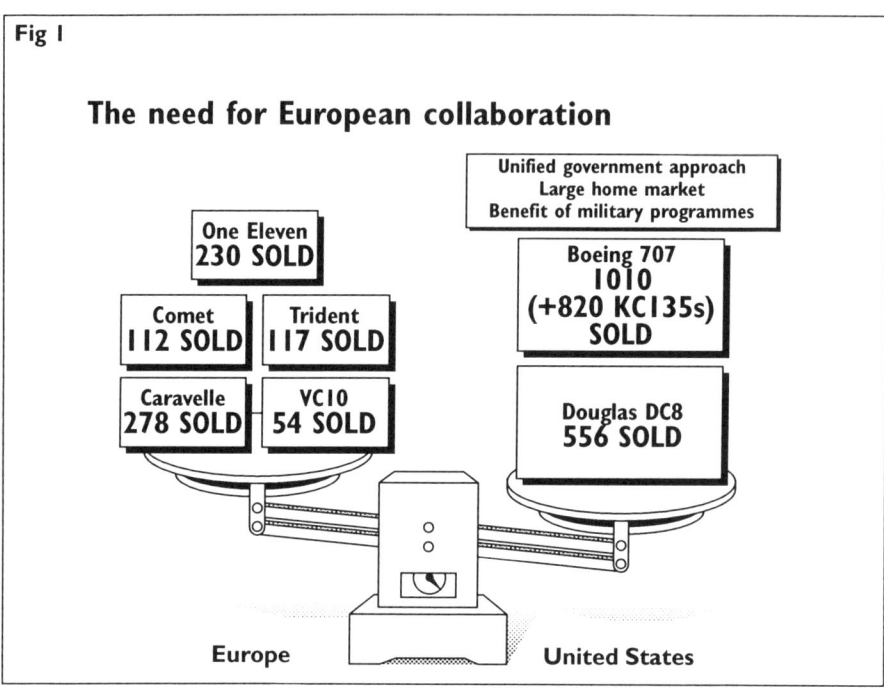

Fig 1

The need for European collaboration

Unified government approach
Large home market
Benefit of military programmes

One Eleven
230 SOLD

Comet
112 SOLD

Trident
117 SOLD

Caravelle
278 SOLD

VC10
54 SOLD

Boeing 707
1010
(+820 KC135s)
SOLD

Douglas DC8
556 SOLD

Europe   United States

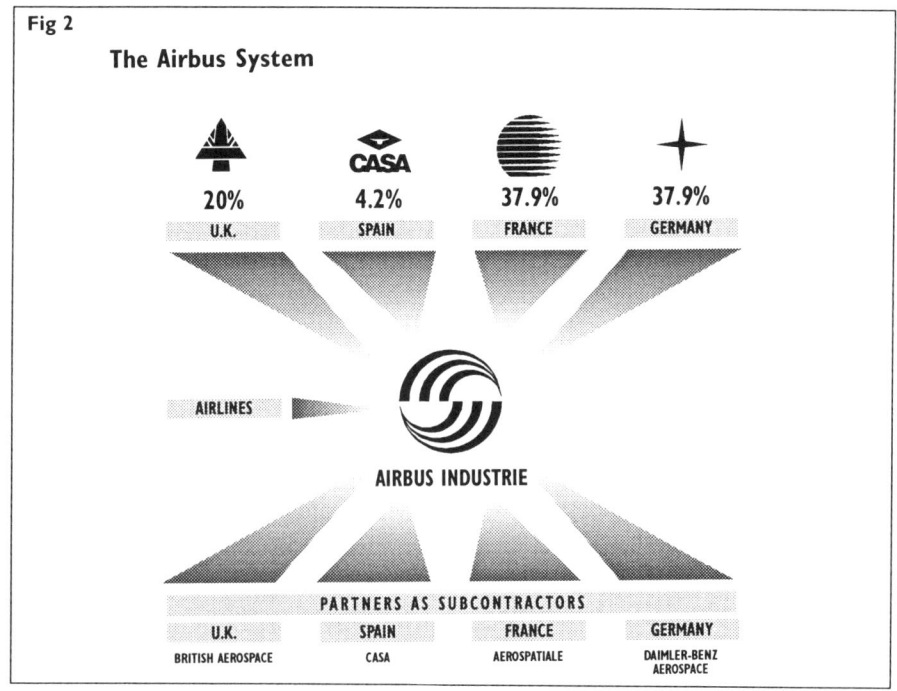

Fig 2

The Airbus System

20%   4.2%   37.9%   37.9%
U.K.   SPAIN   FRANCE   GERMANY

AIRLINES

AIRBUS INDUSTRIE

PARTNERS AS SUBCONTRACTORS

| U.K. | SPAIN | FRANCE | GERMANY |
| BRITISH AEROSPACE | CASA | AEROSPATIALE | DAIMLER-BENZ AEROSPACE |

with the UK providing subcontract support through its Hawker Siddeley wing design expertise and since the beginning of the 1980s as a full partnership between the industries of France, Germany, UK and Spain.

Building an industry was not easy - people were cynical about paper products, about four different European companies with different objectives working together. But build an industry is what we have done (fig 3) - initially through a single product gaining market slowly - 100 aircraft by 1980, development of the A320 in the mid 1980s, and delivering 500 aircraft by the late 1980s leading to an aggressive development programme of the A330/A340 family in the early 1990s - taking us to today's situation where Airbus has a family of products and a forward order book which will take it beyond 2000 aircraft.

A key point to note about Airbus, very different from European collaborative products being developed at the same time in the military market, is that Airbus is a business, not a programme or project office. A business with a proven track record. A business with eight product types and looking at ways of expanding this family (fig 4). A business with a track record of delivering products to the market place on time, to cost and to specification.

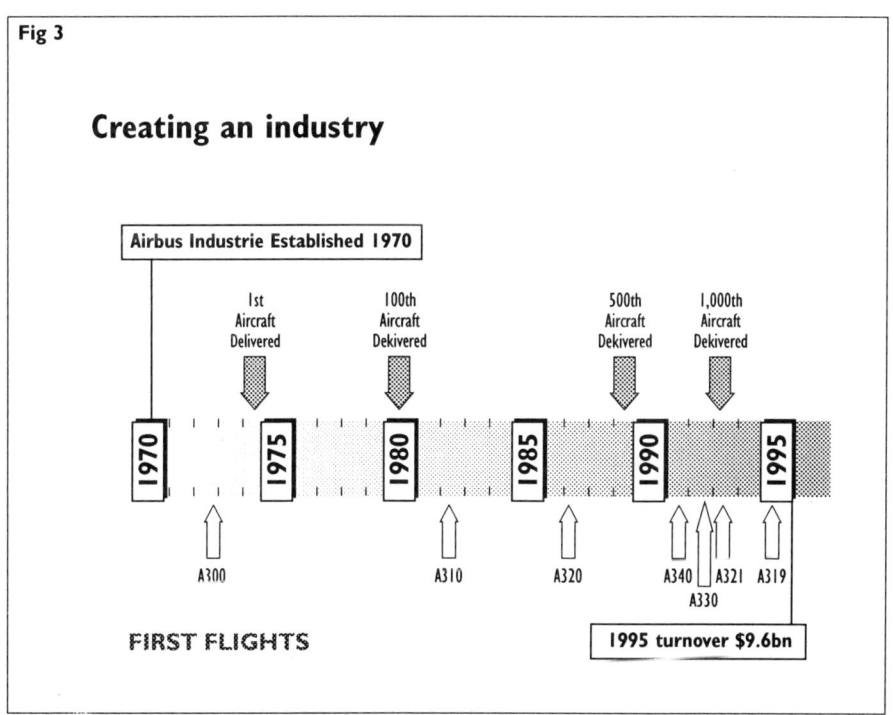

Fig 3

Creating an industry

Airbus Industrie Established 1970

FIRST FLIGHTS

1995 turnover $9.6bn

A business with a global product support network supporting the commercial airlines in their relentless desire for high levels of reliability and maintainability.

Centres of Excellence

This business has been allowed to develop and evolve around a common way of working. Airbus has created and built its industry up around centres of excellence. If we look at the workshare over the development of the product family it is easy to observe recurring patterns. This is in sharp contrast with the changing workshare on many military programmes. This has allowed the partners to focus on core competencies, allowing them to concentrate on cost of leadtime efficiency improvements which can flow through to the customer. The workshare has followed a common approach as the product family has evolved:

Aérospatiale	cockpit/flying control system
Mixture of AS/DASA	fuselage section
BAe	wing design and wing assembly
CASA	horizontal tail

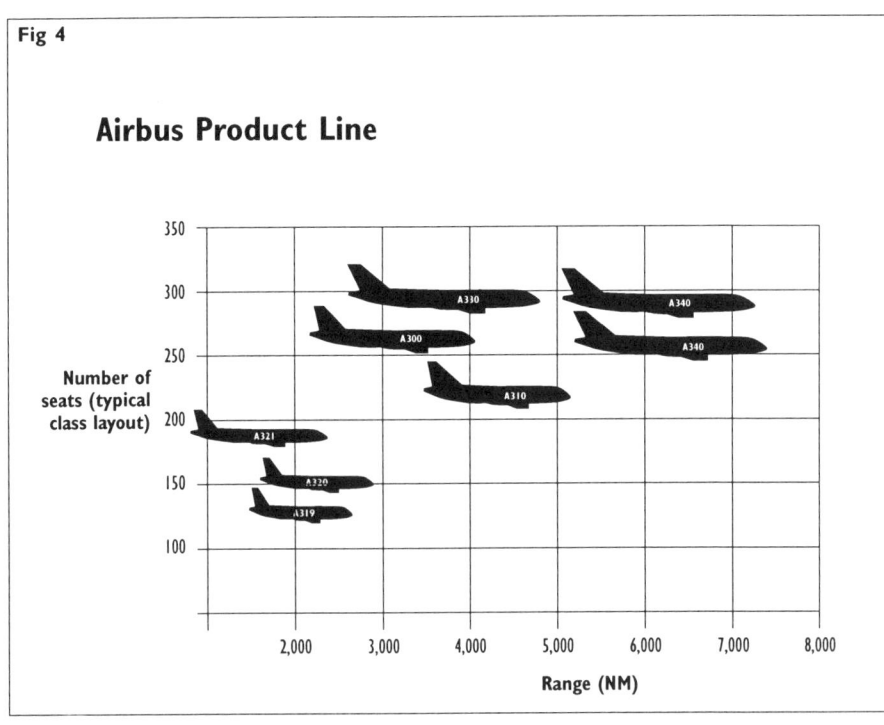

Fig 4

Airbus Product Line

I believe that it is this evolution of centres of excellence which has largely contributed to the success of Airbus.

The results of Airbus, both programme and financial, have been spectacular. But it is probably only in the last couple of years that its significance has really been understood in the UK.

Breaking the US Monopoly

Comparing the value of Jet Airline Deliveries across the Western world in 1974 to 1995 tells its own story (fig 5):

- Lockheed   out of the market sector;
- MDC   very much a third place player and now taken over by;
- Boeing   an uncertain future.

Looking to the future, Airbus now has set its objectives firmly on achieving a 50% market share. The benefits of Airbus to European industry are clearly significant - but the real impact is the benefit to the customer.

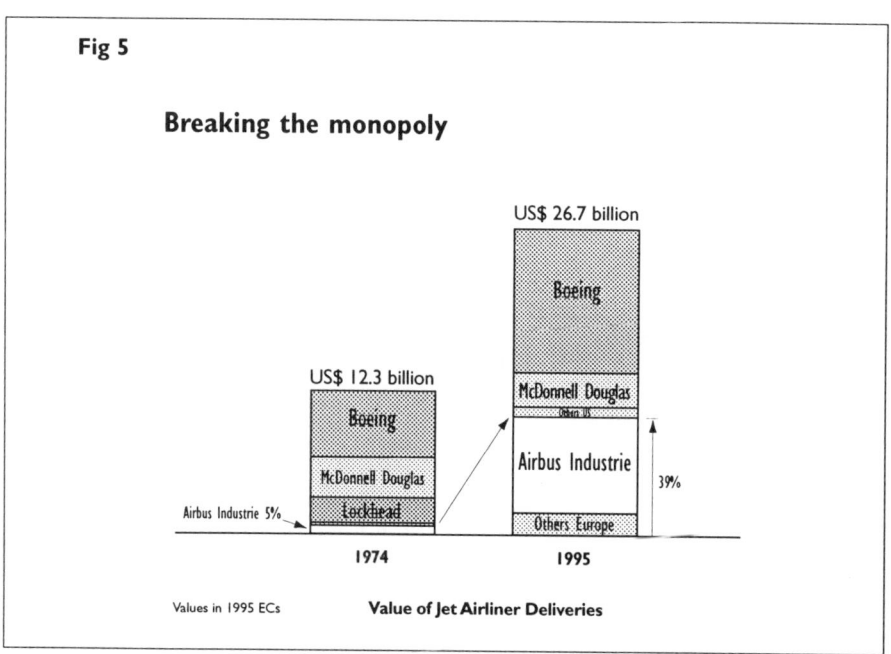

Fig 5

Breaking the monopoly

149

Competition from Europe has helped the customer to get competitive prices, the right technology development and the right products to meet the requirements of the market.

EU Major Defence Procurement Expenditure

Let us now examine the developments in the European defence market within the same time frame. In Europe during the 60s and 70s our defence needs were focused on the potential threat posed by the Soviet Bloc of Eastern Europe. Although "focused" is perhaps an inappropriate description suggesting as it does Europe acting together against a common threat. One can cite dozens of examples of nations and industries producing relatively small numbers of different equipment's and systems to counter similar threats. However the threat was there, and while we were not cooperating across Europe to challenge it, the amount of money being poured into defence research continued to grow and with it technological capability.

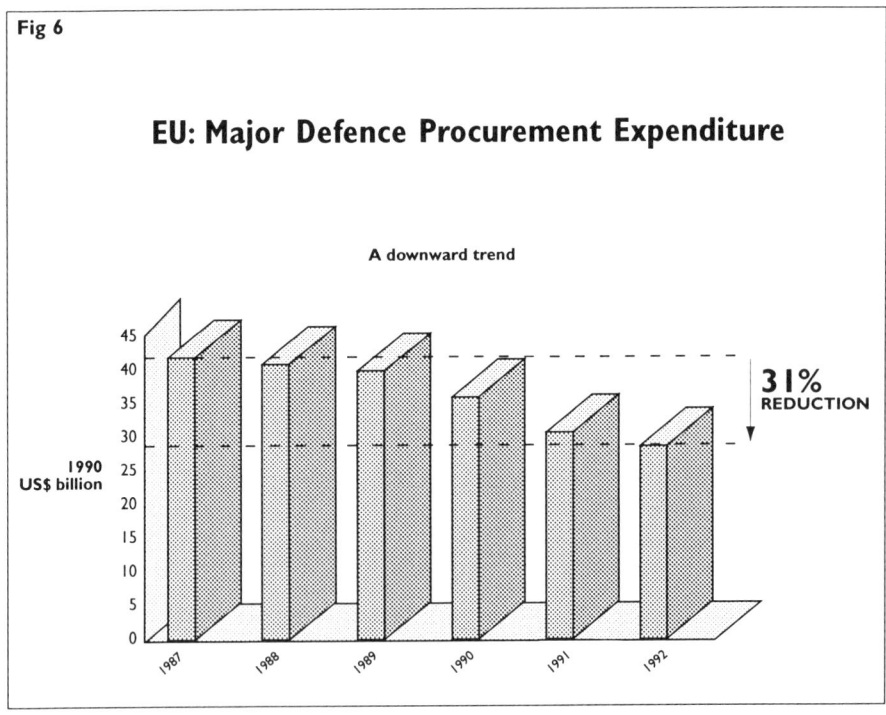

Fig 6

EU: Major Defence Procurement Expenditure

A downward trend

31% REDUCTION

Since the mid 1980s, there has, however, been a downward trend in European defence spending. This trend was accentuated by the end of the Cold War and produced a reduction of 31% in real terms between 1987 and 1992 (fig 6). The expectation of a peace dividend brought enormous reductions in defence spending worldwide. Add to that the recession in Europe and the scene is set for a considerable reduction in the size and capability of armed forces and future investment in defence technology.

Imports

Only in recent years have the nations and industries of Europe begun to realise that our fragmented approach to defence policy, to the specification and procurement of equipment and to industrial strategy is weakening both our military and industrial capability. Recognising that the writing was on the wall, the US defence industry had already commenced a massive restructuring drive. The newly liberated, lean and hungry US arms industry went in search of opportunities everywhere and found them, paradoxically in Europe, among other places. In spite of falling defence budgets, equipment imported into Europe increased its share threefold between 1987 and 1992 (fig 7).

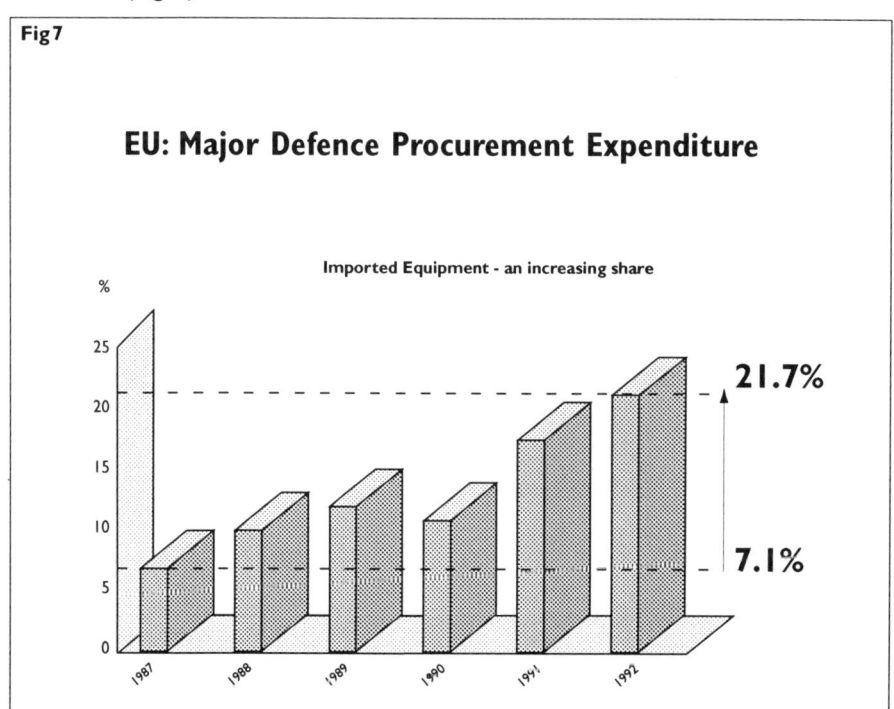

US Consolidation

1996 and the first half of 1997 have witnessed a period of considerable upheaval and change in the US and continues with Boeing absorbing Rockwell and McDonnell Douglas, Raytheon absorbing Hughes and Texas Instruments, and now Lockheed Martin proposing to merge with Northrop Grumman. Now that the necessary regulatory clearances have virtually all been granted, we see a US aerospace and defence industry which is dominated by three companies. This provides a remarkable challenge for the European aerospace industry which will have to compete with these giants upon the world's stage.

In the defence sector, the US defence budget of around $270bn now supports around one third of the number of defence contractors that can be found in the UK, Germany, France, Sweden, Italy and Spain. These countries, which are home to the bulk of the European defence business, have a combined defence budget of $125bn (fig 8).

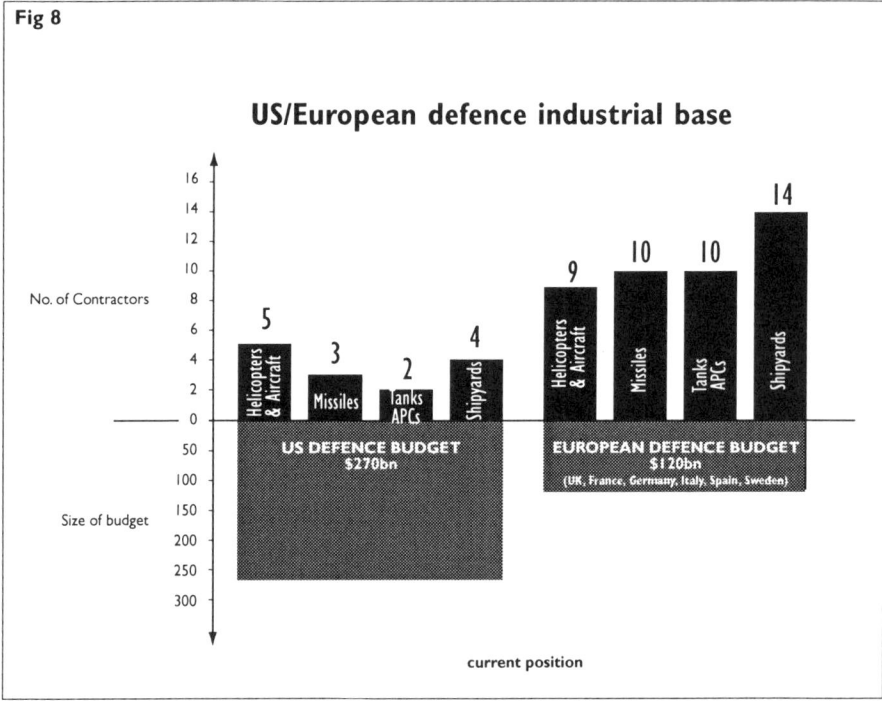

Fig 8

In short, we are trying to support three times the number of contractors on less than half the budget. Further, in the US there is only one customer with one set of requirements. In Europe there are many. Not only supply but also demand is divided into too many parts.

The American aerospace industry also benefits from the Department of Defense's investment in R&D which is three times that of NATO Europe and which inevitably strengthens the technological capability of the industry, civil as well as military. This is the practical reality underlying US government statements about the aerospace industry as a 'key force driving US technology and economic development' which, they say, is 'critical to the American economic future'.

Military

Today, then, we face a similar position in the military transport business to that we faced in the commercial market 25 years ago. If we analyse the value by deliveries Europe has become very much a minority player. (fig 9).

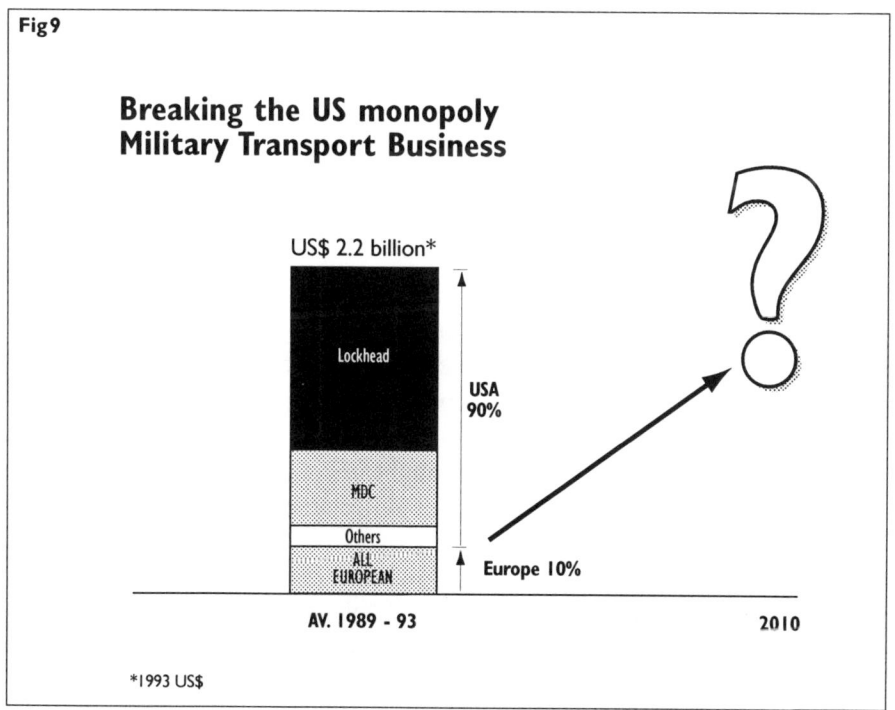

It is recognised that if we do not do something to change this we will be placing ourselves at the mercy of the US in the future, allowing them to control the market, control prices to Europe and control technology. Military transport business opportunities are much more cyclical than in civil aerospace. If we are not part of the next round of military transport procurement in Europe then we will have given our business away to the US. Much worse we will have allowed the US to continue to have the option of cross-subsidising commercial aircraft deals with the proceeds of military transport sales. However, if we can turn it the other way around and succeed in Europe, then I am convinced we can access other markets - we can break the US monopoly and pass the benefits that this will bring back through to industry and through to our customers, both military and commercial.

For Europe this large military aircraft market may be won with a number of possible different Airbus products and derivatives. At one end of the spectrum there is the charter availability of the cavernous Airbus super transporter, the 40t Beluga with its 4,500km range and unique capability. Then there is the military derivative solutions based on existing Airbus platforms. These range from the freighter conversion and VIP aircraft solutions already in service with a number of military customers around the world and through to new applications for AEW and communication aircraft based on the A310 platform and importantly for the UK market the Multi-Role Tanker Transport aircraft capable of simultaneously carrying out air-to-air refuelling and transport operations. Finally, there is our new product being developed for the large military transport market, the FLA, which is the focus of the rest of my presentation.

The large military aircraft market is certainly smaller than the global commercial market, and the potential for growth is no doubt less, but the market is there and is I believe significant to Europe's aspirations to compete with the US. The question before us then is 'can Airbus Military Company, through the FLA, bring about the sort of change in the balance of supply that Airbus Industrie has brought in commercial aviation?' And if it can, would it serve as a model for other areas of defence equipment supply and acquisition in Europe?

For many years the FLA programme (fig 10), under its various descriptions FIMA, EuroFLAg and so on, looked as if it might suffer the same fate as many of the previous joint European military collaborative programmes.

The programme had been severely hindered by a lack of clear common set of requirements. Now this is strange when you consider that the alternative is to buy off-the-shelf already developed aircraft designed to meet a very specific set of USAF requirements. But the fact is that, when you ask a group of end users from eight nations to agree a common set of operating requirements and harmonised mission profiles, the results are either no agreement or a gold plated specification which is hardly affordable in the relatively modest quantities required within Europe and totally unexportable in competition with US alternatives.

Fig 10

FLA Programme History 1983-1995

1983	Aerospatiale, BAe, MBB and Lockheed form FIMA (Future International Military Airlifter)
1987	Aeritalia (now Alenia) & CASA join FLA
1988	Draft Outline European Staff Target (OEST) established
1989	Lockheed withdraws EUROFLAG (European Future Large Aircraft Group) formed
1991	OEST issued
1993	Feasibility Study launched
1994	UK MOD announced C-130J purchase and conditional commitment to FLA
1995	Feasibility Study completed, submitted to European MOD's, EUROFLAG dissolved

---

The European Need is Real (fig 11)

During the late 1980s and early 1990s the defence budgets of all the participating nations were being cut. The high priority items were fighters and attack helicopters; transport and tankers were certainly amongst the last items on the shopping list.

When one considers all these factors together it's easy to see why the FLA was having so much difficulty in getting started and why it gained some very bad press in the process. Something had to change if this aircraft was ever going to fly.

But the requirement in Europe was real - in the form of a substantial, ageing fleet of transports, increasingly called upon to meet international peace-keeping and humanitarian obligations. If Europe did not get its act together, their replacement would form part of the growing US order book.

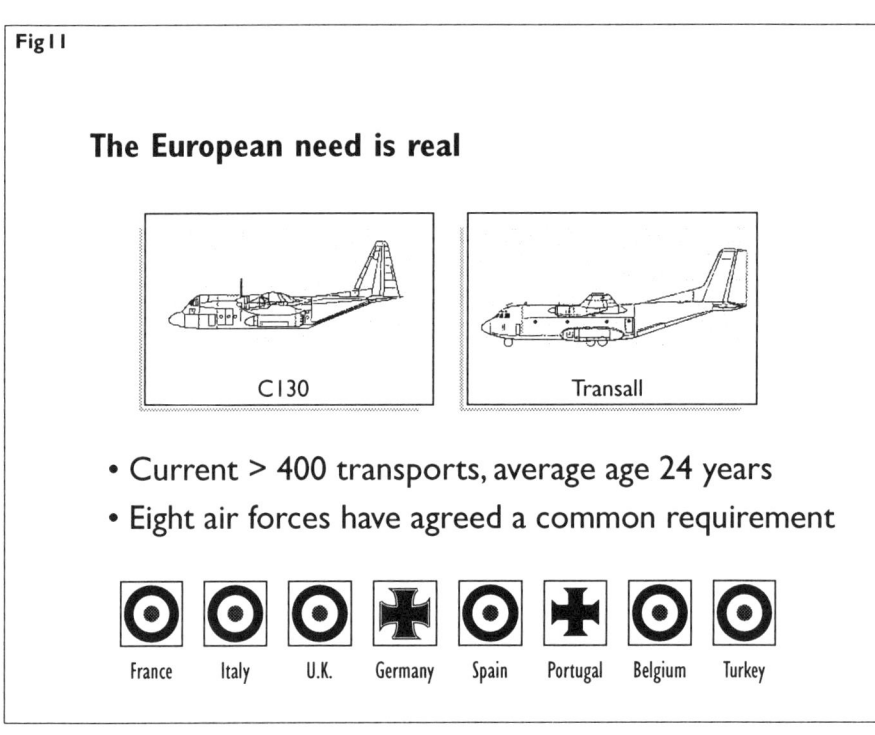

Fig 11

The European need is real

C130 — Transall

- Current > 400 transports, average age 24 years
- Eight air forces have agreed a common requirement

France   Italy   U.K.   Germany   Spain   Portugal   Belgium   Turkey

Traditional Procurement Programme

In the spring of 1995 the Feasibility Study was completed and the work of converting the European Staff Target into a European Staff Requirement had begun. The UK MoD also started to take on a much more active and influential role in the committees that were running the programme.

At this time the programme was still structured along traditional defence programme lines (fig 12).

This meant a multi-phased approach with lengthy industry/government negotiations required between each phase, particularly difficult in the case of international collaborative programmes, each of these negotiation periods can easily become protracted leading to time delays and cost over-runs. Typically, that would mean a Pre-Development Definition Phase lasting about two and a half years, 100% funded by the governments to clarify the ESR and produce the detailed Statement of Work for the Full Scale Development and Production Phase. Each of these phases is preceded by typical workshare/cost share negotiations lasting up to 12 months, and we have seen in the Eurofighter project how tortuous such a process can become.

The partners involved in the FLA programme recognised that if the FLA programme was to succeed then there was a need for change. This was reinforced in the UK by the Secretary of State for Defence's statement in 1994 about the conditions necessary for the UK to rejoin the programme.

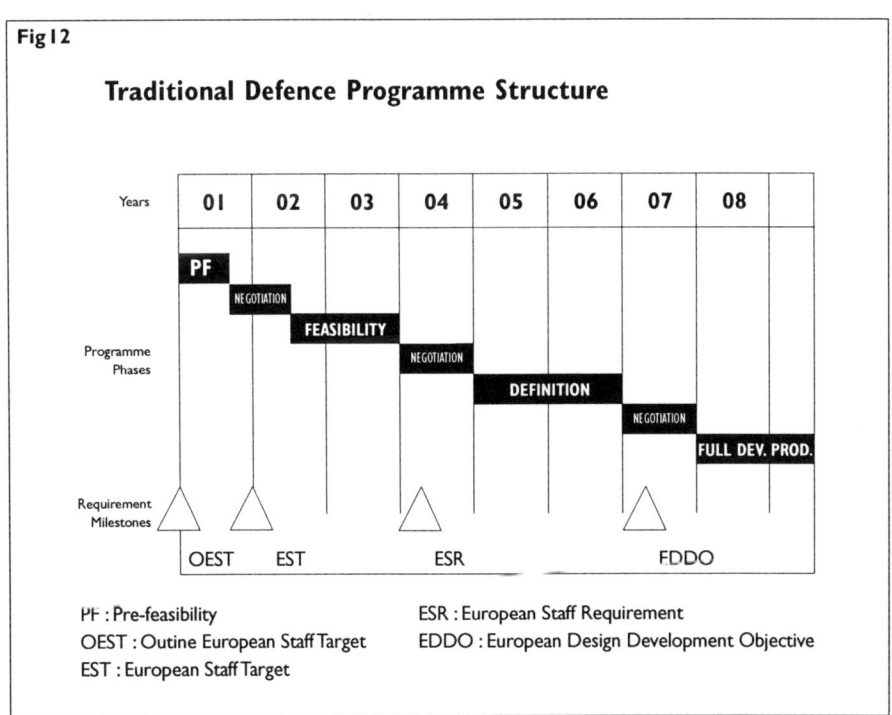

Fig 12

Traditional Defence Programme Structure

PF : Pre-feasibility   ESR : European Staff Requirement
OEST : Outine European Staff Target   EDDO : European Design Development Objective
EST : European Staff Target

Airbus Military Company (AMC) (fig 13)

The first change was in the industrial structure: the previously established programme office, EuroFLAg based in Rome, was dissolved and the programme brought under the umbrella of Airbus Industrie. The project did include additional partners however and a new business solution within this umbrella was required. The existing partners of Airbus Industrie decided to link up with Alenia in a new operating division of Airbus called AI/FLA. This has been up and running with a central team based in Toulouse for over two years. Now with the agreement to issue the RFP, the incorporation of this division into a new company called Airbus Military Company is being progressed.

Dependence on Government

Secondly, the adoption of a commercial approach for a military programme has changed the role for both the government and industry.

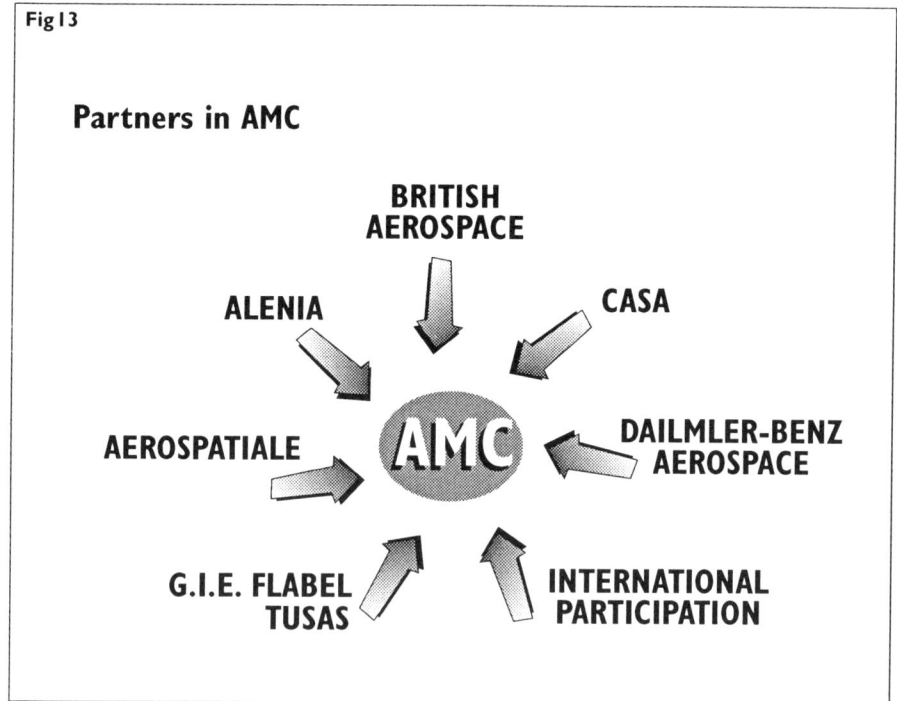

Fig 13

Partners in AMC

BRITISH AEROSPACE

ALENIA

CASA

AEROSPATIALE

AMC

DAILMLER-BENZ AEROSPACE

G.I.E. FLABEL TUSAS

INTERNATIONAL PARTICIPATION

Under the commercial approach, the Programme continues to have a dependence on government for the Staff Requirement formulation and the Specification Agreement, and for providing launch order commitments with associated funding. However, the key change is the separation from government of programme ownership, giving commercial freedom and transfer of risk to industry.

Airbus Technology Transfer

The third aspect was the opportunity to tap into Airbus Industrie's proven technology. The FLA partners considered that a very large percentage of the technological advances in Airbus could be applied and enhanced on the FLA without taking unnecessary technical risk. FLA would not be a technology demonstrator. For the FLA itself, examples of technology transfer can be found in many areas:

- The Cockpit: much work has already been done to demonstrate how the Airbus fly-by-wire flight control system and side-stick controls can be applied to FLA.
- Structures: many of the Airbus structural technology developments using advanced alloys and composite materials can be used directly on FLA to achieve weight savings, while offering high levels of fatigue strength and maintainability at an affordable cost.
- Aerodynamics: the advanced aerodynamic wing design methodologies developed and proven over 25 years on Airbus allows us to design an aircraft capable of carrying twice the payload of a C130J aircraft but with a wing of similar span.
- Production: the production expertise and processes used in the Airbus system are easily adaptable to suit a military transport aircraft and will ensure that the customer realises the benefit of manufacturing cost savings achieved in the commercial business and get 'best value for money'.

Less obvious but equally important are the areas of technology transfer which are related to training and supportability of the aircraft. The advances made by Airbus to support over 1500 aircraft delivered to more than 130 operators are available to support the military customers of FLA.

By application and modest evolution of current Airbus technology, large military transport aircraft will take a significant step forward compared to today's aircraft.

Governments vs Airlines

The nations' governments, in reviewing their own long term budgets, have themselves concluded that only a 'commercial approach' was affordable. To them this meant buying the aircraft from an Airbus type organisation just as the civil airlines do.

But there are some major differences between governments and airlines as customers (fig 14). In particular I note the marked contrast between the change in policy and the wide range of budgetary pressures that can arise in governments compared to the market driven approach of airlines.

Airbus Industrie, while being very supportive of moving FLA into its organisation, does need to look closely at the quality of its potential government customers - just as it would assess a potential civil customer. It is clear that while government procurement agencies have started to change, some nations are further ahead than others, they are all still trying to understand how the 'commercial approach' applies to defence procurement and many are distrustful of 'new' commercial methods.

Fig 14

Governments vs Airlines as Customers

GOVERNMENTS
- Subject to wide range of budgetary pressures
- Likely to change leadership & policy frequently
- Regular reviews of defence requirements
- Relatively short term focus
- Declining defence budgets

AIRLINES
- Market & business driven
- Relatively stable long term plans
- Highly visible market demand – determines needs
- Aircraft seen as commodity rather than long term asset
- Increasing demand driven by economic growth

Single Phase Nations (fig 15)

What was needed was a group of European customers who were no longer constrained by the rules of processes that had hardly changed in 20-30 years.

On the FLA programme, industry and government have worked together to develop what it describes as the 'Single Phase Commercial Approach' to address some of these changes. For the nations this means no international programme organisation. After the specification has been agreed, industry will manage the programme. The nations will behave like Airbus civil launch customers. In return the nations will be expecting to receive guarantees similar to civil customers.

Single Phase Industry (fig 16)

Industry, for its part, expects to manage the programme in a similar way to the way it manages commercial aircraft programmes.

Fig 15

Single phase commercial approach

WHAT IT MEANS... to the Nations

- The Nations behave like Airbus civil launch customers
- No international Programme Organisation
- Development & production of aircraft in a single contract
- Observer role after specification agreed
- Performance guarantees similar to civil customers
- Changes to quantities or withdrawal incur heavy penalty

This involves managing the programme risks related to cost, timescale and performance specification, that it is best placed to manage. It also means that it is the responsibility of industry to resolve workshare and procurement issues within an agreed framework.

To make the aircraft affordable, Airbus and its partners wish to build the FLA using their existing facilities and processes. They want to use existing certification procedures for Quality Assurance and Aircraft certification. Why incur the additional expense of ISO or military certification when JAR approvals and additional Airbus Design Standards are more than sufficient?

Airbus clearly understands the need to make the aircraft commercially competitive as it lives in that world in the civil market every day. It believes that a considerable amount of its return on investment will come from the export market. It knows that the product will have to be sufficiently attractive to be able to take the market away from the suppliers they have used for the last 40 years.

Fig 16

Single phase commercial approach

WHAT IT MEANS... to Industry

- Airbus Military Company manages the programme
- Workshare resolved by industry alone
- Responsible for equipment selection, including engines
- Responsible for export sales
- Industry partly funds development and recovers investment through export sales

---

We still have some way to go yet to the first flight of FLA. But the step changes that have been made in the last 18 months towards the development approach have been quite considerable.

Single Phase Programme

I hope you are starting to see how I believe FLA will benefit from an entirely commercial approach to a defence acquisition need. It should achieve high volumes of European *and* export sales because it is based on an industry-driven specification rather than a customer's inflated vision. Customisation for specific needs will not drive the basic product price too high.

The development and production lead time will be significantly lower (fig 17). The governments' costs of programme management will be almost eliminated. The product will benefit from the enormous previous investments by the partners in the civil transport business.

This process will deliver the most technically advanced and cost effective military transport aircraft ever produced - and it's European!

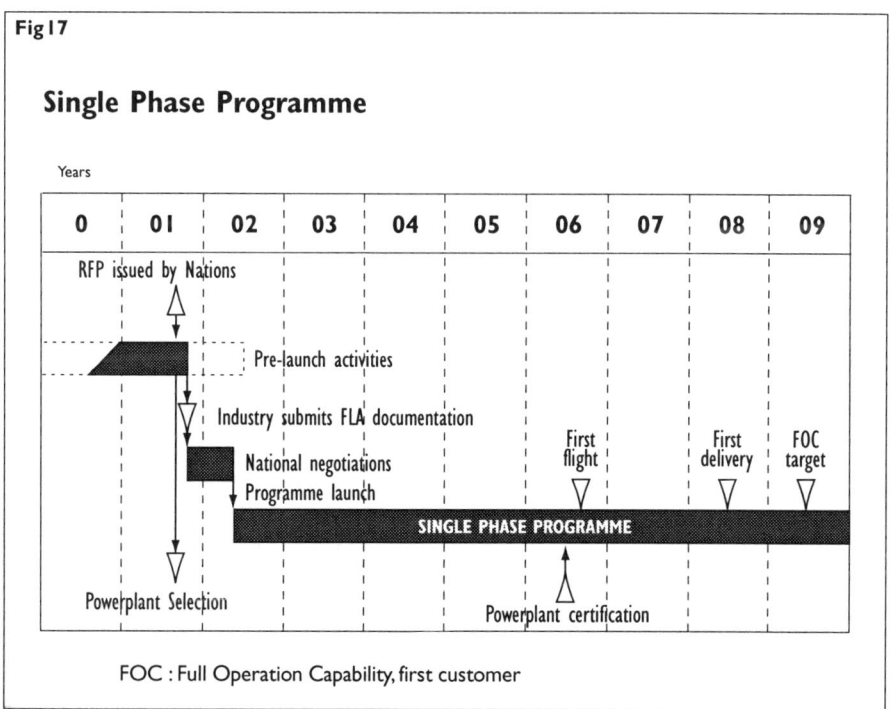

Fig 17

Single Phase Programme

FOC : Full Operation Capability, first customer

Placing development and production contracts at the same time will ensure programme continuity and give the industry the confidence to invest. This may require governments to extend their defence planning cycles from five or six years out to 15 years, but that is something that the US have been doing for several years.

Finally, in the civil business there are no guaranteed home markets and Airbus has to compete against the US suppliers in every deal it does. If industry and governments are able to achieve all of these changes, they will have helped to create a very strong, attractive customer in a 'United Europe'.

The Airbus Military Company will nevertheless have to remain extremely competitive if it is to develop its global market share and replicate the outstanding success of its civil aircraft parent company.

Conclusion

In conclusion I have tried to demonstrate to you how Europe has responded to the US commercial competition over the last 25 years. I believe that Europe is now at a watershed in the large military aircraft business. But I also strongly believe that the Airbus business and business processes are there to support the development of FLA and offer the opportunity to break the US monopoly and bring the same benefits to the military transport customer that we've brought to the commercial sector.

The key benefits come from changing the approach to defence procurement, giving programme ownership to industry, who are best placed to manage programme risks against time and cost targets, taking full advantage of Airbus proven industrial processes and technology and introducing a single phase programme approach with the placement of a single contract for both development and procurement at the same time.

The Secretary of State's announcement in July 1997 that the UK was now ready to join the other governments of Europe and issue the RFP for the FLA to industry has given industry the opportunity to demonstrate why we believe FLA is the right military transport solution for the UK and Europe.

I leave you with this picture of the FLA and the conclusion that not only is FLA the right aircraft to meet the evolving airlift needs of Europe but that FLA can bring about a new approach to defence procurement in Europe.

13 Eurofighter: The New Challenge of Collaboration in Military Aerospace

AIR VICE-MARSHAL PETER NORRISS
UK MOD Procurement Executive

Eurofighter is a single-seat, twin-engine, agile fighter capable of operating in the air superiority, surface-attack and reconnaissance roles. When it comes into service it will provide a significant increase in operational capability as a result of many of the advanced technologies incorporated in both the aircraft and the weapons that it will carry. Special emphasis has been placed on low wing loading, high thrust-to-weight ratio, excellent all round vision, carefree handling, a low radar signature, excellent sensors and the man-machine interface.

In a single-seat aircraft such as the Eurofighter, the man-machine interface has to be particularly well designed to give an acceptable workload and to enhance operational effectiveness. This has been achieved by incorporating the following features:

a. Sensor fusion - Drawing together data from sensors including the radar, the infra-red search and track, a defensive aids sub-system, the identification system and a situational awareness device called MIDS (multi-function information distribution system) and presenting it to the pilot in an easily comprehensible way.

b. HOTAS - allowing the pilot to select and operate most of the navigation attack, weapon, communications and autopilot systems without removing his hands from the throttle or control column, or his eyes from the air around him.

c. Direct Voice Input/Output. Complementing the HOTAS, the Direct Voice input/output facility enables the pilot to give directions by voice to avoid him having to look outside the cockpit or move his hands from controls. The aircraft will also respond by voice to voice questions from the pilot. During cockpit evaluations this device has been shown to be highly effective and easy to use. And increasingly we are talking about the combined HOTAS and DVI capability as VTAS - voice, throttle and stick control.

d. Head Equipment Assembly. The helmet itself represents a leap forward in worldwide helmet technology. As well as providing outside world and aircraft performance cues, the helmet's visor presents comprehensive target and weapon aiming symbology which will enable the pilot to utilise his weapons without having his eyes focused on a particular display inside the cockpit. It allows weapon aiming and sensor monitoring over a wide angle - particularly useful for agile, shorter range air-to-air weapons.

e. DASS. The defensive aids sub system is an integrated internally mounted system which is designed to increase combat effectiveness as well as survivability in a severe electronic environment. It consists of electronic support and protection systems that provide warning of a range of threats such as radar emitters, approaching anti-aircraft missiles and laser energy, and then control the deployment of decoys and chaff to counter those threats in addition to advice to the pilot on how to manoeuvre his aircraft.

f. Radar. The ECR90 radar is a development of the Blue Vixen radar on the recently updated Sea Harrier. It is a multi-mode doppler radar that will enable multiple target air-to-air tracking. The 'radar' picture is computer generated from sensor fusion information, and the internal functions of the radar are highly automated to optimise detection and tracking. In addition the pilot workload associated with radar management will be dramatically reduced compared with that of current aircraft.

g. FLIR/IRST. The combined Forward Looking InfraRed and Infra Red Search and Track System is mounted on the fuselage and can be used in the air-to-surface mode for target acquisition and as a night flying and landing aid. In the air-to-air role it will be used for passive detection and identification of targets. The FLIR imagery will be fused with other sensor information and displayed on the attack and pilot awareness displays and on the helmet.

There are a total of 13 weapon carriage points on the aircraft, including three stations capable of carrying jettisonable fuel tanks. In the air-to air role, a typical weapons load might consist of six medium range missiles, two shorter range infra red missiles, and the internal Mauser 27mm gun, although a total of 10 missiles could be carried. Additionally it may also carry the existing infra-red seeking missile, AIM9L. On entry into service the medium range missile will be AMRAAM, but a competition is currently underway for a more advanced one, known as the Beyond Visual Range Air-to-Air Missile, BVRAAM. In the offensive support role, it would be usual to carry air-to-air missiles for self-defence

166

in addition to offensive weapons such as the Advanced Air Launched Anti-Armour Weapon and the Conventionally Armed Stand-Off Weapon. The Paveway III laser-guided bomb operated in conjunction with the TIALD pod and today's weapons will also feature in the aircraft's arsenal. In flight selection and programming of weapons and delivery modes will permit the pilot to optimise the weapon system to meet a large variety of threat types and scenarios, even within the same sortie, thus offering enhanced flexibility to the operational commander.

As an aircraft Eurofighter will have very high performance and carefree manoeuvrability, by which I mean that a pilot's control inputs will be controlled by computers that will ensure maximum safe performance and no more for any given circumstance. Extensive modelling has been carried out by both the MoD and British Aerospace to compare Eurofighter's performance with that of other advanced fighters. These simulations have shown that EF produces, inter alia, outstanding turning capability and other values which allow it air superiority. When combined with Helmet Mounted Sight Technology and the high manoeuvrability of the BAe Advanced Short Range Air-to-Air Missile (ASRAAM), Eurofighter has the edge in combat. Aircraft agility is supported fully by a new suite of aircrew flying clothing and G protection equipment.

Although highly capable in the close combat environment, it is in the Beyond Visual Range (BVR) combat mission where EF will truly make its mark. The EF airframe, combined with a comprehensive electronic combat suite, presents a small and difficult target to engage, while the long range look-down advantages of the radar, and the inherent high energy qualities of the aircraft will ensure that the pilot can release his missiles before potential adversaries. The much faster and longer range BVRAAM will increase this advantage even further, by greatly increasing an enemy's no-escape zone.

The Eurofighter is capable of attacking ground targets by day or night in very poor visibility and to a high accuracy. Weapon aiming is via visual, radar or electro-optic acquisition of the target. Against planned targets, whose position is stored within the attack computer, the process is largely automated and the pilot's workload is low. Against unplanned targets, the combination of simple moding through the VTAS controls also provides a low workload. Throughout an air-to-surface attack, the pilot can continue to use the on-board sensors (radar and forward-looking infra-red) and MIDS to maintain awareness of the air situation and to identify potential airborne threats. The transition between air-to-air and air-to-surface modes is quick and easy, and the cockpit displays automatically configure to the attack profile selected.

Eurofighter is also planned to have a reconnaissance capability by utilising an externally mounted reconnaissance pod.

Eurofighter will replace the Tornado F3 in the air defence role, and the Jaguar in the offensive support and reconnaissance roles, and both these aircraft types are planned to be out of service by 2010. The Royal Air Force plans to have 232 Eurofighter aircraft to provide an active fleet of around 135 aircraft over 25 years. The active fleet will be split into seven squadrons, an Operational Conversion Unit and an Operational Evaluation Unit. The first aircraft is scheduled to be delivered at the end of 2001.

That's what Eurofighter is expected to look like from 2002 onwards. Let me now go back to the beginning of the project and bring out some of the collaborative issues involved.

History

Five nations, France, Germany, Italy, Spain and the UK began project definition of a new aircraft in the early 1980s, but France withdrew to build the Dassault Rafale, a smaller ground attack aircraft capable of operating off its planned carriers. By 1987 Germany, Italy, Spain and the UK had signed the European Staff Requirement for Development for the European Fighter Aircraft (EFA), and declared a requirement for 765 aircraft, with Germany and the UK each having 250.

Development commenced in 1988, but, in June 1992, Herr Rühe, the German Defence Minister, announced that with the end of the Cold War there was no longer a need for an aircraft like EFA and that as planned it was not affordable to Germany. The partners began a period of consultation during which the operational requirements and the options for cost reduction were reviewed. The four Chiefs of Defence Staff confirmed that in the new environment, a weapon system with the qualities of EFA was still needed, arguing that in fact it was even more necessary when the emerging scenarios for the Rapid Reaction Forces both inside the NATO area and for Out of Area operations were considered. However, recognising the need to meet German political imperatives the programme was reorientated to produce some industrial savings and to allow the costs of each aircraft to be reduced further by omitting some capabilities for those nations that wished to do so.

Ministers agreed to continue with the project, renaming it Eurofighter 2000 and aiming for it to enter service in 2001. A reorientation contract was finally signed in November 1995. Among the detail it was agreed that:

- The Luftwaffe aircraft would be for air defence only, and Germany decided to reduce its initial requirement of 250 aircraft to 140. It has since revised this and now plans to buy 180 aircraft.

- Italy would order 121 aircraft principally in an air defence role but with an air to ground capability.

- Spain would order 87 aircraft to be used in both air to air and air to ground roles.

- The UK would buy 232 aircraft for air to air and air to surface roles, and in the longer term Eurofighter would also be considered as a replacement for the Harrier.

Since reorientation the Eurofighter project has made significant progress in the key areas of programme management, international agreement, technical maturity, definition of support arrangements and determination of prices. In particular, the development programme now meets the demanding set of technical maturity criteria agreed between the four nations. These cover all key systems including the test and evaluation of the Flight Control System and the ECR Radar which has been particularly impressive this year.

By design, Eurofighter is an aerodynamically unstable aircraft. To enable the pilot to control the aircraft, stability is provided by an active, computerised, flight control system. With this design, the quality and integrity of the flight control system is of critical importance. Consequently, it has been necessary to take a cautious, incremental, approach to the development and clearance of the system. The flight control system also has other advanced features such as tailored control response, automatic alleviation from the effects of gusts and automatic protection against loss of control. The flight control system has operated successfully during all of the flight trials carried out to date, and pilots have praised the excellent handling qualities of the aircraft. The next phase of flight trials will demonstrate the carefree manoeuvre capability of the aircraft.

Over the last two years very significant advances have been made in the radar programme; it has completed over 200 hours of in-flight operation in a laboratory aircraft and in Eurofighter. The early indications from the Eurofighter trials are that the installed performance meets or exceeds predictions. The radar is expected to fully meet or exceed its specification, including the requirement to detect and resolve closely spaced targets and to discriminate high priority threats.

As we are entering the later stages of the development programme the risks are diminishing and costs are showing no sign of increasing. Indeed since signature of the reorientation MOU in the summer of 1995 there has been no cost increase to the UK in real terms.

Collaboration

Eurofighter is of course a very high profile example of a military collaborative project. Our experiences in collaboration on this and other collaborative ventures have taught us a great deal about the positive and negative features of collaboration and how we can improve them for the future.

The first, and perhaps the most important, benefit of collaboration is the sharing of non-recurring costs and reduced production costs. Although development among several nations generally means that there is an increase in total costs, the cost to each partner is reduced - common rule of thumb here is that the increase is a function of the square root of the number of partners. In the case of EF, the increase is roughly double, (the square root of 4) so the UK is paying 2/3 of the estimated cost of going alone. Shared tooling costs and larger production runs lead to economies of scale but consideration does need to be given to nations' desires to have their own assembly, production and test facilities which can lead to diseconomies.

Interoperability is the major operational gain from collaboration. A common requirement and common solution mean that it is much simpler to use allied nations' facilities and bases and for coalition forces to operate more cohesively. The force commander's task is radically simplified, and many more STANAGS can be introduced - a benefit which has not always been fully exploited in the past. Although the airframes may have appeared to be similar, they have had a lack of commonality in systems such as the defensive aids suite, weapons and associated software, stores management and ejection release units. This was the case when Tornado entered service in three partner countries with limited ability to carry one another's weapons, or even to maintain one another's aircraft, some equipments being national solutions.

Collaboration, whether it is within Europe or transatlantic, enhances NATO and political cohesion. Our NATO partners are keen to collaborate and indeed the US now places collaboration above single and joint service solutions.

History has shown that there are political and industrial advantages to collaboration. Collaborative projects are less likely to be cancelled by individual nations - loss of credibility as a partner within the international arena is a powerful driver which helps to ensure that the Armed Forces concerned do finally get the equipment they are planning for. In the wider political field, collaboration, such as for EF, has been a means of bringing countries and companies together, a crucially important factor for the aerospace industry. There may be elements within some countries who do not want this to happen, but EF will certainly be one of the major catalysts for restructuring within the European aerospace industry. With the continuing shrinkage in the defence industries, collaboration allows companies to work together and pool their strengths, bring in and keep hi-tech business within Europe and not have to resort as a matter of course to buying off-the-shelf.

But, of course, there are disadvantages and problems associated with collaborative working. For example, such projects are prone to slippage for a number of reasons:

- it is occasionally difficult to get a consensus from nations, and when it is achieved it invariably represents a compromise; that said, compromise does not infer a reduction in specification requirement;
- nations have different perceptions about their needs over time, for example the end of the Cold War and the German perception that EF was no longer needed nor affordable;
- differing political timescales, usually driven by general elections. Major projects can also pose difficulties for small majority governments and affect their timetable and political manoeuvring concerning the project. For EF there are four national timetables and the result is inevitably a slowing down in the overall programme;
- budgetary pressures can also cause nations to modify their position and a project may therefore be prone to the impact of budgetary problems.

Diseconomies can occur because of national image and perceptions. Let me give you two examples. Each nation understandably wants to make sure that its voice is properly heard, and so international management structures in both government and industry are generally larger than they would be for a purely national one. And each of the four Eurofighter nations will have a national assembly line for building and testing its own aircraft; while this leads to higher overall costs, it provides nations with higher capability in responding to export requirements.

Additionally, national motives for joining a collaborative project may vary and impact on the progress of the project. Some nations may join to meet a real requirement, and others may join for other reasons such as technological gain. This may result in some companies having to transfer technology to their competitors. Moreover, the quest for a selfish and prescriptive share of both quality and quantity of work can lead to complex, costly and technically sub-optimal solutions.

Jobs are crucial to each nation, and so there has been a tendency for nations to overbid for development workshare and then, to reduce the eventual number of aircraft that they will purchase, but with the hope of retaining a larger share of the work. This leads to tensions with those who believe that the share of work should be related to offtake. On EF this has been circumvented through territorial funding, a system whereby national governments pay only for the work done in their own country. This brings discipline on the nations not to seek more workshare than their offtake and encourages them to drive down the prices of their industry's work on the project whilst retaining the benefits of scale.

Workshare can be problematical; within the Eurofighter project each aircraft system is broken down to give the specific workshare for each partner nation on the basis of their entitlement, which may not always be commensurate with a nation's contribution to the programme. In development the breakdown of Eurofighter work was. 33% to Germany and the UK, with the balance split between Italy and Spain.

When the entitlement changes, for example on transition from development to production because of changes to the number of aircraft to be ordered by each nation, work for the production phase has to be physically moved from one nation to another. This can cause technical and attitudinal difficulties, and in some cases it is physically impossible to do without really major upheaval and much slippage to the programme. In the case of Eurofighter, the UK share has gone from 33% in development to 37.5% while Germany's has dropped from 33% to 30%. As each percentage point broadly equates to £150 million, you can understand the scale of the difficulty, particularly if you want to move work economically and secure timescale and technical standards.

Exchange rate variations can cause budgetary problems in some nations. During the nine years of the development programme so far, there has been massive fluctuation in the exchange rates and this has had a real impact on the aircraft's costs to us. But territorial funding in production will virtually eliminate the exchange rate problem.

Management authority is a major consideration in the organisation of collaborative projects. Where there is one customer, one procurement authority and one supplier, the line of authority is simple. But EF has a management agency, NETMA, which operates only with the authority of the four nations, and there are two consortia producing the aircraft - Eurofighter GmbH for the airframe and Eurojet for the engine. These consortia have little authority themselves - this is vested in the eight partner companies that provide the resources and overall expertise to them. Forthright management in this situation is very difficult to achieve. This leads me on to consider the differing industrial arrangements and philosophies in different European countries.

Some nations rely almost entirely upon market forces to shape their defence industry, whereas others maintain their defence companies in public ownership and take a very dirigiste approach. Others have said that they wish to privatise their industries but this has not occurred in practice. This leads to difficulties in establishing a level playing field for competition or to incentivise those who think that they have an entitlement regardless of the cost of their product. Where such procurement policies differ, achieving a consensus on a procurement strategy can be very difficult. Moreover, the act of establishing a NATO project and generating a consortium such as EF can make one feel rather like the inventor of that terrible but effective monster, Frankenstein. For these consortia are in reality enormous monopolies that make it very difficult for the nations to derive or establish value for money in support, in follow-on activities and in later upgrades.

But there are other ways of collaborating and the Procurement Executive is employing some of these, and learning from the lessons of the past, in projects such as FLA and JSF. The days of projects based on rigid workshare, taking no account of competitiveness and technological capability are over, and there is a clear imperative to exploit the advantages and minimise the disadvantages of collaboration.

The FLA model is designed to maximise the commercial approach to avoid wrangles over workshare, the emergence of differing requirements, delays in government decisions, and a top heavy collaborative structure which could prevent the UK from attaining the benefits of competition. This is being achieved through a partnership of nations working to a common requirement (expressed in the FLA European Staff Requirement) and an agreed set of principles under which the procurement process will be conducted. Nations have issued a Request for Proposals (RFP) to Airbus Military Company (AMC) and will negotiate a common core contract with AMC in the knowledge of the likely production offtake of the other partners. Each country would then be responsible for its own procurement decision and placement of contract with the prime contractor (AMC) on the basis of its assessment of the proposals received. Each country has the option of asking for its own equipment options, for example, role equipment, to be defined in national annexes to the RFP. This allows economies of scale with the minimum of bureaucracy and avoids the need for cash flow across European borders. Coordination between the partners will be achieved through an over-arching MOU which will enable the setting up of a Joint Steering Committee to resolve any common difficulties and manage such areas as joint trials and data exchange. The aim is for nations to achieve partnership through a commercial approach with a prime contractor responsible for the design, manufacture and production.

The JSF model is an example of transatlantic collaboration. Collaboration with the Americans is very different from that between European nations in that it is inevitably a leader-follower relationship with the US very much in the driving seat. This is not necessarily a bad thing; the price advantage that can be gained from economies of scale and the amount of work which UK industry gets by participating in fulfilling the US requirements as well as export orders, might well be greater than it would have been in a European collaboration. Decision-making is swifter, if rather less consultative, and so far slippage has been avoided - a remarkable achievement given the technical complexity of the project.

But with collaborations such as this there are also disadvantages. For example, if during the aircraft's service life you wish to maintain the economies of scale, you really have to hang on (and that means pay your share) during the leader's updating and development of his product. If you don't, you will alone have to support the legacy systems, and that is expensive.

Moreover, whatever the wishes of the US Government it is a simple fact that the US Congress can greatly influence the future, budget, shape and scope of military programmes on an annual basis and do!

The Future For Collaboration

Difficulties generated by present collaborative methods are such that I for one favour change, from the current model employed on EF, towards some form of partnering and a model which gives authority to management decision-making by the customer and industry concerned. It is strategically and economically important to have a strong, soundly-based and competitively viable indigenous defence industry. But the UK would be unable to sustain the industry at anything like its current level of capability on the back of its own armed forces' peacetime requirements. So, larger orders, based on joint requirements and exports are vital. That means, increasingly, cross-border industrial partnerships in the defence sector. Decisions must be based on good commercial sense founded on the central criteria of performance and effective project management and the notions of *juste retour*, workshare and national preference must be eliminated. This is particularly relevant in the context of a US defence industrial base with a domestic budget more than twice that of Europe - we simply do not have the resources to pursue this fragmented approach within the European defence industry. However, it is essential to underline that European collaboration in no way presupposes a European preference. Our essential procurement criteria of competition and value for money can be fully realised only in the context of international as well as European or domestic acquisitions. It is only through open defence markets that European industry can flourish. By keeping our defence industry competitive, and at the cutting edge of technology, we sharpen the European defence industrial base as well as ensure its commercial viability.

But that is easy to say and much less easy to effect. Europe is moving far too slowly in its restructuring of the defence industry, and the slowing down of privatisation in France has been a complicating factor here. It would be a catastrophe if national parochialism undermined overall European competitiveness as a result. But mergers and rationalisations will not occur in a vacuum. Large defence projects are undoubtably one of the major catalysts that drive such changes, although there are only a few projects that generate significant clout to force the pace. Airbus and its products are clearly one such catalyst. Apache and Storm Shadow, ASRAAM and BVRAAM offer a weapon catalyst; and Eurofighter, building as it does on Tornado experience, offers a powerful one in the military aircraft sector.

One possible opportunity to break from the past and deliver best practice procurement is the Organisme Conjointe de Cooperation d'Armement or OCCAR. This is the new armaments agency linking France, Germany, Italy and UK. This organisation is still in its infancy and realistically cannot be expected to deliver improvements for some years, with the next tranche of projects. It must also be recognised that OCCAR is only a mechanism; no matter how efficient its practices without new collaborative programmes it can achieve little. With our major European partners dealing with constrained budgets and under the additional pressure of EMU convergence criteria, the ability to launch new collaborative projects even pre-supposing an improvement to Europe's track record for agreeing collaborative requirements must be problematic.

Whilst OCCAR offers an opportunity to achieve best practice procurement and deliver value-for-money through competition and working in an efficient manner, there are also risks. Beyond the rhetoric there are still differences between the partners, and the potential exists for the organisation to promote protectionism and to be overly bureaucratic. It will take very hard bargaining without partners at all levels - from politicians to officials - to achieve the UK vision of OCCAR delivering efficient collaborative programmes. Without such resolve the chances are that many bad, old habits will persist.

Finally, Europe alone does not have the market volume to sustain these industrial sectors, and so the products will have to compete in overseas markets against the mega companies of the United States. Current collaborative arrangements are unlikely to deliver competitive products in the future unless those collaborating, in industry and in government, find more efficient ways of working together and closing a potentially widening competitiveness gap between Europe and the USA.

Part IV

Technology Development Issues

14 The Strategic Significance of R&T Strategy

DAVID MARSHALL
Director General, SBAC

Introduction

The latest data on the UK aerospace industry shows that the position of the UK as a dominant force in the world aerospace market was strengthened in 1996 (figs 1 & 2).

Putting the UK in a Wider Picture: Europe

Aerospace is a highly competitive global business in which technology plays a vital part. It is dominated by the US and Europe. Even though the European industry is only half the size of the US it is successful nevertheless and is one of Europe's most important industrial assets. The UK aerospace industry has an important economic influence on Europe.

Fig 1	SBAC DATA FOR THE UK AEROSPACE INDUSTRY		
		1995	1996
Aerospace Turnover (unconsolidated)		**11355.10**	**13066.26**
	Civil Turnover	5212.13	5782.07
	Military Turnover	6142.97	7284.19
	Airframes Turnover	5006.88	6044.43
	Engines Turnover	2231.32	2749.80
	Equipment Turnover	3677.74	4089.30
	Space Turnover	439.16	182.73
Exports		**8007.76**	**9702.53**
	As a percentage of Turnover	70%	74%
	Civil Exports	4020.22	4602.68
	Military Exports	3987.54	5099.85
Employment		**110549**	**92749**
	By Activity		
	R&D	18936	12992
	Production	62496	55806
	Rest	29117	23951
Turnover figures measured in £m		Employment figures are absolute	

179

Fig 2   **THE UK AEROSPACE INDUSTRY**

World wide sales of aircraft and equipment will exceed £160bn per year (European Aerospace Industry - Trading Position and Figures 1996)

UK Aerospace contributed £2.9bn net to the Balance of Trade in 1996

The UK sector comprises 1,000 firms and employs 230,000 people directly and indirectly

It has the second highest value added per employee in high tech manufacturing, employing some 40,000 graduates

HOWEVER, UK SHARE OF THE MARKET HAS SLIPPED FROM 13% TO 9% OVER THE LAST DECADE

Fig 3   **1995 AEROSPACE R&D**

                    UK   **US**

                             SOURCES

HMG	25%	**FEDERAL 62%** (c.f.36% across all other sectors)	
INDUSTRY OWN FUNDS	41%		
OVERSEAS COMPANIES INVESTMENTS	24%	**INDUSTRY 38%**	
OTHER UK BUSINESS	10%		

180

The European industry directly employs 350,000 people with approximately a further 700,000 indirectly employed, and involves over 7,000 firms throughout the EU.

The industry exports more than half of its turnover to areas outside the EU, earns approximately 20bn ECU per annum and produces a positive trade balance of approximately 8bn ECU per annum.

1995 Aerospace R&D (fig 3)

The US invests more in R&T ($2bn per annum) than the total given by all of the European governments ($1.65bn pa). There needs to be rationalisation in Europe. The money that is invested is not spent effectively as there is duplication of activities by the competing companies, and internal competition between the companies in the EU. In order for European companies to be able to effectively compete with the US, there is a clear need for European investment in aerospace R&T to more closely reflect that of the US.

Technical Capability

One of the key characteristics of the industry is a high dependence on technology. The cost of which is high, but not as high as the financial costs of developing and launching a major new product.

Technical capability can be broken down into a number of factors, all of equal importance:

- technology development;
- engineering and management staff;
- the right institutional structures and management organisations;
- both government and industry facilities;
- the required funding from government contracts and private venture.

Successive US administrations have believed that aerospace is of vital strategic importance from both an economic and military perspective. The US administration has recently reaffirmed its commitment and the current level of US government support for aerospace R&T acquisition is more than the equivalent total support given by the EU governments.

The current conclusion being drawn by the aerospace industry is that the European aerospace technology base will become progressively less competitive unless there is urgent investment in technology. There is an urgent need to rationalise R&T investment at a European level, which is dependent on, and subject to, national agendas.

Little or no investment of this kind will increasingly affect the saleability of European products and make European companies and consortia less attractive partners to non-Europeans for collaborative projects and have major adverse effects on employment levels and the European balance of trade.

The United Kingdom

The UK aerospace industry has had notable successes over the past 15 years or so, but its share of the global market has been declining. Further improvements in technology and competitiveness are critical to the future of the industry.

Government (DTI) funding for civil research and demonstrator programmes in aerospace has declined. There has been a similar pattern of decline in government expenditure on defence R&D (fig 4).

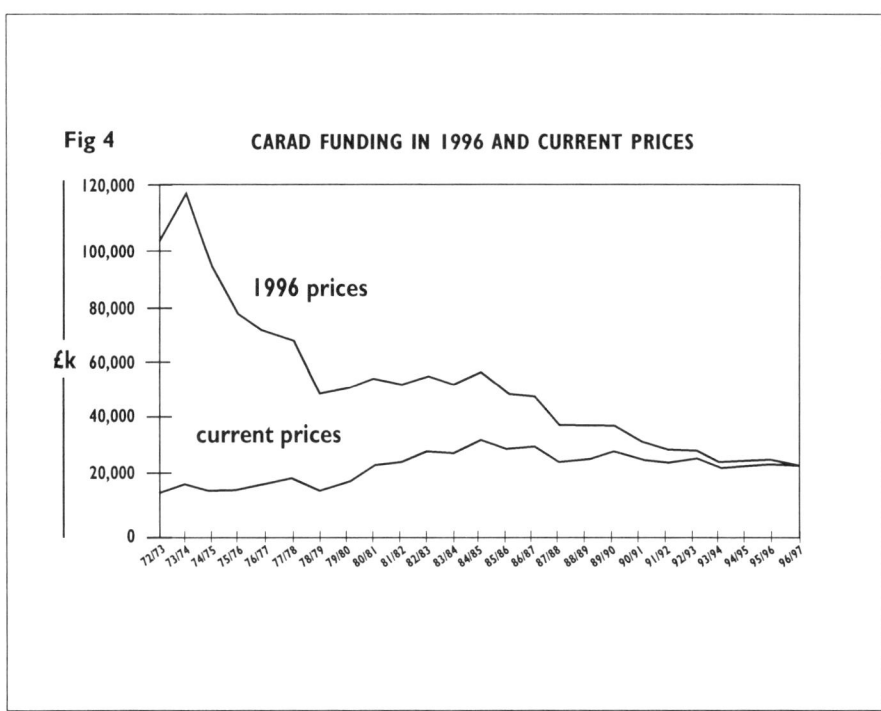

Fig 4   CARAD FUNDING IN 1996 AND CURRENT PRICES

Embedding Foresight

The lack of money invested in R&T is not only a government issue. Industry has had to invest in restructuring, new plant and R&T through periods of recession as well as growth. In this industry there is no quick return on investment - the return could be 20 years away or more.

It is important that investment is applied throughout the whole supply chain, and not just to the Primes, as technical capability is created throughout the supply chain (fig 5).

Products that are selling well now are the result of 'old' technology. Some aircraft still in service today have been manufactured with technology that is anything up to 50 years old (fig 6).

The health of the UK's future aerospace industry largely rests on investment in technology. The UK's technology base is ageing and needs urgent investment. The UK is currently living off its technological inheritance.

Historically, technology has been led by developments in the defence arena. This is no longer the case and industry cannot rely on military budgets and subsequent investment in R&T. The UK aerospace industry is a dual industry and is no longer civil following the lead of defence.

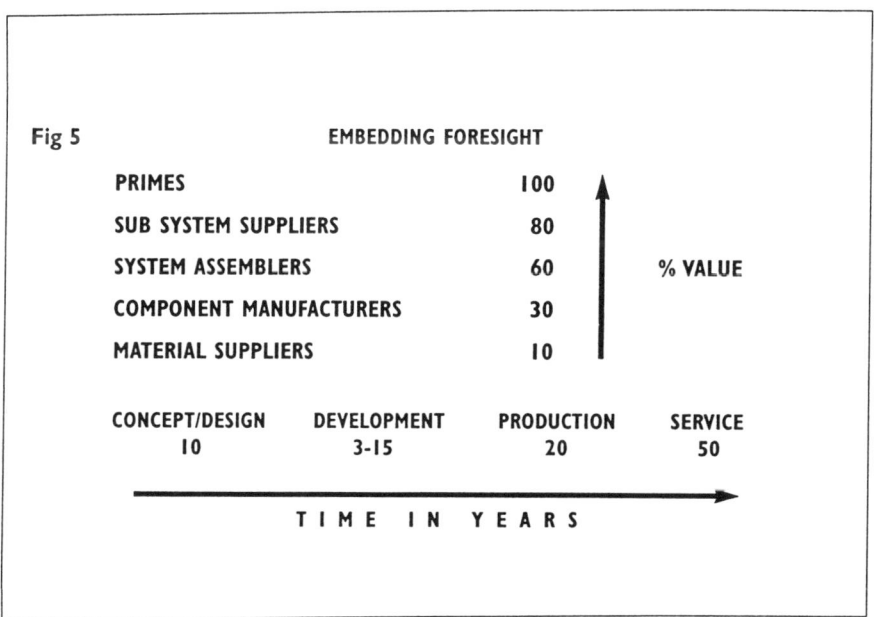

Although the UK market share of the global market has been declining, a reversal is possible as UK industry has already laid the groundwork:

- Structure of the industry has been rationalised, workforce reduced and manufacturing productivity increased
- UK has low labour costs (in relation to some competing nations) and
- The problems have been identified and those within the industry have recognised the need for urgent action

If the UK aerospace industry does not strengthen its technology base, then notwithstanding its strengths, its market share will continue to decline.

The government's Technology Foresight Programme provides the opportunity/impetus for the industry to reverse the decline and recover some of its market share.

Fig 6	CIVIL AIRCRAFT IN SERVICE 1940's - 1960's		
1940's			
Vickers Viscount	13		Total = 13
1950's			
Boeing 727	992		
DC-8	256		
Boeing 707	125		
BAC 1-11	108		
Lockheed Electra	57		
Concorde	13		
Handley Page Herald	9		
Vickers Vanguard	1		Total = 1,561
1960's			
Boeing 737-200	934		
Boeing 737-100	19		
Airbus A300	386		
Boeing 747-100	173		
DC9-10\20	98		Total = 1,610

Source: Flight International census, October 1996

Foresight Action

The SBAC has launched a national technology programme, *Foresight Action.*

Foresight Action provides the vital link between concepts and ideas, and proven, saleable products. It is the direct result of a government-industry initiative to identify wealth-creating technological investments for the UK. *Foresight Action* is a nationwide programme involving the whole spectrum of companies in the industry, plus government and academia with the common aim to promote technology acquisition through capability demonstration.

Each programme is market-focused and covers all of the major technology sectors needed to maintain the UK's position in the world market and to remain an important and valued partner in collaborative ventures.

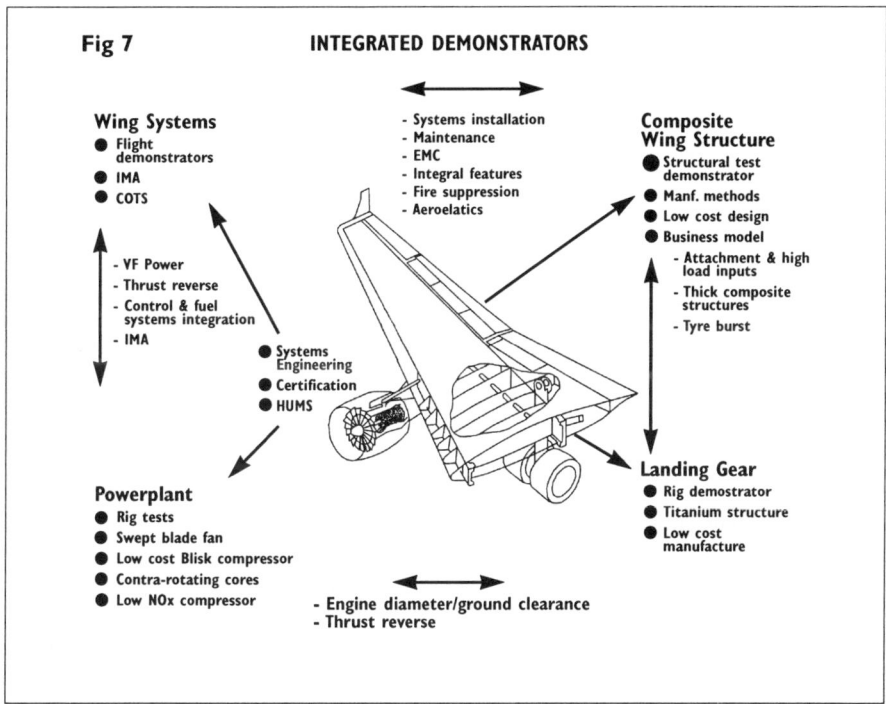

Fig 7   INTEGRATED DEMONSTRATORS

Wing Systems
- Flight demonstrators
- IMA
- COTS

- VF Power
- Thrust reverse
- Control & fuel systems integration
- IMA

- Systems installation
- Maintenance
- EMC
- Integral features
- Fire suppression
- Aeroelatics

- Systems Engineering
- Certification
- HUMS

Composite Wing Structure
- Structural test demonstrator
- Manf. methods
- Low cost design
- Business model

- Attachment & high load inputs
- Thick composite structures
- Tyre burst

Powerplant
- Rig tests
- Swept blade fan
- Low cost Blisk compressor
- Contra-rotating cores
- Low NOx compressor

- Engine diameter/ground clearance
- Thrust reverse

Landing Gear
- Rig demonstrator
- Titanium structure
- Low cost manufacture

The Pilot Phase

The Pilot Phase of *Foresight Action* was launched in early 1996. Three pilot projects exist:

- Powered Wing
- Flight Crew Environment (FCE)
- Ultra Reliable Aircraft

Powered Wing (fig 7)

This will provide UK companies with the capability to design and manufacture all elements of future powered wings for airliners launched from the year 2000. The wings will deliver competitive advantage to the Aircraft Supply Chain and the airline customer.

FCE Content (fig 8)

Fig 8   **FCE CONTENT**

- **Human Factors in Cockpit Equipment Design**

- **Understanding how HCI Error Arises and can be Controlled**

- **Technologies (inceptors, displays etc)**

- **Systems (flight control, flight management etc)**

- **Techniques and Algorithms (sensor fusion etc)**

This project will demonstrate UK capability and improve competitiveness in flight crew, mission and passenger systems, on which all types of aircraft (military and civil, fixed and rotary wing) rely in order to carry out useful tasks, cost effectively and safely.

Ultra Reliable Aircraft (fig 9)

This will enable the UK aerospace industry to maintain or increase market share by becoming the global benchmark for affordable life cycle costs. The project aims to increase availability and reduce the cost of unreliability through the elimination of unscheduled maintenance.

Foresight Action - The Business Case (fig 10)

Foresight Action has to be a partnership between industry and government if aerospace is to flourish as a national asset furthering wealth creation in the UK. The full programme has to be big enough to make a difference to the prospects of each sector of the industry.

Fig 9   **ULTRA RELIABLE AIRCRAFT**

- **Objective**
  To increase availability and reduce the cost of unreliability through the elimination of unscheduled maintenance

- **Key Targets are:**
  The production of an industry wide 'Design for Reliability' process
  The development of a product reliability model
  The identification of the key reliability drivers
  The identification of the technologies to improve reliability

---

Starting the main phase would cost £80 million a year, split 50/50 between industry and government. This will need to rise to £200 million by the year 2000 if the UK aerospace sector is to remain world-class.

If this expenditure is related to sales then there will be a substantial return. Applying this new technology will open the UK to a potential £90 billion of sales.

Consequences of Inaction

If *Foresight Action* is not successful or no/low government funds are received, the outcome would be that the nation will lose one of its chief industrial assets. The most likely eventual outcome is that the UK will become a net importer of aerospace products ending up as a subcontractor to the more advanced companies overseas, up to 35,000 direct jobs (plus 150,000 indirect jobs) will be lost over the next decade, and there will be a trade deficit in excess of £3bn.

Fig 10   FORSIGHT ACTION - THE BUSINESS CASE

The Business Case for Foresight Action:

- A significant demonstrator programme is essential for UK industry to maintain competitive military and civil capabilities, reducing risk on next generation programmes

- The UK needs to provide an environment which is attractive to large new projects to secure jobs and attract investment

- A funding partnership between government and industry is essential to match initiatives in competitor countries

- Foresight Action provides the opportunity to gain best value from the national investment in technology

- The returns for investment are likely to be substantial (a potential £60billion of sales over the next decade)

If *Foresight Action* is successful/receives the required amount of government funding, the result will be a prospering world-class manufacturing industry employing over 300,000 people either directly or indirectly, generating a positive trade deficit in excess of £3bn with technology capabilities spinning off into other UK manufacturing industries.

The Ministry of Defence (MoD) has recognised what *Foresight Action* is working towards, and is already funding a programme of defence-related research in recognition of this. Although some of this does 'spill over' into the civil sector, it is crucial that the government gets involved and on board with a dedicated source of finance for civil technical development.

Conclusion

The UK has one of the most significant aerospace industries in the world, and is determined for this to continue.

It is important for a country to own its Intellectual Property Rights (IPR). The aerospace industry is the only industry in the UK that has British ownership. It is a direct mirror image of the car industry whose IPR is based in the US.

The principal requirement for maintaining competitiveness is a substantial increase in investment in R&T acquisition activity. The amount of investment in R&T will determine how far and fast the industry will go.

Investment will enable the UK to develop cheaper more efficient technologies to take the aerospace industry into the 21st century and beyond.

15 Beyond Technology Foresight: European Aerospace Research and Technology in the 21st Century

ANDERS HANSSON
Senior Science Consultant
Reaction Engines Ltd

Credo

The central theme here is that the present strong positions of Airbus and Arianespace are at risk unless our political masters in the EU understand that a total integration is underway in aerospace systems. Let me give two examples to illustrate this point.

Firstly, there is the increased information that will be exchanged between aircraft and ground, both in the form of technical data and from customer demand. In the future this could include optical laser systems and with them new cockpit designs.

Secondly, there is the possibility that Arianespace's position will be overtaken by a US spaceplane. Both examples could even involve the same US company, Boeing, which is strong in laser systems as well as space. Hence, the EU could find that the monopolistic situation that existed in the past will return but this time on a more permanent timescale. Furthermore, Boeing's 'rent' would continue, even if Airbus introduces an alternative to the B747. The cost of apathy among the EU leadership is thus likely to be high, turning the continent to a subcontractor for the biggest industry of the 21st century.

Background

In the UK aerospace community, the term Foresight has come to be identified with *Foresight Action* and its aim to show a return on national investment. Here, Foresight has a much wider implication. It is impossible to discuss technology in a meaningful way without an idea of the mission the technology is aimed for. Hence to address the challenges in research and especially the verification/demonstration of its results we need to look at the re-structuring of aerospace and its changing missions. Having discussed that, it becomes possible to ask if the present research is keeping pace with the industry's needs for growth?

Some may be surprised by the assumed growth as the natural state of an industry which many in the media consider to have fulfilled its economic role, and which is to be continued only by replacement and gradual improvements, mostly to be performed by future generations of aeronautical engineers. The outlook behind these remarks is different. The idea is that if we in the aeronautical industry are able to conceptualise new products and to demonstrate their viability, only the time limit of our civilisation will limit what we can do in the future.

The corollary of this view is that the term 'research' will have to become a broader subject in aeronautics than investigating, for example, lift-and-drag matters. Let me take one example. The all wing aircraft has been the object of speculation since the 1940s but mainly as an aerodynamical problem. Such a new type of aircraft cannot be introduced without a social agent that can solve all the operational issues associated to the integration of the wing in the existing air transport infrastructure. To identify such a social agent it is not only vital to know the number of passengers and the size of the cargo needed to make the wing aircraft superior to the conventional aircraft but also to embed this knowledge in the operations of today. Many technological improvements in reducing wing drag can at present disappear much faster than the research can be introduced in aircraft by changes in the fuel cost. Thus we should look at the issue as one of fuel and drag. Also, the lifevest concept is based on Second World War ideas, perhaps it is time to come up with a better concept involving new structural ideas?

At Manchester's new airport it appears that kerosene as a chemical is becoming a problem to the same degree as the change to the landscape. Now we know that there are alternatives to kerosene, some have even been tested on aircraft, but does the travelling public know this? Methane is a possible step from kerosene to hydrogen as it is cryogenic but not as low as hydrogen and it performs better then kerosene. With hydrogen being about four times the volume of kerosene, its introduction will change the shape of aircraft and will require more investments on infrastructures. EU studies indicate some Cryogenic Planes by 2010.

Engineering is difficult to bring to the public because of its trade-offs, but this fact should not really prevent us from broadening the visibility of the technological options that are available and consequently to the debate on which technologies we should make further investments in. A related issue is the question of whether the Mega Mergers we have seen are driven by industrial needs, stakeholders interests or short-term financial asset values. It is not possible here to answer this question but, hopefully, it is clear to all that the role of research and the type of research funded is different in the different situations. At present, only 3% of the total atmospheric pollution is attributed to aviation in spite of its visibility in the media. What role would it have in the different forms? In 'industrial needs' air transport is regarded as a public good, providing military capabilities and mass transport for work and tourism. In my limited understanding of the 'stakeholder', the aim would be more social, with possibly an increasing importance given to environmental impacts over the traditional research areas set by industrial needs. The asset value model is even more difficult to summarise mainly because we have very little historical experience of it. Its foundation is the cost-benefit analysis and the concept of global welfare maximisation as the norm. A recent example in education is physics where the closure of physics departments it is argued is based on a 'market assessment' of the subject's importance for industry and students. We are not really concerned with whether education should be regarded as a 'market'. What matters is that medical research charities, pharmaceutical companies, etc., are now setting the research agenda in the UK, with the result that while aeronautics is paying back historical support, it gets less and less from the government. It is obvious to me that we should include this payback in any 'market testing' the government wants to do and therefore we should claim that there are significant reasons to support aeronautical research. This is a local UK issue but perhaps a trend-setter if the world continues down the road of deregulation and welfare mathematics. Note, for example, that 'in constant dollars air travel is practically free compared with its cost 40 years ago'.[1]

The European Bank for Reconstruction and Development is applying the 'least cost' principle for its investments and 'profitable' assumptions of demand. This is very different from the 'R and D cult' transformation in the 1960s USA where 35% of research was invested in aerospace that had 4% of value-added, while mining, food, textiles with 60% of value-added got 8% of R & D.

Andy Grove, chief executive of Intel, defined a so-called 'strategic inflection point' when the fundamental nature of the business changes in such a way that it is necessary to focus on one product and 'to building, popularising them and making them useful'. In one sense, this implies that Intel creates the demand itself. Is this a viable strategy for aeronautical technology as well? Are there the financial resources within the industrial manufacturers to achieve this? Furthermore, a bureaucracy stores extant knowledge and creates new knowledge with great hesitation. Compare this with engineering as a self-correcting process of observations, analysis/synthesis design and test. How can this process be maintained in an industry increasingly dominated by giants?

The answer could be to fragment the market via technology and expand demand in that way, reproducing the same situation surrounding information. But with a less atomised market, aeronautics is unlikely to be capable of doing that. After all, the equivalent product of the car hoped for in the 1920s is still not here for air travel, disregarding for the moment new attempts in the USA.

The vitally important point is to make sure that a new experimental phase is set off in aeronautics. Hence, we need new applications. Of course, in some applications aeronautics is what economists call 'mature' but the subject is not a monolith, as most economists appear to think. In fact, its development is more a question of technical difficulties for a product and the amount of suitable scientists and engineers, thus the connection with educational aims. Also, some 30 states now have programs designed to capture part of the aerospace market, suggesting that the sector may be a source of significant trade conflict in the future, and on a much broader scale than the recent EU-USA one over the Boeing McDonnell Douglas merger.

If we assume that we are moving towards both an OECD wide industry, with even more global supply chains and the truly aerospace firm covering both air and space products, what technology will be critical? I limit myself to three:

I. Microsystems

Microsystems will impact all areas of aerospace from recording actual aerodynamic performance, via boundary layer control and supercritical wings, to distributed Microsystems in space launchers.

II. Software

This is partly related to I and is in some respects a limiting step. In the USA, there is a Software Engineering Institute in operation and Australia has got a Software Verification Research Centre. What role should the EU have? Integrated testbeds are important here, both in computers and as physical vehicles in air at different Reynolds numbers.

III. New framework for production development
Bill Livingstone, an industry consultant from the USA, put it like this: 'Our nation's technological leadership is dependent on advances in new materials. Commercial space research and manufacturing have the potential to revolutionise American industry'.[2] With the Title 3 System where the US government guarantees to buy new materials for evaluation in industry, i.e. 100% return to material supplier, the significance given to new materials in the USA is clear.

Probably only Japan operates a similar support with national programmes in, for example, high strength nanogranullar quasicrystalline Aluminium based alloys as a new lightweight structural material.

Livingstone also advocates the view that the so-called International Space Station is a step in this support system. It would not appear that ESA takes the same view even if DASA has offered to become a partner in operating the station along industrial lines.

For manufacturing itself it appears that robotic-based manufacturing will increase as our understanding of how to manipulate materials increases. The precision by design is already better than the precision by skill of hand.

The Integration with Space

Space is becoming central to Boeing. 'Boeing has always had a toe in the space business, but I think they're looking at a long term strategic investment to get away from being a one-product company' Walter Morgan, from Communications Center, Clarksburg, stated in Space News, 15-21 of September 1997. The one-product company, in short, can be Airbus. Or, as Alan Mulally, President of Boeing Defense and Space, put it at the 1997 Sopwith Lecture at the Royal Aeronautical Society, London, UK: 'Within five to six years one third of all the company's dollar revenues will come from information communication, one third from aeroplanes and one third from space vchicles, and that will gradually move more and more to information'.

While Airbus will have to focus on the aeroplanes, the EU must consider the other two aspects mentioned by Mulally or all the investments and technology success that is within Airbus will gradually become dependent on the Boeing aerospace system. It is possible to argue that this three legged Boeing, would constitute a policy problem, even for the Lockheed-Martin-Northrop Grumman Group, and if it is so, what would it be for the EU? So far the debate has centred around navigation satellites but the impact will not be restricted to that area. Returning to AlanMulally: 'the infrastructure that we thought of as aeroplanes travelling around the world, is going to move up to be space based'. Here, the concept is Teledesic which includes both Boeing and Bill Gates, as well as Sea Launch. The Marrakesh Agreement of April, 15, 1994, changed the future, especially for Europe, since it made no exception for space services and products, from a commercial framework, apart from civilian aircraft with over 100 seats, defence and non-industrial research.

With the abandonment of the HOPE project in Japan,[3] a tragic waste of international resources in space transportation development is finally coming to an end. Its Second Coming (Boeing X-20 Dynasoar was the first) began with Aérospatiale's HERMES, from 1985. Then, France gradually convinced the members of ESA to support a combination of Ariane 5 and HERMES. Britain did not join this ESA project but the HOTOL study was terminated because of lack of government support in 1987. If it had continued HOTOL would have had its first flight in 1997. Unfortunately, political considerations became more important than engineering arguments and thus it took many years and many re-designs before HOTOL finally ended as a collaboration with Russia in 1992.

In the USA, President Reagan launched the X-30 under the name Orient Express, in 1986, later renamed National Aerospaceplane Program (NASP). In the end of 1992, after $3bn for general tools, no detailed design had yet appeared. Meanwhile, a refined design of a spaceplane SKYLON, had been developed by Reaction Engines Ltd (REL). Studies both at REL and at the Aerospace Corp in USA show that with 30 of such craft operating commercially the present cost-barrier will be broken and a new industry in space can be generated.

This will have significant implications for aerospace that go beyond the present definition of Foresight in the UK. Hence, we should not debate any longer whether wing manufacture or design is better supported in the UK or Germany but whether the EU can provide the necessary technological infrastructure to maintain Airbus and hence space transport, in the future. Two elements of such an infrastructure that are vital signs for survival are lasers and computers.

Lasers

The laser is becoming a multi-functional tool for aerospace, covering a range of roles from micromachining and imaging to information transfer and power. A statement by Sheila Widnall, USAF Secretary, in 1996 illustrates this point. 'From what I've seen, the airborne laser could be in the same league as the invention of stealth, the development of GPS and the Manhattan Project. These are not just words. Boeing's Defense and Space Group is contracted for $1.1bn to build a prototype laser on the B747 and a $5bn is estimated for seven such vehicles by 2008. Hence, even if Boeing lost out in the micromachining facility in Virginia their involvement would still remain significant.

In the information field the development of free air communication will revolutionise the air-to-air and ground-to-air links, often with a space segment in-between. The Japan's Optoelectronic Industry and Technology Development Association has made free-space light transmission the second of five priorities in optical communication systems. Concepts like air tubes are thus possible but whoever designs the framework will set the standard as in GPS. Gradually, power may even be provided by solar pumped lasers in high orbit with an information network spanning the Earth.[4]

Computing

The virtual design facility will be necessary to attract end users as partners. It will however also require new computing hardware such as quantum based systems. Again this cannot be an issue for Airbus as it is for Boeing with the predicted one third of the activities being on information, but the EU must provide the capabilities. Lee Holcomb, NASA Director of Information Technology Strategy calls the aim of such capabilities as a move from 'fly before you buy procurement to simulate before you buy'.

Instead of Conclusions

With a theme such as aims and objectives for the 21st century, it is not possible to make any real conclusions. On the other hand, it is possible to identify some trends:

- For the first time, the USA appears to be serious about developing a spaceplane and not a generic support program. This would create a new monopolistic vehicle as the B747 is challenged by A3XX.

- Space will become integrated with the present internet and with air vehicles. Different types are likely here, i.e. hybrids of air vehicles (balloon, UAV, etc.) and space vehicles, but the system will gradually act as one setting the standard.
- The laser will become central for handling information especially if free air communication can be scaled up economically.
- Microsystems will be central and they will increasingly be manufactured in laser facilities, with one testbed being under construction in Virginia, USA.
- New types of computer hardware, based on quantum concepts, will enhance the depth of the calculations and the visualisation of projects, especially for aircraft.

Finally, as stated above, such issues are not for Airbus (in its present form) even if they are for Boeing. If the EU leadership wishes to maintain the success that Airbus represents, it must provide a cluster of support infrastructure that it needs. If not, Airbus will only be a short lived flower in a desert and Europe will have given up the largest industry of the 21st century: aerospace.

Notes and References

1   *Scientific America*, (February 1995), p77.
2   *Space News*, (28 July - 3 August 1997), p15.
3   *Nature*, (1997) vol. 388, p615.
4   *Quantum Satellite Networks: Some Comments*, at the UK-Japan High Technology Industry Forum, Kobe, Japan, (30 September-2 October 1997).

16 Propulsion Research and Technology: The Power to Compete

MIKE J GOULETTE
Project Director Advanced Engineering, Rolls-Royce plc
and
GROUP CAPTAIN J K NEWTON
UK MoD Procurement Executive

Summary

To compete successfully any business must provide what the customer wants, when they want it, at the right price and of suitable quality. This is as true of aero engines as high street retailers.

The aero engines market is international and the needs of our worldwide civil and military customers, shaped by political and economic events around the globe, are reviewed. Translating these needs effectively into products requires an appropriately structured business. The radical organisation changes within many aero engine businesses over the past decade are described. Technology has a vital part to play in providing competitive performance, cost and environmentally acceptable engines. Demonstration of new technology, however, is traditionally a slow and costly process although essential to reduce risk. Ways of reducing cost and time whilst maintaining or improving demonstration quality are being adopted, such as dual civil and military demonstration and financial or technical partnerships. Such developments are essential if, in the increasingly demanding markets of today and tomorrow, we are to retain the power to compete.

World Political Situation

On the civil side one of the greatest effects on the business has come from airline deregulation. This started 25 years ago, in 1972, when the UK granted Laker Airway's application for a cut-price Skytrain service from

London to New York. In 1978 the US became much less regulated, and now within the European Union the process is almost complete. The impact on the airline industry has been profound (fig 1). This has put immense pressure on the aero engine industry to provide cost effective propulsion systems.

The increasing volume of air travel has increased the pressure on international air traffic control. In 1989 a quarter of flights in Europe were delayed by more than 15 minutes. This was the era of the holiday at Gatwick Airport. It occurred when an unforeseen consumer boom coincided with lack of investment in air traffic control. For a time it seemed as if the best way out would be larger aircraft such as the proposed 600 to 1000 seat Boeing 7XX and Airbus 3XX which could cope with increasing demand without the need to increase the number of flights. However, current and future improvements in air traffic control have largely eliminated the problem. Passengers' preference to fly directly to their destination, rather than to a hub airport has also reduced the pressure for such large aircraft. The major manufacturers' policy in this market is quite different, Boeing has shelved its large aircraft project, however, Airbus is still preparing to launch its A3XX.

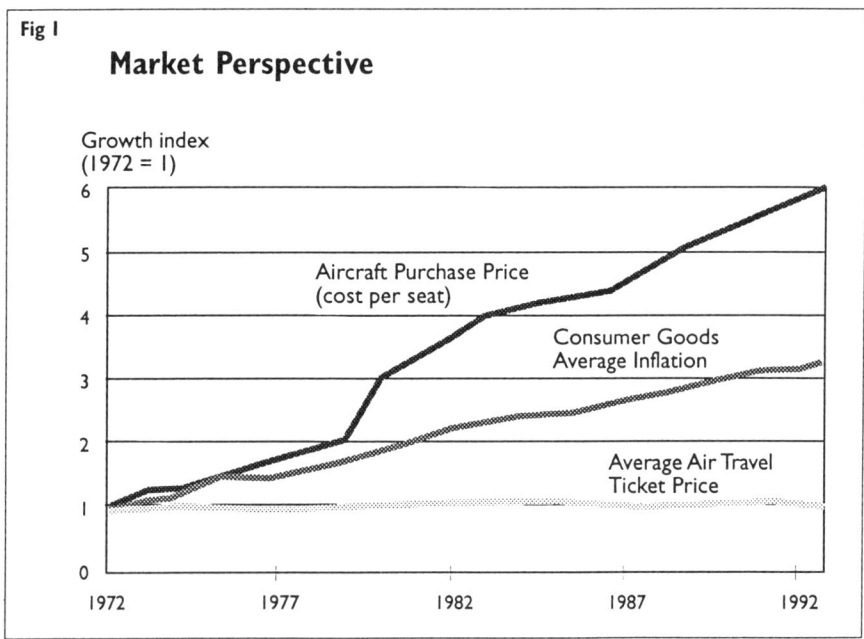

Fig I

Market Perspective

Growth index (1972 = 1)

Aircraft Purchase Price (cost per seat)

Consumer Goods Average Inflation

Average Air Travel Ticket Price

Environmental issues are increasingly important. The first noise limits were imposed on civil aircraft in 1968 and more stringent limits followed in 1976. Since the 1960s aircraft noise levels have fallen by 75% due to design changes, for example increasing engine by pass ratio (fig 2).

We are now at the stage where airframe noise, particularly on approach to landing, is starting to become as significant as engine noise. Although there have been no new noise limits agreed since 1976, airports are increasingly imposing operational restrictions which will result in only the quietest designs being acceptable in the US and Europe by 2002. This means a high proportion of older aircraft will be retired as they no longer meet airport noise limits.

Aircraft emissions have been regulated since 1974. These first limits covered smoke alone but were followed in 1984 by hydrocarbon limits, and in 1986 by CO and NOX standards. Modern aero engines are much cleaner than early engines. Hydrocarbon and carbon monoxide emissions per passenger mile are less than for a car with a catalytic converter and an order of magnitude less than for a car without a catalyser.

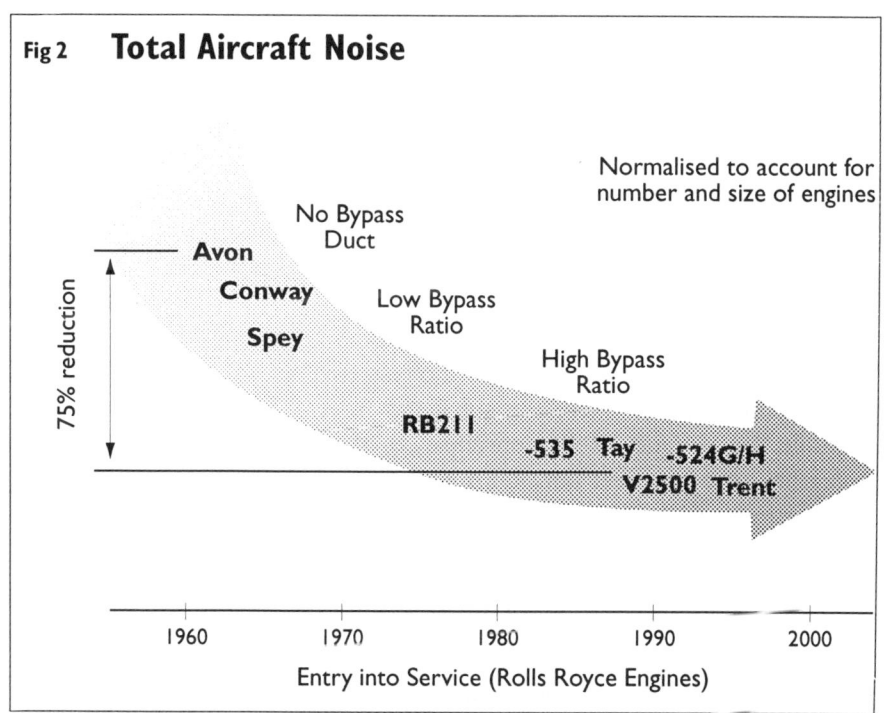

Fig 2 **Total Aircraft Noise**

The prime concern nowadays for subsonic civil engines is NOX which, when released at high altitude, produces ozone which contributes to the greenhouse effect. NOX is not easily eliminated and sophisticated combustor technology is therefore a key requirement for future civil engines. Emissions of the greenhouse gas, CO_2, is also a concern, particularly with the projected growth of air traffic. This can only be addressed by continuing improvements in airframe and engine efficiency. Military engines are not exempt from the need to become more environmentally friendly, particularly during peacetime training flights.

Future military aero engine requirements are changing in response to the changing political climate, particularly in Eastern Europe as a result of the breakdown of the Warsaw Pact. This has removed the large and familiar threat of the USSR, against which plans had existed for many years, and replaced it with any number of smaller, more unpredictable threats we are still coming to terms with. In addition, satellite communication has made local conflicts highly visible to the whole world. Iraq and Bosnia are two such examples. This has prompted individuals and governments to provide humanitarian aid to troubled areas. Peacekeeping is a relatively new role and strategies are still evolving.

In this new political climate flexibility is a key demand. The old network of strategically located bases is not appropriate when the number of potential trouble spots is high and advance warning of problems may be short. Hence it is necessary to be able to send equipment anywhere in the world at short notice and with the minimum of ground support. Once deployed, aircraft and engines must operate reliably with limited logistical support. Military customers now require a minimum period of maintenance free operation.

The high cost of defence is prompting increased collaboration between countries in order to share the burden. NATO is expanding and Western European Alliance, as a sub set of NATO, is starting to become a workable unit. One likely consequence of such organisations is inter operability of equipment between member countries although this is at a very early stage. Another consequence is that internationally agreed limitations on arms sales become easier to agree and control.

World Economic Situation

The total value of the civil aero engine market world wide between 1995 and 2014 is forecast to be worth $370bn. Demand is greatest in the Asia

Pacific region, and will be supplied largely by companies in North America and Europe (fig 3).

The increase in new aircraft is half in response to increasing air traffic and half due to retirement of aircraft currently in service due to a combination of age and inability to meet noise and emission regulations existing aircraft.

On the military engine side it is difficult to accurately predict future demand but reductions in defence budgets a result of the "Peace dividend" are largely complete and the market is stabilising, albeit at a lower level (fig 4).

The consequence for future military engine programmes is fewer, larger programmes with bigger technology jumps compared to civil engines (fig 5). Economic pressures also make a reduction in life cycle cost (purchase price + fuel + maintenance) a long-term aim for all military aircraft, including combat aircraft with demanding targets set for future military development programmes.

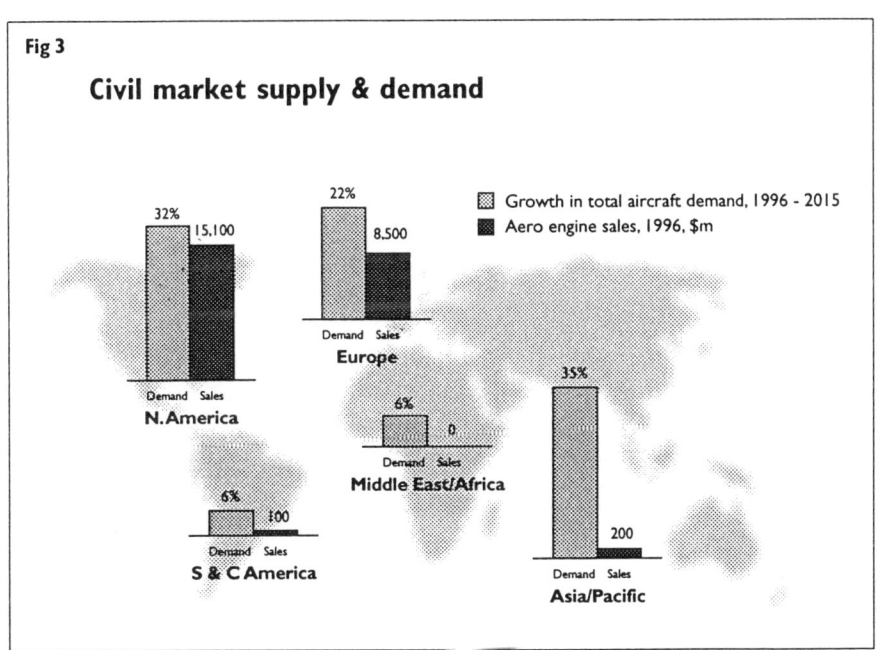

Fig 3

Civil market supply & demand

- Growth in total aircraft demand, 1996 - 2015
- Aero engine sales, 1996, $m

N.America — 32% / 15,100

Europe — 22% / 8,500

Middle East/Africa — 6% / 0

S & C America — 6% / 100

Asia/Pacific — 35% / 200

In the nearer term there is a trend towards using civil engines where possible, e.g. military transport and reconnaissance. An example of this is the proposed re-engining of B52 bombers with RB211 civil engines.

There is intense competition in the aero engine and airframe business (fig 6). This has led to a number of recent changes, such as the merger of McDonnell Douglas with Boeing. Another example is the purchase by Rolls-Royce of the Allison Engine Company to provide access to the US market and programmes like JSF as well as broadening its product range. Further take-overs and mergers are anticipated.

At the same time existing companies are consolidating, developing countries want to get into the aero engine business. One reason is to offset their spend on airframe and engine purchases with a corresponding level of inward investment in component manufacture or component definition technology. At present they are relatively small players with limited capability but this is likely to change.

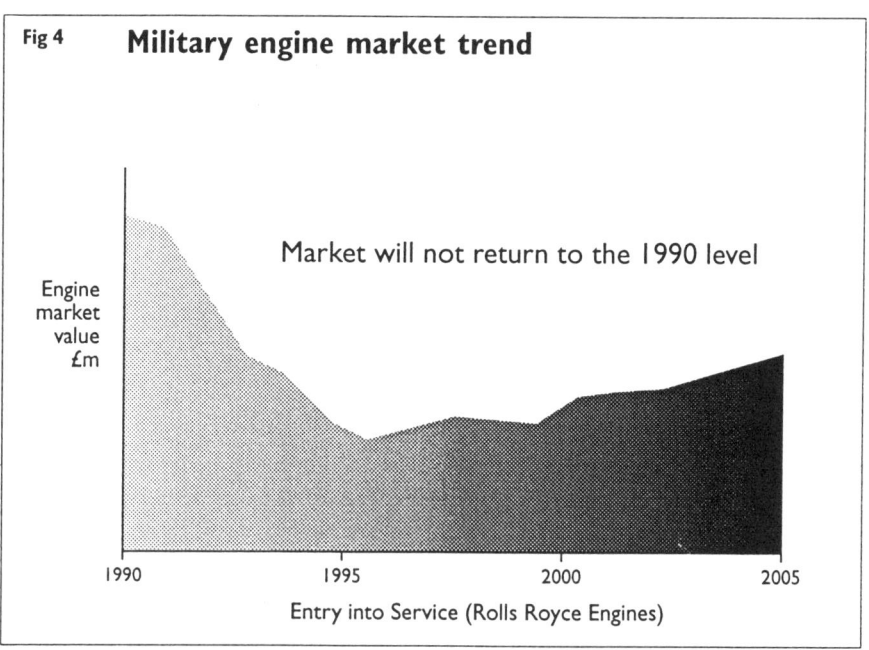

Fig 4   Military engine market trend

Engine market value £m

Market will not return to the 1990 level

1990   1995   2000   2005

Entry into Service (Rolls Royce Engines)

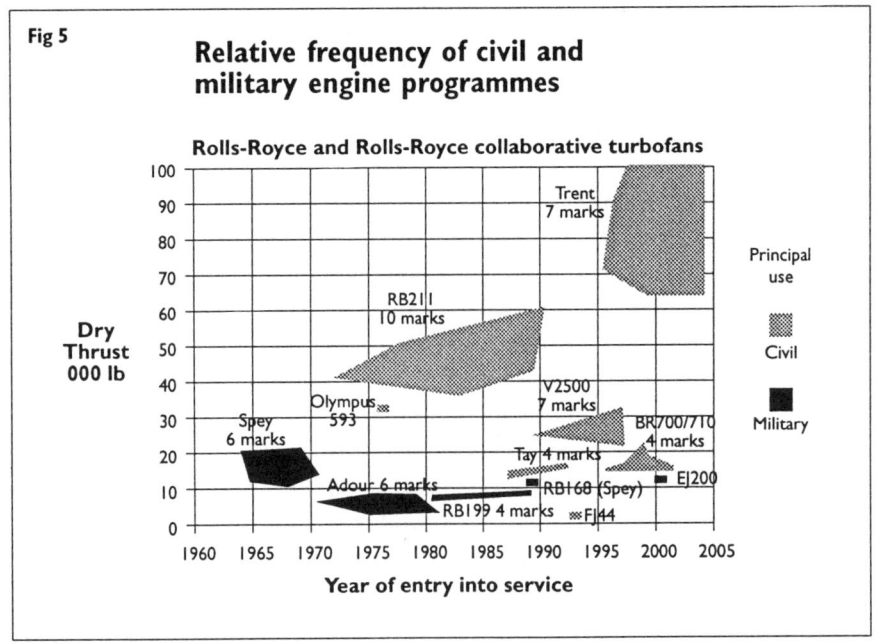

Fig 5

Relative frequency of civil and military engine programmes

Rolls-Royce and Rolls-Royce collaborative turbofans

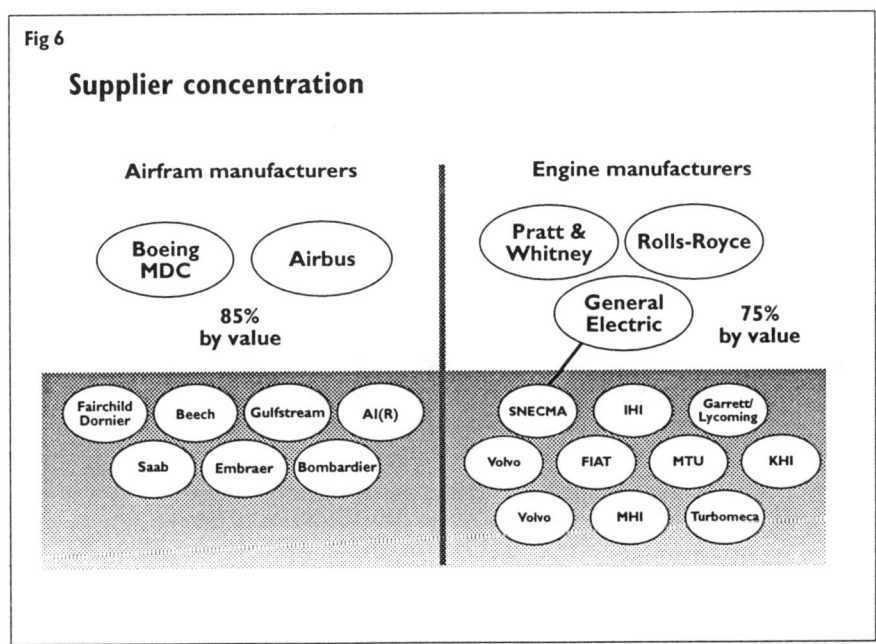

Fig 6

Supplier concentration

205

For both civil and military engines the aero engine companies are being squeezed between the high and increasing cost of research and production technology and decreasing government funding. For new products the high initial company investment is recouped over a period of time via engine sales and spares. The spares market is significant since engines may remain in service for up to 40 years. Future military engine sales may be constrained as the political climate means we may become even more selective about military sales to certain foreign regimes. Laudable as this is, it does eliminate a potential source of profit.

Business Organisation Trends

The development of new products requires very high levels of investment and the payback periods are long. Project failure in such an environment has major financial, social and possibly public safety impacts. The capability to manage new product introduction effectively is, therefore, vital for an aero engine company.

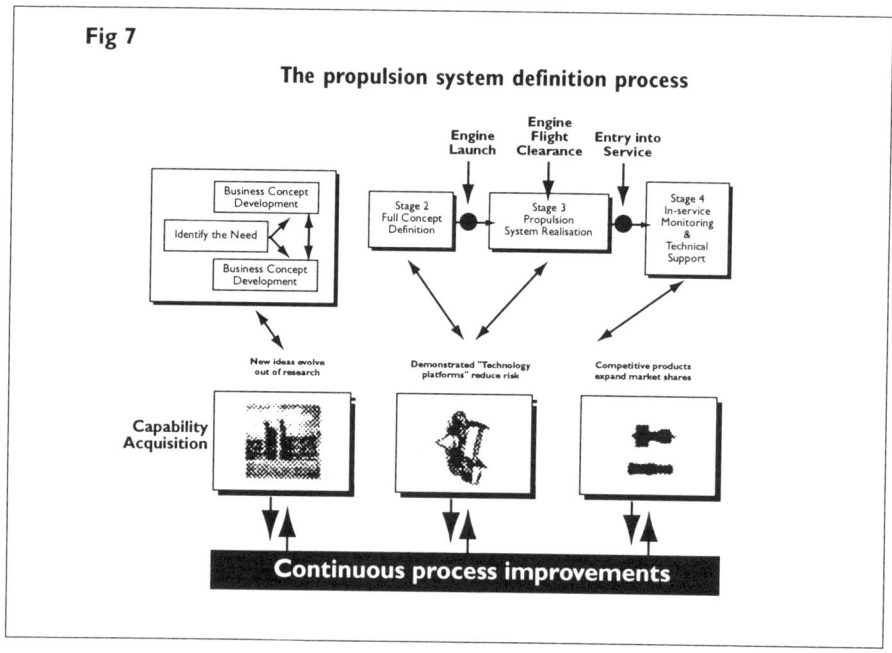

One aspect of this is the ability to reduce the time to design and certify an aero engine. In the past this took about five years, i.e. three years longer than to design and certify an airframe. Hence, costly engine changes were inflicted as the airframe took shape.

One response to the problem has been to identify and optimise the processes involved in aero engine technology acquisition, development, design and production.

Adoption of a four stage propulsion system definition process (fig 7) has the potential to reduce non-recurring costs by 30%, and more importantly, to cut by 40% the time taken to design, make and certify a new engine, hence bringing engines within airframe development time scales. Achievement of both these improvements is within sight.

Fundamental to shorter engine time scales is access to competitive technology already demonstrated in a realistic environment and therefore available "off the shelf", rather than being developed in parallel with the engine as has often been the case in the past. Supplementary benefits come from more efficient working practices such as the use of integrated teams to eliminate boundaries between different departments with different disciplines and taking account of supplier expertise at the design stage via simultaneous engineering and sharing product data throughout the supply chain.

Another business trend is the move towards sharing risk and revenue, and sometimes also technology, with other partners (figs 8 & 9). This trend started back in the 1970s with the Adour and RB199 military engines, has continued with more recent military engine projects such as the BR710 and EJ200 and looks set to continue for the foreseeable future. Civil engine partnerships have also been employed to reduce non recurring costs and minimise commercial risk to the individual partners.

All the most recent RR engines have some degree of partnership, either via a collaborative company like the BR700 or via risk and revenue sharing of specific components within the RR engine such as in the Trent and Tay. Such partnerships are not without their problems. Geographical location, language, culture and different technical backgrounds and experiences can all provide challenges.   However, the problems are generally felt to be outweighed by the advantages, providing the relationships in the partnership are clearly defined and a compctent company has responsibility for propulsion system integration.

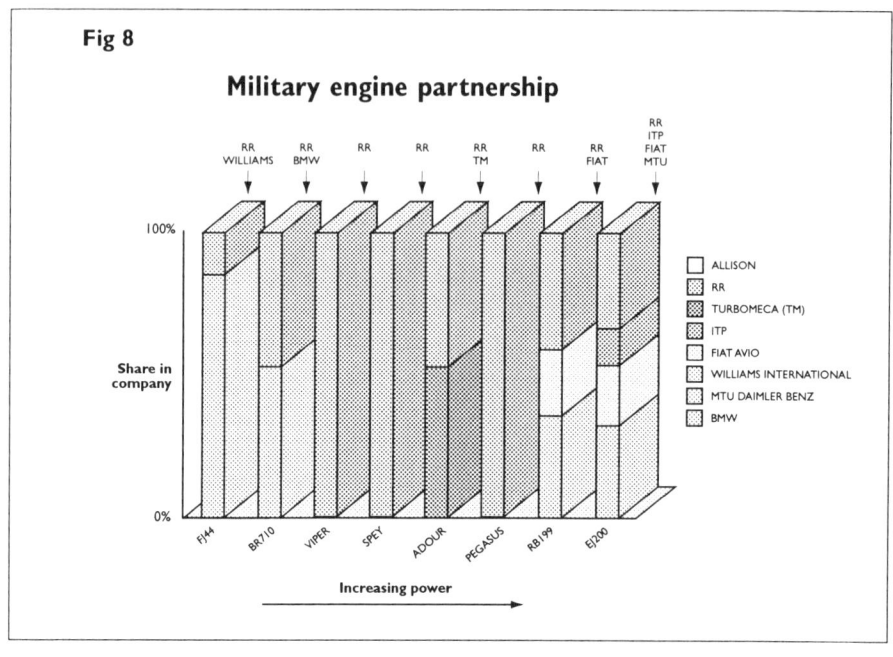

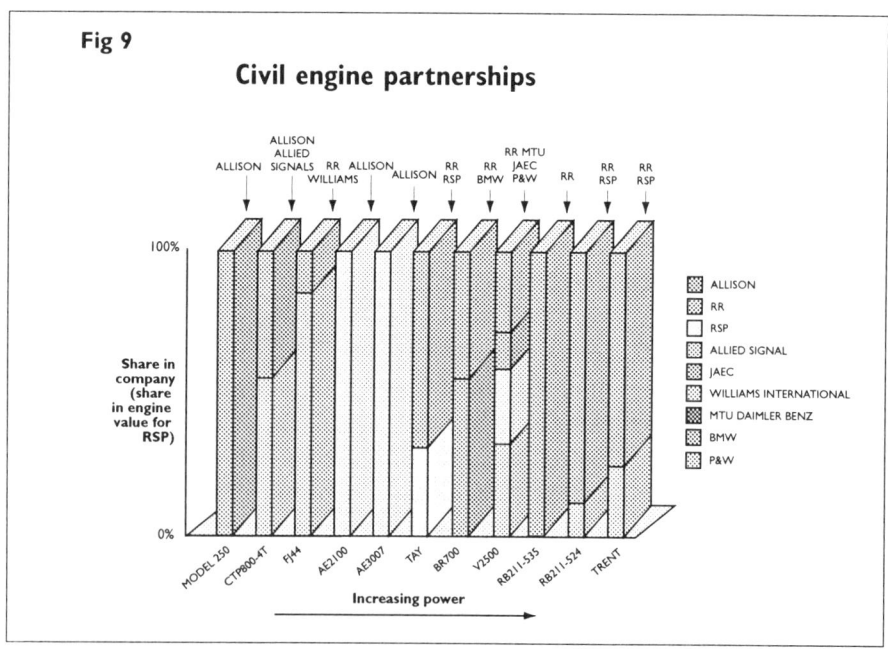

Technology Requirements

As we have seen, the political and economic drivers may be different for civil and military engines, but the aims of competitive performance at lower cost and risk are common.

A comparison of the total life cycle cost for civil and military engines shows purchase price comprises around 30% for both, fuel is 56% for civil engines but only 18% for military engines whereas for maintenance the situation is reversed at 14% and 52% respectively.

The technologies necessary to reduce civil engine purchase price and improve fuel efficiency, or reduce thrust/weight, as well as improving reliability and minimising maintenance are also generally similar. The key areas are higher temperature materials and high efficiency cooling configurations to improve temperature capability, higher overall pressure ratio and higher aerodynamic efficiency together with modelling and prediction of component behaviour and failure. Often these technologies interact and the maximum benefit is only realised with the availability of a 'matched set' of complementary solutions. For example improved fuel efficiency is promoted by higher thermodynamic efficiency which depends on higher overall pressure ratio and turbine entry temperature, hence higher temperature capability materials and better cooling. It also depends on high aerodynamic efficiency via modelling and close tolerance component manufacture, as well as low weight via light materials.

The need to reduce time scales for civil engine development to within those of the air framers, and to produce robust, low maintenance designs for both civil and military applications necessitates adequate prior validation of technology via demonstrator rigs and engines.

The concept of simultaneous demonstration of technology for both civil and military engines, i.e. dual use demonstration, has a number of advantages. For the civil business it provides funding support for technology validation, reducing risk and the burden on limited R&D funds. For the military business and customers, even if they are in a comparatively stable period between new engine developments, it ensures that advanced technologies are 'pulled through' and verified in the civil marketplace before they are needed for military applications. Consequently the technology base is maintained and refreshed during the long, 20 - 25 year, intervals between major military programmes. Overall the cost of technology validation through demonstration is minimised, making best use of government and industrial funding. The application of common design tools, techniques and technologies to civil and military products will also reduce development times and costs and in the production phase economies of scale will reduce manufacturing costs.

Where a technology has future application in civil and military engines the dual use concept requires it to be developed with both these uses in mind from the start (fig 10).

The need to cover dual applications may require some compromise or extension of testing in the demonstration phase but the additional cost of this pales into insignificance compared to the benefits described above.

Demonstration must be sufficient to allow the technology to be included, at acceptable risk, into any future development programme and hence production engine. It may be carried out using a civil or military vehicle, whichever is the most appropriate. Dual use technology may enter service first in either civil or military applications, depending on the timing of new engine projects.

Dual use technology is not the answer in every case. There are still some purely military needs, such as signature management and reheat, and some purely civil needs such as large diameter fans. But the area of dual application is large and the concept will play a large part in making our future technology cost effective both in its acquisition and in production.

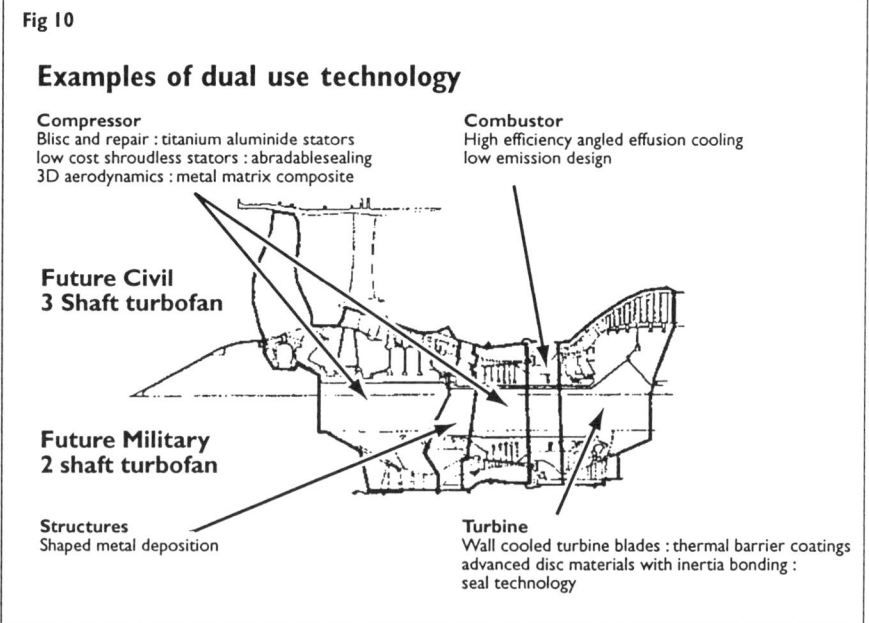

Fig 10

Examples of dual use technology

Compressor
Blisc and repair : titanium aluminide stators
low cost shroudless stators : abradablesealing
3D aerodynamics : metal matrix composite

Combustor
High efficiency angled effusion cooling
low emission design

**Future Civil
3 Shaft turbofan**

**Future Military
2 shaft turbofan**

Structures
Shaped metal deposition

Turbine
Wall cooled turbine blades : thermal barrier coatings
advanced disc materials with inertia bonding :
seal technology

The Way Forward

It is essential to have the ability to look far enough ahead to identify innovative long-term technologies and design concepts. These are usually prompted by long-term military engine goals such as those set by the US and UK air forces. Civil engine horizons are usually much shorter, less focused and hence less conducive to such thinking.

Dual demonstration and application of technology to civil and military engines as described above will remain a key success factor in the future.

Technical and financial partnerships to reduce cost and share the risk of technology acquisition are expected to increase. Recently in the UK there has been a major initiative called Foresight Action led by SBAC on behalf of the Defence and Aerospace Foresight Panel. This is developing a national Aerospace Technology Demonstration programme coordinating the activities of the airframe, propulsion and equipment sectors. Within the European Union collaboration at the research level is well established through the Framework programme and it is intended that this will extend to larger demonstrator programmes in the upcoming Framework 5. In the specifically military field, helicopter propulsion technology has been jointly acquired by RR and Turbomeca within the ASTEC programme and RR is also working with SNECMA on future combat engine concepts in the programme called AMET. There is also significant US/UK activity in the materials and manufacturing area through CAESAR and more generally through the collaboration on JSF.

Such partnerships will increasingly engage the total supply chain, from airline or armed service down through component makers and material suppliers. In doing so we will develop and demonstrate the soft technologies of business processes and their accompanying information technologies as well as the harder technologies of aerodynamics, mechanical and manufacturing engineering.

The aero engine market is flourishing but will remain highly competitive. Only the fittest will survive. Cost effective technology acquisition and demonstration will remain key to any company's power to compete.

17 A New Perspective on Aeronautics R&T for Europe

PROFESSOR DIETER SCHMITT
Lehrstuhl für Luftfahrttechnik
University of Munich

Introduction

In previous times a group of specialists from aircraft design, aerodynamics, structures, production, avionics and systems could sit around a table and define a 'new aircraft concept'. The project leader (today referred to as the chief engineer) was very experienced because typically he would have overseen several projects during his career and he would always push his project team to new and innovative configurations. In the main, market requirements were not so important as long as each new aircraft had considerable advantages in speed, range, size, comfort or cost against the existing competitive aircraft. Technology was the driver!

However, with fuel prices remaining fairly constant and benefits from new technologies only being introduced with higher risk and costs, the cost issue became the dominant yardstick for the development of a new aircraft. The GATT dispute – triggered by the American industry against the upcoming European competition – started a dramatic rethinking about the aircraft design process in Europe. The main focus of this chapter will be to outline the new approach to the definition and development phases and the related processes in the launch of new aircraft projects. However, the chapter will also analyse some aspects of development funding.

Typical life cycle of a civil aircraft programme

The typical life cycle of a civil aircraft programme is shown in fig 1, highlighting the four basic technical processes which are split into:
- Research and Technology
- Development and Product Improvement

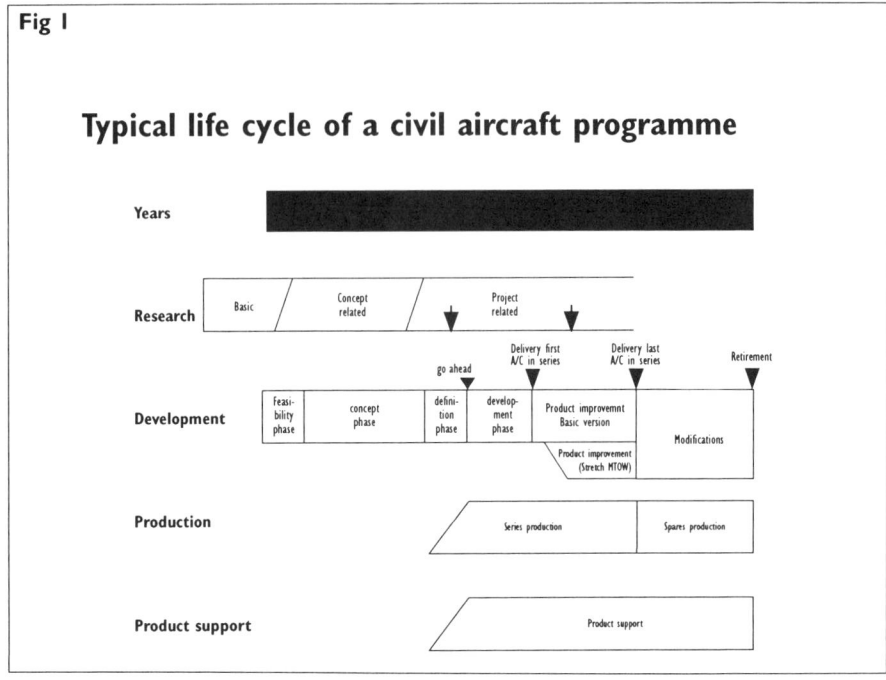

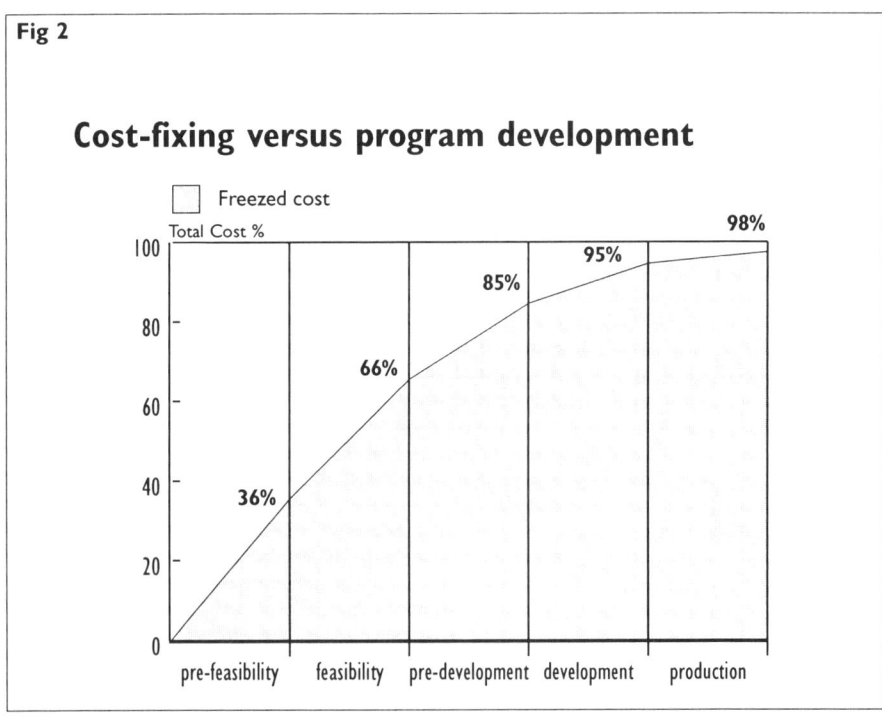

- Production
- Product Support

The corresponding critical milestones are:

- Go Ahead
- Delivery of first aircraft
- Delivery of last production aircraft
- Retirement of last aircraft

As I have indicated the main concentration here will be on aspects of the definition and development phases.

Fig 2 demonstrates the well established fact that the costs for production and maintenance are fixed early in the definition phase by the technology and technical solutions which are selected at this period.

The traditional method in Europe of funding the development of a new aircraft has been different from the American way, as revealed in fig 3.

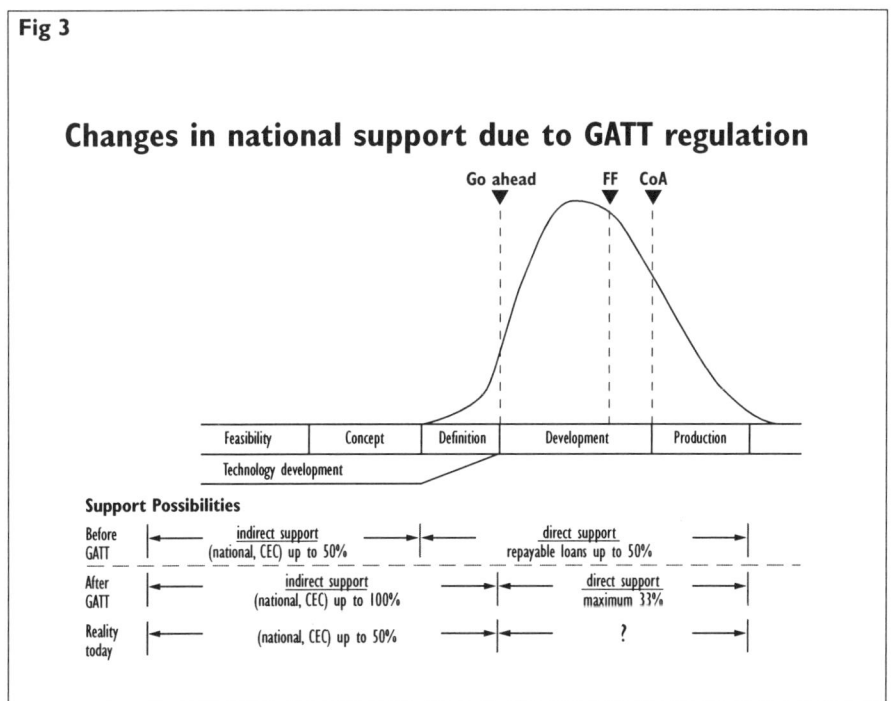

Fig 3

Changes in national support due to GATT regulation

In Europe, technology and research programmes are only supported to a maximum amount of 50% from government agencies. The other 50% has to come from industry to assure the technological relevance for a possible application. For the development of a new aircraft programme, repayable loans of up to 90% have been granted by some European governments to support their national aeronautical industry. Because of this arrangement the industry has been able to reduce the amount of money spent during the definition phase and especially before 'Go Ahead' (typically only 2 to 4% of overall non recurring costs) but this has led to large expenditure after the 'Certification of Aircraft' milestone, as major modifications still have to be incorporated in the production process due to late corrections of aerodynamic and/or performance characteristics.

The introduction of the GATT regulation is officially harmonising the international support system (indirect support up to 100%, direct support limited to max. 33%, with additional restrictions) as shown in fig 3. But as chapter three of this book clearly shows in reality the American government and industry have imposed their support system on the European aeronautical industry. Unfortunately for the European industry, the European governmental agencies have not increased their indirect support to 100% to keep the industry at the same level as their American competition. This has led to a major rethinking of the processes and workflow during the definition and development phases. Business re-engineering is the new management method.

A new process structure

If the milestone 'Go Ahead' is the critical point which differentiates between the impact of direct and indirect support there may be new possibilities for rearranging the workpackage allocation around this milestone:

- Shift the milestone backwards by one year (fig 4)
- Rearrange the workflow between definition and development phase (fig 5)

Option 1 will be difficult to achieve. The Milestone 'Go Ahead' is market driven and depends on clear launch conditions (see below). Therefore the realistic way for a restructuring of the technical re-engineering on a programme is option 2. In an internal study within DASA Airbus, the NRC distribution for the A320 was analysed and all possible engineering tasks, which could have been completed earlier in the design process, were identified. In particular aerodynamic related work and windtunnel tests were identified as activities that could be undertaken before the 'Go Ahead' milestone. In addition to achieving a better aerodynamic standard earlier in the process, the study also found that aerodynamic loads data could be more accurate and that less duplication in detail design could have been achieved. A better definition standard at 'Go Ahead' leads to a better product at 'Entry into Service' and will reduce the money needed for refurbishing of the early series aircraft considerably. A 30% reduction in NRC seems possible. In addition a reduction of the development time is feasible. But more money has to be spent before the milestone 'Go Ahead', about 15% of the overall NRC (see fig 6). This means that a much better project definition before 'Go Ahead' has to be achieved. But this also has consequences for the management and will require the introduction of new technology items with demonstrated benefits and reduced risks. As a consequence important technology items must be tested in a demonstrator programme.

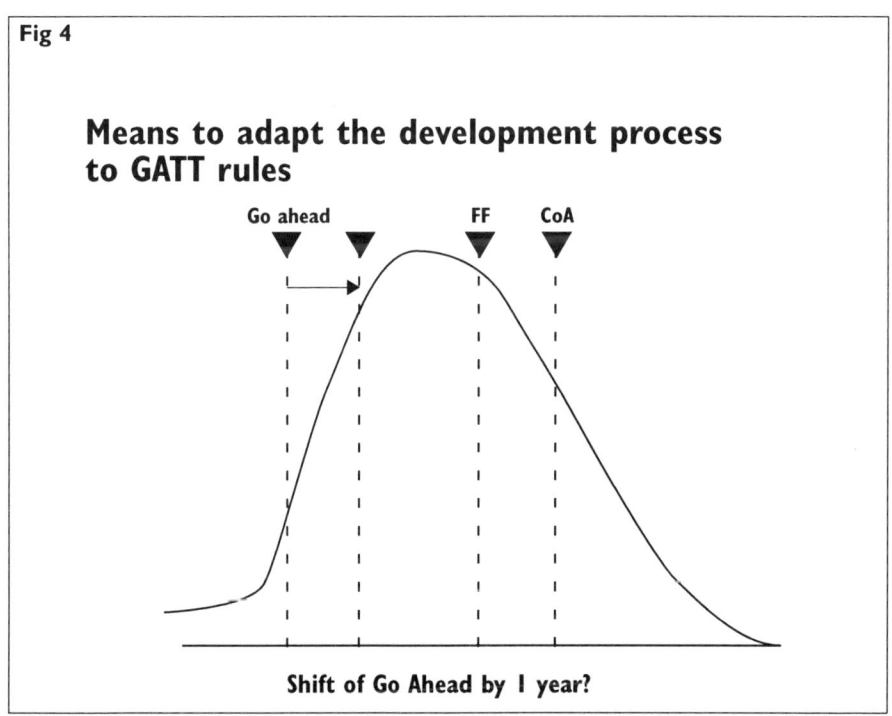

Fig 4

Means to adapt the development process to GATT rules

Go ahead   FF   CoA

Shift of Go Ahead by 1 year?

Fig 5

Means to adapt the development process to GATT rules

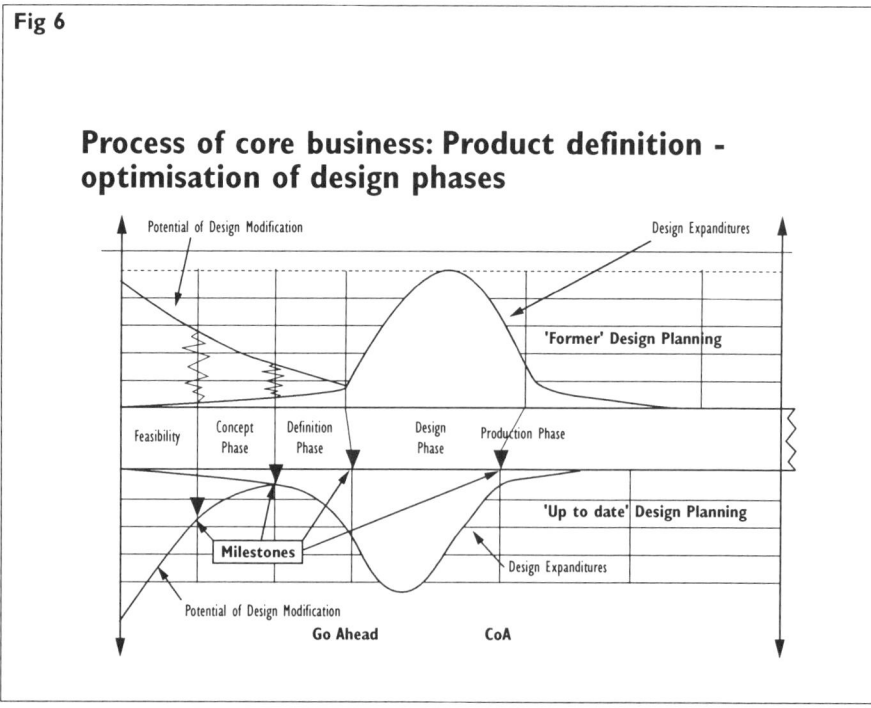

1) Transfer of work packages from development to definition phase
2) Better A/C definition leads to snowball effects in development phase
3) First time right

Fig 6

Process of core business: Product definition - optimisation of design phases

Potential of Design Modification

Design Expanditures

'Former' Design Planning

Feasibility | Concept Phase | Definition Phase | Design Phase | Production Phase

'Up to date' Design Planning

Milestones

Design Expanditures

Potential of Design Modification

Go Ahead   CoA

Milestone 'Go Ahead'

The 'Go Ahead' milestone is critical for an aircraft programme. If the programme is launched the airframe manufacturer commits to produce an aircraft to a given specification with performance guarantees within a margin of 2% to 5%.

To do this the firm must spend several billions dollars for the development and production of the aircraft. The risk is enormous as the break even point in the cash flow will be up to 12 years later. All aspects of the three major processes (market, business and technology) have to be fulfilled at the decision point for 'Go Ahead', as shown in fig 7. I would like to call this the 'magic triangle'.

Now I shall turn to review the three process elements in more detail. The key process here concerns the market. Launch criteria must be defined early in the programme and should include a clear statement about the number of aircraft and number of different customers required for a launch. The launch criteria can only be fulfilled if precise aircraft specification, performance guarantees, contract conditions, prices etc are in existence at this point.

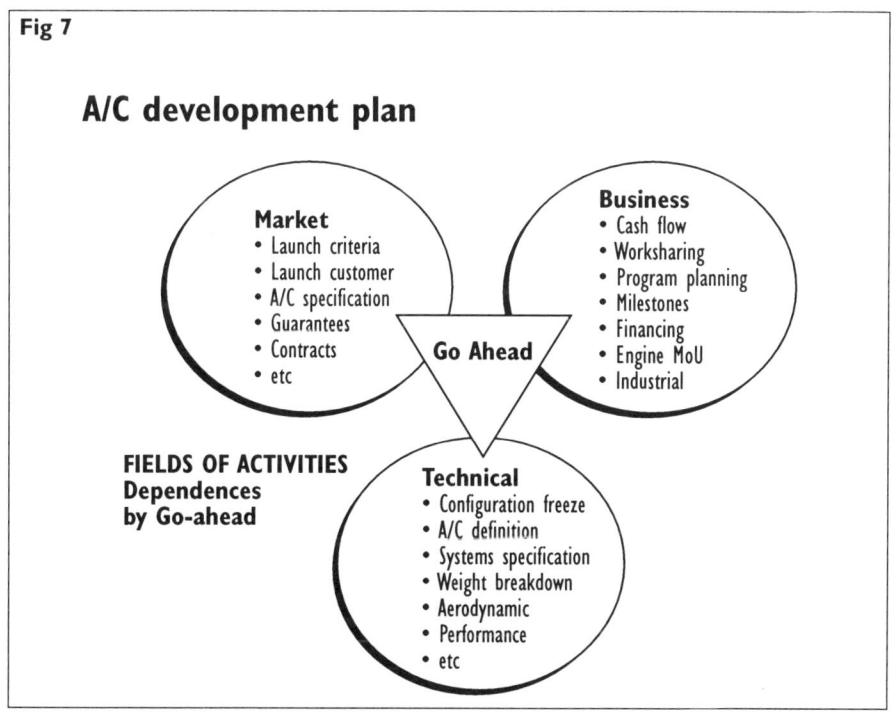

Fig 7

A/C development plan

Market
- Launch criteria
- Launch customer
- A/C specification
- Guarantees
- Contracts
- etc

Business
- Cash flow
- Worksharing
- Program planning
- Milestones
- Financing
- Engine MoU
- Industrial

Go Ahead

FIELDS OF ACTIVITIES
Dependences
by Go-ahead

Technical
- Configuration freeze
- A/C definition
- Systems specification
- Weight breakdown
- Aerodynamic
- Performance
- etc

On the business side the following are pivotal:

- clear worksharing definitions between partners and subcontractors ;
- cost estimations and cashflow calculations must show a profitable programme;
- an engine manufacturer must have given a commitment to deliver an engine with a clear specification for weight, thrust and fuel consumption;
- programme planning must be agreed between all industrial partners.

All these market and business activities are based on technical work. But the technical process is not the driver. The project is driven by market and business requirements, which has not always been sufficiently understood in the European aeronautics industry.

As a response to this issue a major initiative by Airbus to rearrange the design process has been underway for several years. The main business re-engineering process is called ACE (Airbus Concurrent Engineering). In the ACE process all major milestones have been defined and the necessary workpackages between the milestones have been identified, with deliverables specified for the end of each phase. As we are all aware it is all too easy to do process planning and put attractive ideas on paper. However, the most critical issue for success is effective management performance.

For a programme such as ACE to be effective a clear management decision at each milestone is mandatory. Our slogan could be: either continue or stop the programme!

If the management is not able to decide, cost will increase and progress of work will be small and the possible reduction of 30% in NRC will not be achievable.

Product Definition Process

The product definition phase is fundamentally different from the other processes, such as product development, product support or production. At the end of product definition a 'Go Ahead' decision will be required. But as far as the technical definition is concerned the target is not clearly fixed. As has been highlighted before, the market process is the driver. The engineering team has to define an aircraft which is marketable and for which the launch conditions can be fulfilled. But what does this mean in engineering terms?

- The payload/range capability is fixed from the marketing side, but there is rarely a market specification signed by the marketing group!
- The technology level should be high, but cost efficient for the user!
- The aircraft configuration must show a significant market benefit relative to existing products
- The schedule for 'Go Ahead' will be fixed in advance, but will depend in reality on the market situation
- The competitor will not wait for your "final product definition" and will act on the market
- The management is normally reluctant to spend the necessary money in advance of a 'Go Ahead' decision

The history of the A330/A340 programme is a typical example of how market requirements will change with time (see fig 8).

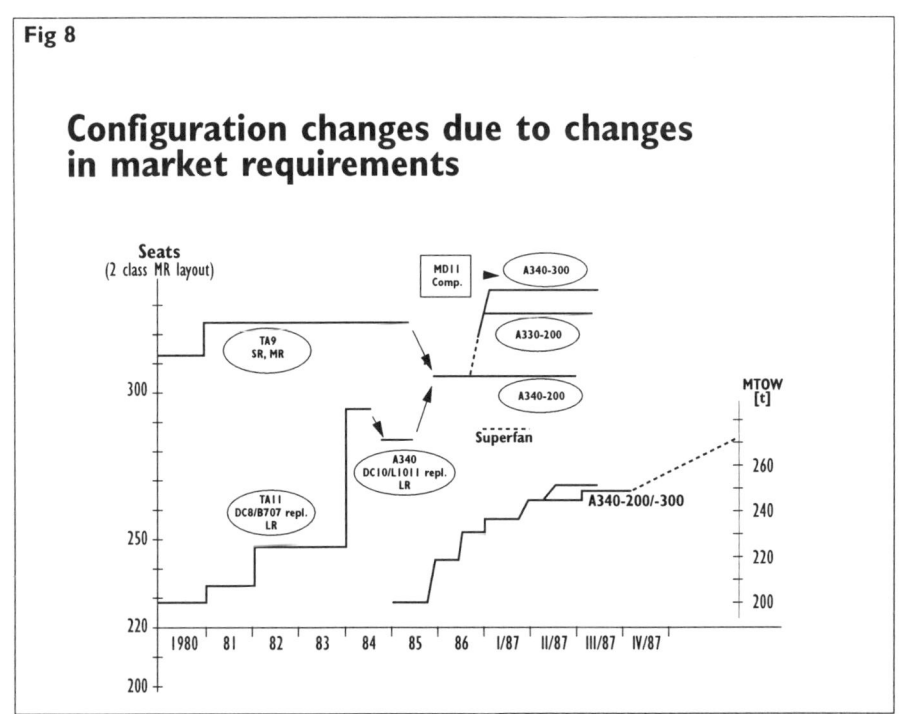

Fig 8

Configuration changes due to changes in market requirements

When the concept for this double aircraft programme emerged in 1976, the A340 (at this time designated the TA11) was defined as a replacement for airliners such as the B707 and DC8. In 1984 the fuselage length had to be increased considerably, as the aircraft was then remodelled as a replacement for the DC10 and L1011. A further change in size was endorsed by the marketing team in 1987 when, prior to the launch of the A340, the MD11 appeared on the market and it was decided that the A340 had to be competitive in size and range to the McDonnell Douglas product. This led to a new aircraft definition which required a new engine. The 'Superfan' appeared on the scene only to disappear some months later when the final configuration could be defined and fixed. As can be imagined the situation was a nightmare for the technical project team.

As outlined above the timing of the 'Go Ahead' milestone is difficult to predict at the beginning of a new aircraft programme. But this milestone is the critical one for each aircraft programme because all the technical, commercial and business related issues (activities and deliverables) must be clearly defined in order to achieve the launch conditions.

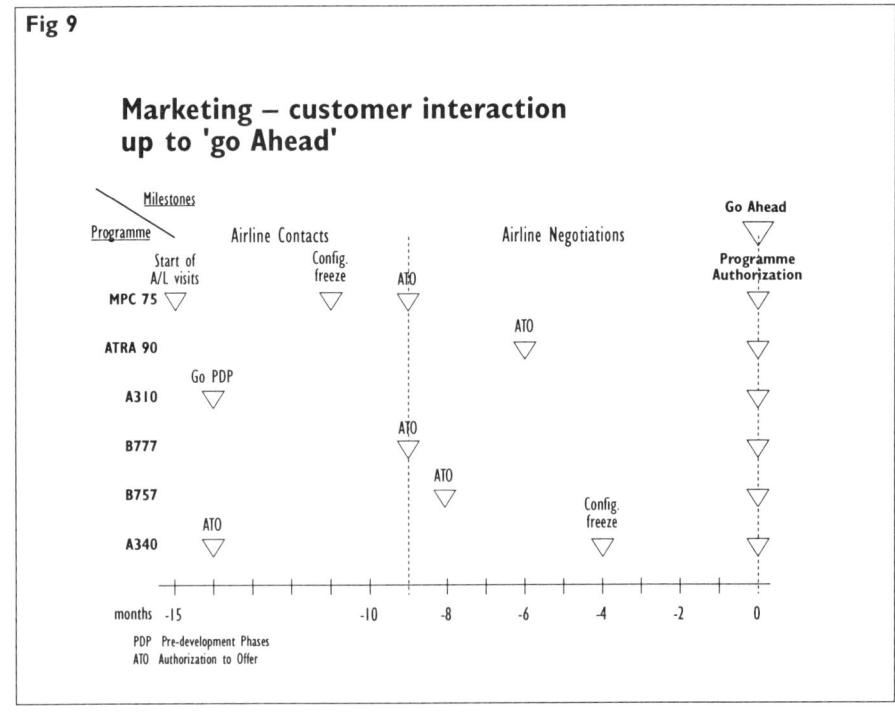

Fig 9

Marketing – customer interaction up to 'go Ahead'

This requires business re-engineering which will now be done by Airbus in the ACE project. All other prior and related milestones can be defined more accurately by working backwards from the 'Go Ahead'. From Airbus's experience and information from other programmes, the milestone ATO (Authorisation To Offer) is normally between six to 15 months before 'Go Ahead' (see fig 9). The other milestones (ACE designates them from zero to five) have to be defined and adjusted to support the aircraft definition in a consistent and cost efficient manner (see fig 10).

The Need for Technology Demonstrator Programmes

As is illustrated by the difficult situation before 'Go Ahead' and during the definition phase a very experienced design team is needed and a series of proven and mature technologies must be available to assure market acceptance for the new programme. This is clearly recognised in the USA. The American aerospace industry is perceived as a strategic industry because it combines military and commercial applications and also makes a major contribution to the overall health of the US economy.

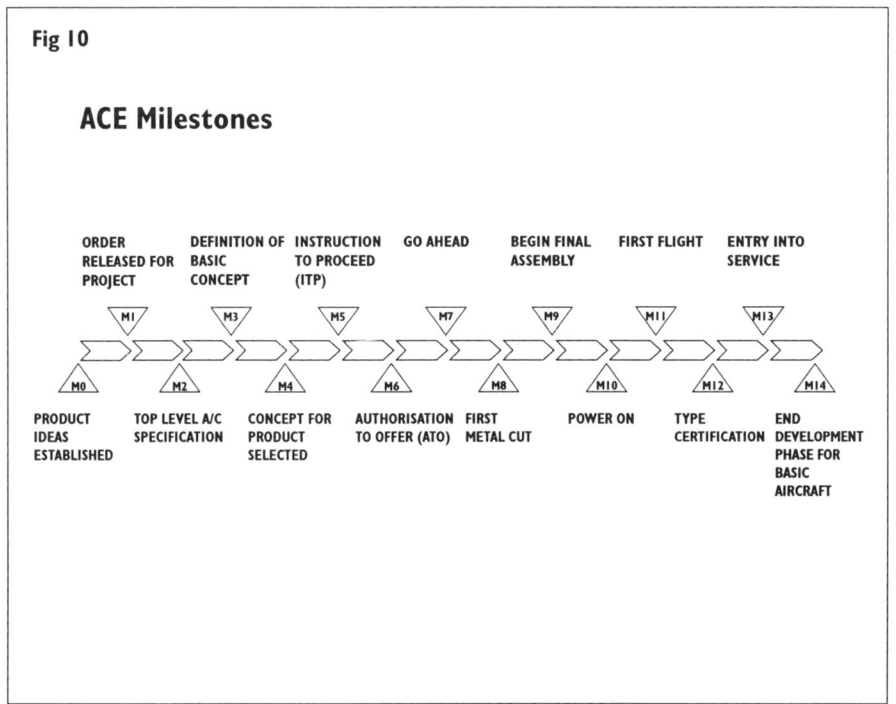

Fig 10

ACE Milestones

As a result the US government wants to retain the strategic lead in aeronautics and space.

A similarly clear policy position from European governments is rare and only France seems to have a strategic conception of the aerospace industry. Returning to the GATT agreement and the related changes for the European aeronautical industry in comparison to their competitors in the US, there are two major deficits in the European system:

- The European system – in particular the aeronautical research programmes at European Commission level and at national level (Germany and UK) – only allow an indirect support of 50% maximum for the industry. But the US can give 100 % research contracts to the industry.
- Europe has no large-scale technology demonstrator programmes. In fig 11 a comparison of NASA's and Europe's demonstrator programmes is shown.

Fig 11

NASA demonstration programs compared with Europe

Experimental Demonstrators USA (1993)	Experimental Demonstrators Europe (1993)
B-757 Hybrid laminar flow testbed (subsonic) B-737 High lift flap technology F-18 High angle-of-attack research vehicle SR-71 Flight research testbed for high-speed civil transport UH 60 RASCAL Helicopter, nap of the earth fight guidance, GPS precision navigation flight system XV-15 Certification profiles for noise abatement, failure modes and handling qualitities F-15 Highly integrated digital electronics control 2F16-XL Hybrid laminar flow control (supersonic), for civil transport X-30 National Aero-Space Plane	F-100 Technology Demonstrator for laminar flow research **?** *National Denmonstrators,* *which are not comparable* *with US Experimental Demonstrators*
X-31 Strike fighter technology demonstrator	

The mere quantity of US programs shows a further distortion in competitiveness

Based on a study, conducted in 1993 by DASA, a clear deficit in technology demonstrator programmes is shown.[1] In addition the indirect support for aeronautics in the year 1992/93 shows a clear advantage for the US industry. Twice as much money for research contracts is spent in the US compared to Europe (see fig 12).

Nevertheless, US public opinion is still persuaded by their government and technical press that Europe is subsidising its aeronautical industry, whereas the US industry is only market driven and independent of any governmental support. But the figures in fig 12 prove the contrary. A typical statement to support the Anti-European position in the US with respect to the subsidised European aeronautical industry has recently been published in an article by 'Aerospace America' and is given in fig 13.

Conclusion

Boeing and the US Government have imposed their support system for the aeronautical industry as a world standard.

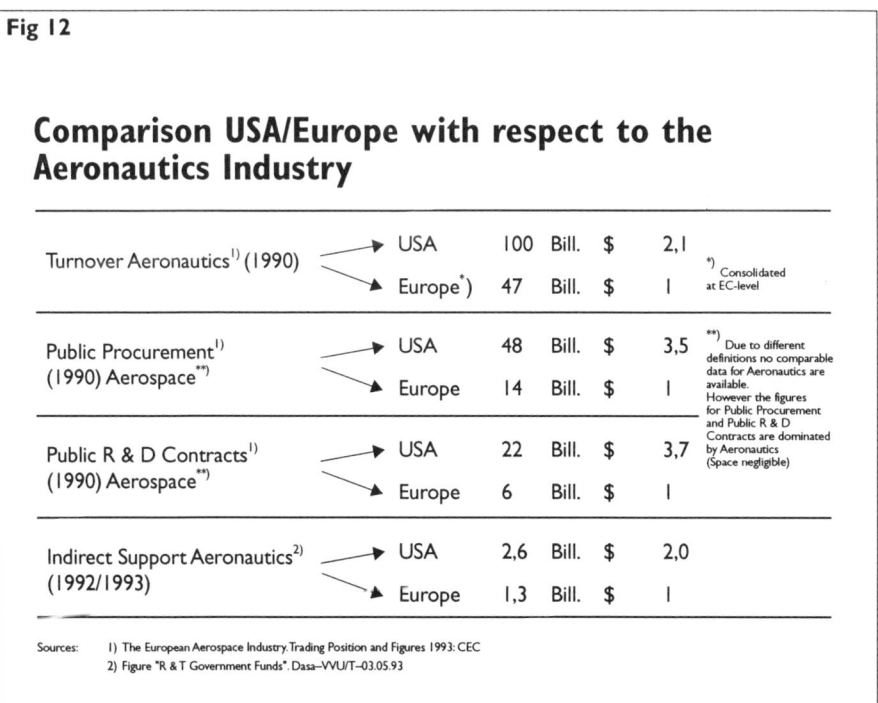

Fig 12

Comparison USA/Europe with respect to the Aeronautics Industry

Turnover Aeronautics[1)] (1990)	→	USA	100	Bill. $	2,1
	↗	Europe[*])	47	Bill. $	1
Public Procurement[1)] (1990) Aerospace[**)]	→	USA	48	Bill. $	3,5
	↘	Europe	14	Bill. $	1
Public R & D Contracts[1)] (1990) Aerospace[**)]	→	USA	22	Bill. $	3,7
	↘	Europe	6	Bill. $	1
Indirect Support Aeronautics[2)] (1992/1993)	→	USA	2,6	Bill. $	2,0
	↘	Europe	1,3	Bill. $	1

*) Consolidated at EC-level

**) Due to different definitions no comparable data for Aeronautics are available. However the figures for Public Procurement and Public R & D Contracts are dominated by Aeronautics (Space negligible)

Sources: 1) The European Aerospace Industry. Trading Position and Figures 1993: CEC
2) Figure "R & T Government Funds". Dasa–VVU/T–03.05.93

When European governments have given loans to their aeronautical industry, the American companies and press call it 'subsidies'. But when NASA gives a 100% contract to the US industry to develop, for example, a new composite wing, which by chance fits to an existing aircraft programme, the American side call it 'technology development'.

European administrations have accepted the GATT agreement and have reduced the support for the aircraft development phase accordingly, but have not adopted the 100% contract possibility for component development. To secure equal economic conditions, Europe needs an equivalent 'aeronautical support system' to match the US system, i.e.:

- 100% funding for new technology programmes;
- Large demonstrator programmes for proof of concept for new technology features.

CEC aeronautical research programmes are useful for standardisation and technology transfer in Europe, but are not equivalent to NASA programmes.

Fig 13

AEROSPACE AMERICA Interview
with Jonathan Schofield

Airbus Industrie, a consortium of Aerospatiale, Daimler Benz Aerospace, Airbus, British Aerospace, and CASA, was created in 1970 and delivered its first aircraft in 1974. Since then Airbus has sold over 2,000 airliners. It has about 35% of the world market.
How did Airbus get started, and what role did government subsidies play?

I am extremely proud as an American that we are one of the leading countries in the world that makes R&D a top priority and spends sizeable amounts of money each year on contracts to industry to conduct it. That's hy we're a leading economic power in the world today. We do not call it subsidy, but I would say it is. Our government supports R&D differently than the Europeans, but it amounts to the same thing. McDonnell Douglas, for example has $160-million contract with NASA to develop a composite wing. The results will be directly transferred to other U.S. aircraft companies.
There are numerous other examples. There's nothing wrong with this. But let's call it what it is, a subsidy. This way we support our industry. The commerce Dept., with whom I debate this issue all the time, would not call them purchases of goods and services. These are not loans.
No monies for these goods and services need be paid back to our government.

The national aeronautical R&T programmes are small and not comparable to NASA programmes.

In order to be effective a combined effort of the Airbus partner countries (Spain, France, Germany and the UK) is needed to agree upon a common aeronautical research initiative.

Europe and Airbus learned much from the 'commercially unsuccessful' Concorde programme. But Concorde was the 'technology demonstrator' for Airbus for more than 20 years (A300 concept, A320 Fly-by-wire, etc). But today Europe needs a new 'technology platform'. I pose the question: where is the new European technology demonstrator programme?

Notes and References

1   Prem H, *'Analysis of Indirect Support for the Aeronautics Industry in Europe and the USA'* , (DASA, Munich, 1993).

18 Technology Diffusion and Globalisation in Civil Aeronautics

Dr STEVEN McGUIRE
Loughborough University

It has become commonplace to describe important sectors like aerospace as 'globalised'. Quite what is meant by this is often unclear. Aerospace has always been global - in the sense that aircraft are sold to customers around the world. However, if the criteria of development and production is used rather than the geographic spread of the product, then the industry is not highly globalised. The same North Atlantic nations which gave birth to the industry some 70 years ago remain the dominant players. However, new work in economics has made a variety of states look at the aerospace industry as a source of high-technology, high skill jobs. Thus, European and American firms face more and more competition from nascent aerospace states. For these emerging states to be successful, they will have to master one of the most technologically demanding industries in the world. Thus, an examination of the links between technology diffusion and aerospace is in order.

This chapter will examine the process of technological diffusion and its role in the globalisation of the aerospace industry in three sections. First we consider the economic rationale for developing an indigenous aerospace industry. In the second section, we outline the process by which nation-states acquire advanced capabilities in high-technology industries. Thirdly, utilising the framework set out in the previous section, I will look at the process of building an aerospace industry.

The Attractions of the Industry

Globalisation is often considered to be a firm-centred phenomenon; that is, the process can be grasped by understanding how firms react to economic incentives to internationalise their activities. This chapter - while not disagreeing entirely with that view - argues that given the pervasive government involvement in the aerospace sector the correct actor to study is the state, not firms. As such the sections below examine technological diffusion in aerospace by placing political economy, rather than corporate strategy at the heart of the analysis. Moreover, this chapter assumes that in developing an aerospace industry, a state will wish to produce an aircraft rather than components. This is because there is still a perception in the industry that to become a 'full member' of the sector, it is simply not enough to make parts - even important ones.

Aside from government's historic concern for aerospace (largely for national defence reasons) new work in economics has provided intellectual justification for continued - indeed strengthened - government involvement in the sector. Theories of strategic trade have been developed to explain trade in high-technology sectors like aerospace. But while trying to explain existing or historic patterns, this economic literature has, in some cases quite unintentionally, provided governments with intellectual justification for intervening in the aerospace sector.

New trade theory seeks to explain trade in situations where the traditional tenets of free trade do not apply. Neo-classical economics grounds its explanation of trade on the theory of comparative advantage: that states trade goods on the basis of specialisation that flows from factor endowments. Comparative advantage, at its simplest, expects a world where countries and their firms tend to specialise. International trade is thus a harmonious affair, since nations can sell their goods for others they need. To a great extent, the model does describe the international trading system pretty well. Canada, with its vast mineral wealth, does tend to trade more in primary products and extractive industries, just as neo-classical theory would predict. Comparative advantage continues to shape the thought of business and government leaders. When a Boeing vice-president said, 'Every country does not have to build every product it consumes. You build good train systems in Europe and we [US] do not', he was giving eloquent - if controversial - expression to the theory.[1] As powerful as neo-classical economics is at modelling international trade, there are several phenomena which are not accounted for by the theory and it was these lacuna which led to the development of new trade theory in the early 1980s.[2] These phenomena include: barriers to entry; externalities and spillovers; relief from low-wage competition.

Neo-classical economics assumes that entry into an industry is relatively easy. This assumption is important as it conditions expectations about profit levels in the sector. Imagine a situation where a new product in the international market takes off in popularity. Firms in the sector enjoy great profitability. However, new entrants come in and the level of profitability falls. Eventually, the enormous profits which the 'pioneer' firms enjoyed - called rents - are competed away. But what if entry into the industry is not easy? What if aspiring entrants face formidable technological or financial barriers?

High technology industries like aerospace or biotechnology are not easy sectors to enter. There are several reasons for this. For example, research and development costs are enormous; developing a new, large civil airliner can cost anywhere from $3-10bn. Much of this cost is in production costs, but a substantial proportion is tied up in research on new materials, computerisation for the flight controls, technology for in-flight entertainment systems. For example, Boeing's R&D spending in 1996 was £701,221,000, representing 5.3% of sales.[3] As substantial as this figure is, it represented a drop of some 20% from the firm's R&D spending in the early 1990s, when its new 777 model was still in development. In short, developing products in the aerospace sector is so expensive that new entrants simply have to have government support - a point made by the success of the Airbus consortium. Since barriers to entry are high, new trade theory expects that existing entrants will enjoy considerable profitability. This point can be argued, but the perception that major aerospace firms are comfortably profitable can lead to politicians arguing that their government ought to support entry into the sector to gain a share of these rents.

Another argument used to support investment in high-technology industries like aerospace is their spillover effects. Spillovers occur when activity in one economic sector leads to changes in another. The advantage of having a high-technology firm in your locality is that other firms benefit from having to 'raise their game' to supply the high-technology company. Boeing makes great demands of its local suppliers in terms of the cost-effectiveness, performance and quality of their components. Supplier firms thus tend to be pushed up to new levels of technological and production sophistication by the high-technology firm. In sum, a locality ends up with a more capable and sophisticated economy than otherwise.

As more and more states develop economically, knowledge-intensive sectors like aerospace are regarded as being havens from international competition based on low wages. Japan, for example, has long held the view that it must create national capabilities in aerospace, biotechnology and advanced materials precisely because of the threat of NICs in medium-technology industries like automobiles or shipbuilding.[4] Thus, moving up the value-added ladder is seen as a key state goal. Knowledge-intensive industries are thought to be less prone to competition precisely because of the central role of ideas, of tacit knowledge that undergirds them. This tacit knowledge accrues to highly-trained individuals and cannot be appropriated by unskilled, low-wage workers. Thus, states lacking the necessary technological infrastructure will not be able to enter the market and compete away the economic rents captured by the first-movers.

If states have a particular set of reasons for accelerating the globalisation of the industry, firms in existing aerospace powers also have reasons. There are two principal rationales: market access and financial risk. Firms which sell civil or military aircraft have long been used to offering incentives to potential customers as a way of gaining sales. Offsets are one such incentive. Offsets are agreements whereby an aircraft firm agrees to locate certain production functions in a country in exchange for that country placing an aircraft order. The long history of offsets has convinced firms that developing relationships with foreign firms offers an opportunity to influence future business. China, for example, has over the past several years used its large market to gain a variety of business from US and European airframe manufacturers.

Firms also choose to globalise as a way of spreading risk. As the figures from Golich illustrate, the real cost of producing a large civil aircraft has shot up over the past decades; the pattern is similar in civil engine and military programmes.

With programmes costing billions of pounds and with pay-out periods now extending into decades, fewer and fewer firms possess the financial resources needed to develop, produce and market a commercial airliner. The Boeing 777 programme, for example, saw Japanese firms attain 'programme participant' status, a position which involved Japanese firms in some design decisions as well as more traditional subcontracting roles. Japanese firms also provided funding for both recurring and non-recurring programme costs.[5]

In sum, for both governments and firms, there are important reasons for the globalisation on the industry. For existing aerospace firms, the need is essentially a defensive and conservative response to the increasing risk which characterises the sector. Governments, especially those of developing countries, as well as their domestic firms, see in aerospace an inviting sector where prestige, profit and high-technology combine. The view that aerospace is an attractive sector to enter is at odds with the financial structure of the industry which, if anything, ought to deter entry. The international industry has been characterised by a contraction in the number of firms operating, not an increase.

Table 1 - Aircraft development costs (1991 US dollars [millions])

Aircraft type	Entered service	Development cost	Development cost per seat
DC-3	1936	3	0.1
DC-8	1959	600	3.75
B-747	1970	3300	7.3
B-777	1995	4300*	14.0*

* - estimate

Source: Golich in Talalay *et. al*, table 13.1[6]

It is in fact a sector where, to paraphrase Wolfgang Denisch's famous remark, failure is the norm and success the exception.[7] But clearly many states wish to gain a foothold in aerospace. With that in mind, we turn now to a consideration of the process of technological diffusion.

National Innovation Systems

Technology is the application of scientific developments to economic life. While we live in the age of high-technology, there is a rich historical literature examining how technological change affects the international economy. Some of this work has strong links to the discussion of new trade theory above. German mercantilists of the 1800s such as Friedrich List noted the important role of technology in the economic development of the British economy and argued that Germany needed to acquire British technology to push its economy to higher levels of growth. The British sought to limit German access to technology by restricting the export of machine tools - an early illustration of the trade-related nature of technology.

As it was in Imperial Germany, as it is for Malaysia, Taiwan, Chile and other states seeking to gain entry into the exclusive club of economically leading nations. To do so, they must tap the technology of the leaders and then gradually develop their own. Perhaps they will emulate Germany and overhaul the heretofore-leading state. In any event, the efforts of these states positively require a degree of technology diffusion. How does technology diffuse around the globe?

For neo-classical economists, technology is much like any other good - its existence is governed by supply and demand - and the issue is at what price the technology will be transferred from seller to buyer. Technology was thus appropriable, that is, a buyer would be able to put the technology to immediate use in the same way he or she might be able to consume a meal. It is also assumed that 'the opportunity costs of abandoning older existing technologies and knowledge, including the human skills which embody them, are relatively negligible'.[8] If this was true, then economic development, at least from the standpoint of technological change, ought not to be a problem: states could tap a pool of internationalised technology and apply it easily to the economy where it would smoothly supersede existing technologies and their associated workers and industries.

But this neo-classical world view of technology is clearly untenable and is sliding into 'merciful oblivion'.[9] In its place is much more nuanced, more realistic understanding of technology diffusion which sees technology transfer as an uncertain, highly differentiated process. Technology does not flow like water from one point to the next. Instead, the diffusion process may be relatively smooth in one case, and immensely difficult in another. Some states may adapt to new technologies easily, while for others, new technologies fail to enter the economy, either through indifference to the possibilities they offer or outright hostility. The receptiveness of a state to new technologies is a function of societal values and culture as well as institutional conditions such as the mode of governance, economic infrastructure, capabilities of domestic firms, and the research infrastructure (universities, schools, research institutes).

With so many factors seeming to condition the ability of technology to diffuse, it is not surprising that an adequate model of diffusion eludes us. What can be done is outline a series of broad characteristics which seem to distinguish successful adapters of new technology from those states and firms which fail to appropriate new knowledge into their economic development efforts. Successful countries seem able to develop their own national system of innovation (NSI). NSIs can be defined as the nation-specific factors which develop and condition a state's ability to advance technologically, either through the successful absorption and adaptation of foreign technology, or its indigenous generation.[10] In respect of diffusion, a successful NSI is one with significant 'absorptive capacity', that is, the ability to take foreign technology and see it utilised by domestic firms. Three components of an NSI are: educational infrastructure; structure of domestic firms; governmental structure.

Technology must be assimilated by a country for it to be put to use. This implies the existence of an educated workforce capable of absorbing the new technology and then applying it. Recent debates about the importance of education obscure education's long historical role in international technology transfer. That both Germany and the United States were able to eclipse the British as leaders in technological industries by the end of the nineteenth century was due in no small part to the higher levels of education enjoyed by their workforces. As Mowery and Rosenberg have argued, the early expansion of the US university system provided firms with large numbers of skilled workers.[11] A virtuous cycle was created: firms with skilled workforces could develop more advanced products and processes, thereby increasing the demand for yet more skilled workers.

The lessons of the US and Germany have not been lost on some NICs, which have invested heavily in expanding their education systems. At the university level, several developing countries have placed a special emphasis on scientific, engineering and technical training. These results seem to be paying off in that more R&D is being done in these countries. One piece of evidence comes from the increasing (although still small) role of affiliates of MNEs which are conducting R&D in host countries. Judging from US corporations, 'the proportion of R&D scientists and engineers in total employment in foreign affiliates overall, and in particular, in developed and some developing countries, including countries in the Asian region, is increasing'.[12] Skilled workforces are a virtual prerequisite for any country contemplating an expansion of its aerospace sector.

Research and development capabilities are also an important feature of a state's NSI. These capabilities include physical research establishments, such as university and government laboratories, as well as monetary capabilities in the form of state funding as well as corporate research funding. In Western countries, comparing R&D expenditures across nations has become a growth industry. What underlays this concern is the view that investment in R&D can permanently increase the long run growth potential of the economy.[13] Yet in spite of these concerns there is little evidence that - beyond a certain level - countries are able to dramatically increase their expenditures on research and development. As the accompanying chart shows, developed states cluster around a level of 2.3% of GDP as an expenditure on gross (business and government) research and development.

Table 2 - Science and Engineering education - selected countries (per million population)

Country	Year	R&D scientists and engineers	R&D Technicians
China	1992	1129	428
Indonesia	1988	181	na
Korea	1992	1190	349
Taiwan	1991	1673	573
Japan	1992	5677	869
Germany	1989	10701	5115

Source: UNCTAD 1996, adapted from Table VIII.5[14]

Table 3 - Gross Expenditure on R&D - selected countries

Country	Year	GERD (% of GDP)
USA	1994	2.54
UK	1994	2.19
Germany	1994	2.37
France	1994	2.38
Japan	1993	2.73
Taiwan	1993	1.70
Korea	1992	2.30
Indonesia	1993	0.20
China	1992	0.50

Source: ONS, 1994, and UNCTAD, 1996, Table VIII.4[15]

As can be seen, nascent aerospace countries like China and Indonesia do not match the spending levels of leading countries, although

China has committed itself to a dramatic increase in its aerospace R&D budget. Recent currency turmoil in SE Asia may limit the ability of Indonesia to follow suit.

Indeed, the difficulties experienced by Asian states point out the hazards in moving up the value-added ladder. These states hoped that acquiring foreign, especially Japanese, technology in areas like semiconductors would allow them to develop indigenous technological capabilities. These may yet come but, as early as 1994, a UN study pointed out that wage demands in export sectors like consumer electronics vastly outpaced productivity gains. For example, between 1985 and 1990, real wages in Singapore rose by 36% while productivity grew 18%.[16] This provides a powerful incentive to substitute more capital-intensive industries for labour, either via attracting FDI or using R&D to upgrade industry. However, as the report implies, with so many Asian states attempting to move up the value ladder at more or less the same time, competition damaged the ability of states to attract the requisite levels of investment. Allied with weak indigenous research infrastructures, the result was economic damage.[17]

In respect of firms, work drawing largely from the Japanese experience shows that the structure of domestic competition is vital for spurring high-technology industries. MITI oversaw competition among Japanese firms in sectors like semiconductors, while protecting these producers from international competition. Having honed their competitive skills behind these barriers, the firms were then 'unleashed' on American and European competitors. Internal competition among firms obviates a problem with national champion strategies like those employed in Europe in the 1960s - as the chosen instrument in a particular sector, the champion has no economic incentive to increase its international competitiveness.

Economies are also thought to need complementary industries for the one being developed. These are sectors whose products, processes or technologies can contribute to the other sector's development by providing, for example, a skilled workforce or vital components. Thus, technological diffusion is an interdependent process, where progress in one sector relies on developments in another. Countries looking to develop in aerospace would do well to have capabilities in, for example, electronics, automobiles, and heavy engineering.

A final, and often ignored, component of technological diffusion concerns the ability of the state to develop a stable political and economic environment that allows the diffusion to take place. While frameworks of technological transfer seem to believe that the process occurs without government involvement, more recent work has highlighted the damage that corruption and political instability can have on economic development. When Western firms seek partners in developing states they must consider whether the political risk is intolerably high.

Rise of New Competitors

The emergence of new competitors to challenge the traditional dominance of Europe and the United States in aerospace provides us with an opportunity to apply insights gleaned from the diffusion literature to a specific sector. Numerous countries - from Brazil to Indonesia to Japan - are making concerted efforts to develop advanced capabilities in aerospace. These new competitors are mounting a varied assault on numerous market segments and seek to gain access to aeronautical technology through one or a combination of offset agreements and willingness to join in collaborative ventures with established firms.

China represents a quickly emerging player. Its strategy is to use its expanding passenger market as a lever to draw Western firms into alliances with Chinese partners. On one estimate, China will account for some 11% of the global aircraft market by 2014. While this is still some way short of being the world's largest national market for aircraft - a distinction which belongs to the US - China's market has hardly been developed and will be a source of significant orders for years to come. With this in mind, Boeing and Airbus are exploring a variety of relationships with Chinese firms. The Chinese, for their part, fully expect to learn from these arrangements many of the skills of successful aircraft development. Production of some B737 fuselages will now be done in China. Airbus, in a 1994 agreement, undertook to develop China's service infrastructure with the manufacture of a flight training centre.[18] In 1997, Airbus also succeeded in gaining a £1.5 billion order for aircraft from the Chinese. In military aircraft, the Chinese are building Russian-designed Su-27s for the Chinese air force. In sum, China has skilfully used access to its large aircraft market to 'buy' production capacity from existing aerospace states.

However, as our framework above suggests, there will be limits to the ability of Chinese firms to move up the technological ladder without greater investment in research and development. Two features are worth noting here. First, the Chinese have indicated that they will dramatically expand their aerospace R&D funding. Second, the Chinese do have an existing complementary sector in the space launch industry. The country does have a considerable number of scientists and engineers. However, there is the consideration of political risk. While Jiang Zemin has indicated that economic reform will continue, the lack of a clear process of selecting leaders may yet cause severe political instability and economic disruption. In short, Chinese efforts to develop in aerospace may be limited more by the potential for political instability than by any other element of its national system of innovation.

Korea is another example of a state with great ambitions for its aerospace industry. Indeed, the Koreans have been so aggressive in wanting to enter commercial aerospace that potential agreements with overseas collaborators have not come to fruition partly out of overzealous demands from the Korean government about workshare and technology transfer.[19] Under government auspices, 14 firms have formed the Korea Commercial Aircraft Development Consortium (KCDC) with Samsung Aerospace as the lead partner. Korea has followed the lead of Brazil, Indonesia and Canada in developing products for the regional jet market. The Korean government pledged $4.73 billion to underwrite the plane's development.[20] KCDC has tried various approaches for launching the jet. Talks with the Chinese about an 'Asian Express' regional jet foundered when the parties could not agree workshare. Samsung also failed to obtain regional jet capacity 'off-the-shelf' when it refused to pursue a plan to rescue the Fokker aircraft company. In the wake of these failed efforts, some Koreans questioned the business logic of the enterprise, and suggested that the government was interested in developing aerospace for its prestige value rather than out of any economic logic.[21]

Nonetheless, Korea has other elements of the absorptive capacity. It has a strong education system, which produces a steady stream of engineers and scientists. Crucially, it also has 'complementary' industries that can aid in the development process: two key sectors are electronics and automobiles. Samsung is currently the world's largest producer of memory chips. The Korean car industry - now the world's fifth largest with annual production above two million vehicles - may also provide assistance to the nascent development in aerospace.[22] Global aerospace has seen the gradual erosion of the craft aspects of the industry and instead seen a move toward the 'commodification' of production in the sector. This has seen final assemblers seek to improve productivity and cut costs by the adoption of lean manufacturing techniques associated with the car industry. Korean car firms, spurred on by competition with the Japanese, have increased their share of the Japanese car components trade: a reflection on their competitiveness.[23] Car production provides states with experience in large-scale manufacturing and its concomitant need for sophisticated inventory and production control.

However, the framework developed above does need to grapple with some characteristics specific to the aerospace industry, traits which may alter expectations about the ultimate scope of state-led globalisation in the sector. In terms of the framework outlined, it is clear to one familiar with the industry that internal market competition as a preparatory step to international trading is not possible. Minimum efficient scales of aircraft production simply preclude the option which appeared to be so successful in automobiles and semiconductors. Thus, developing nations looking to advance in aerospace confront the national champion problem - why should a protected firm seek to become more competitive?

There are additional factors which are not quite captured by the mainstream framework described above. One factor is the enormous cost of production, as opposed to R&D; the other concerns the important role that tacit knowledge plays in the aircraft production process. It is commonplace to regard aerospace, computers, telecommunications, pharmaceuticals, biotechnology and advanced materials as more or less identical 'strategic' industries sharing common competitive characteristics. But this may be very misleading as, aside from high levels of R&D, the sectors differ dramatically. One area of difference is the high costs of production - particularly the up front costs of developing manufacturing facilities - associated with aerospace. Firms already in the sector gain enormous economies from operating only a handful of production facilities. While acknowledging the increasing commodification of the sector, it is not at all clear that developing states will be able to generate the necessary production runs to recoup massive investments in plant. Thus, in contrast to the semiconductor sector, there may be significant first-mover advantages in aerospace.[24] The enormous costs of producing - then financing and servicing - commercial aircraft make it difficult for new entrants to sustain themselves. Payback periods for new products may stretch out past 10 years. Airbus' success came after billions of pounds and years of waiting for the consortium's commercial strategy to come good. Does Indonesia possess the financial muscle and patience to see its regional aircraft dream through?

A second important limit to technology diffusion in aerospace is the key role played in the production process by tacit knowledge. Tacit knowledge is uncodified know-how acquired via experience.[25] Such knowledge is not written down in a firm's training manuals, nor can it be learned by rote; it exists in employees' particular 'ways of doing things', or 'tricks of the trade' that develop over years of trail and error.

While it is difficult to measure tacit knowledge (it is by definition non-quantifiable) it is axiomatic that aircraft production embodies a great deal of learning by doing. We see this in the enormous decline in the number of hours it takes to develop the early versions of an aircraft relative to later ones. Airbus estimated that the first A300B fuselage took some 340,000 hours to build, the final figure was 43,000.[26] In short, early production will be inefficient - and very costly - as the firm develops the tacit knowledge needed to move down the learning curve.

But tacit knowledge does not just mean that firms need to absorb costs in the early stages of production. It also means that firms may never acquire the skills needed to build aircraft. If the secret to success lies in the very experience of building, then developing states will be at more or less permanent disadvantage. The technology - the hardware - of aircraft production may reach them, but lacking the uncodified knowledge of experienced workers, the technology may not be appropriable.

Conclusion

Aerospace is a seductive blend of glamour and economics. As we have seen, some economic theory suggests that states ought to enter the industry for the sake of general economic development. However, developing the technological capabilities to do this is not easy. For developing countries, the desire to move beyond the stage of a junior partner - building offset packages or providing components - and on to that of a platform builder may be too great to resist. But doing that requires a fertile education and research system, an already high level of economic development and the political stability to see through a long-term commitment to the sector.

Moreover, even if these things are in place, formidable barriers remain. Development costs of aircraft seem ever increasing, and break-even points for new aircraft move ever further out. Utilising alliances or offsets to gain access to some needed technologies may not be enough; the catalyst to success lies in the tacit knowledge of established players who may not wish to share these secrets.

Notes and References

1   McGuire S, *Airbus Industrie: Co-operation and Conflict in EC-US Trade Relations*, Macmillan/St Martin's Press, London and New York, 1997, p124.
2   Krugman P (ed), *Strategic Trade Policy and the New International Economics,* MA: MIT Press, Cambridge, 1986.
3   *Financial Times*, 26 June 1997, p 23.
4   Hayward K, *International Collaboration in Civil Aerospace*, Pinter, London, 1986, pp 4-45.
5   Ibid, p181.

6   Golich V, *Aviation's Technology Imperative and the Transformation of the Global Political Economy*, in Talalay, M. *et al.*, *Technology, Culture and Competitiveness:Change and the World Political Economy*, Routledge, London, 1997, pp 180-195.

7   Rodgers E, *Flying High: The Story of Boeing and the Rise of the Jetliner Industry*, Atlantic Monthly Press, New York, 1996, p 5.

8   Talalay M, Farrands C, Tooze R (eds.), *Technology, Competitiveness and Culture: Change and the World Political Economy*, Routledge, London, 1997, p78.

9   Archibughi D, Michie J (eds.) *Technology, Globalisation and Economic Performance*, Cambridge University Press, Cambridge, 1997, p140.

10   Ibid, p3.

11   Mowery, D and Rosenberg N, *Technology and the Pursuit of Economic Growth*, Cambridge University Press, Cambridge, 1989, p117.

12   UNCTAD, *World Investment Report, 1994*, United Nations, New York and Geneva, 1994, p237.

13   Crafts, Nicholas, "Deindustrialisation and Economic Growth", *Economic Journal*, 106(January), 1996, pp172-183.

14   UNCTAD, *Sharing Asia's Dynamism: Asian Direct Investment in the European Union,*: United Nations, New York and Geneva, 1996.

15   Office of National Statistics, "Research and Experimental Development (R&D) Statistics 1994", *Economic Trends,* No 514, August 1996.

16   UNCTAD, *World Investment Report, 1994*, United Nations, New York and Geneva, 1994, p67.

17   UNCTAD, *World Investment Report, 1994*, United Nations, New York and Geneva, 1994, p71.

18   *Financial Times*, 7 November 1994, p20.

19   *Aviation Week and Space Technology*, 28 October 1996, p26.

20   *Aviation Week and Space Technology*, 9 December 1996, p32.

21   *Aviation Week and Space Technology*, 28 October 1996, p26.

22   World Trade Organisation, *Trade Policy Review: The Republic of Korea*, WTO, Geneva, 1996, p84.

23   World Trade Organisation, *Trade Policy Review: The Republic of Korea*, WTO, Geneva, 1996, p83.

24   Mowery, D., "Does Airbus Industrie Yield Lessons for EC Collaborative Research Programmes?", in Humbert, M (ed.), *The*

Impact of Globalisation on Europe's Firms and Industries, Pinter, London, 1993, pp45-55.

25   Howells, J, "Tacit Knowledge, Innovation and Technology Transfer", *Technology Analysis and Strategic Management*, 1996, p92.

26   McIntyre, I, *Dogfight: The Transatlantic Battle Over Airbus*, Praeger, Westport, 1992, p36.